The Best I.T. Sales & Marketing BOOK EVER!

MW01110320

What's being said about MSP University?

"…to find a company other than MSPU that provides this type of support for our industry specifically is nonexistent. I am currently using MSPU's CEO Support and would not hesitate to recommend them to anyone with a new business or even an established business looking to grow. It's an invaluable service that has been meeting my expectations each month plus more."

- Jamie Williams, President, Effective Technology Partner, Illinois

"During the three-day boot camp it was obvious to me that I was learning cutting-edge information that would make me successful. I was so impressed that I signed up for the CEO Program and the Marketing Program and I gave notice to my employer. It was that clear, how I would be able to succeed, in a relatively short period of time, at realizing my dream of turning my side consulting company into a full-time, full-service Managed Services Provider. I know my business will be successful and I owe a large part of that success to the training and mentoring provided by the MSPU staff. Keep up the great work"

- William Davis, President, Technology Consulting Services, LLC, Washington

"…the tools that you give us are incredible, and the way you've put this together to go out and do a presentation is the best I've ever seen.."

- Pam Tappan, Director of Sales, ANS Solutions, California

The Best I.T. Sales & Marketing BOOK EVER!

What's being said about The Guide to a Successful Managed Services Practice?

"This book sits on my shelf and my service manager's shelf. You can't get $99 worth of consulting this valuable. It's a great reference, a great start, and worth looking at for everyone looking at managed services."

- Dave Sobel, President, Evolve Technologies, Virginia

"Every Small Business consultant needs to read this book. Yes, it's an awesome guide to managed services. But it's also a great guide to deciding which services to sell, how to price them, how to sell them, and how to "deliver" after you've inked the deal.

Did you need to know how to run a help desk? Or how to create an escalation procedure? It's all here.

You'll save literally hundreds -- maybe thousands of hours of work by reading this book. I run a very successful managed services business and I learned a great deal from this book. Simpson deserves a big hand for putting together such a valuable guide."

- Karl W. Palachuk, President, KP Enterprises, California

"...a "must-have" for any organization considering offering proactive, flat-rate I.T. Services"

"Packed with lots of valuable tools and other information that would have likely taken years to acquire on our own."

- Kurt Sippel, President, Applied Tech Solutions, Wisconsin

MSP University's

Managed Services Series

The Best I.T. Sales & Marketing Book EVER!

Erick Simpson

The Best I.T. Sales & Marketing BOOK EVER!

MSP University

7077 Orangewood Avenue, Suite 104

Garden Grove, CA 92841

www.mspu.us

Voice: (714) 898-8195

Fax: (714) 898-8194

10 9 8 7 6 5 4 3 2

Printed in the United States of America

ISBN 978-0-9788943-1-3

The Best I.T. Sales & Marketing BOOK EVER!

Table of Contents

The Best I.T. Sales & Marketing BOOK EVER!

Table of Contents

The Best I.T. Sales & Marketing BOOK EVER!

Table of Contents

The Best I.T. Sales & Marketing BOOK EVER!

Table of Contents

About the Author – Erick Simpson

As Vice President and CIO of Intelligent Enterprise and MSP University, Erick Simpson has experienced first-hand the challenges of growing an I.T. Business. Intelligent Enterprise has been providing Information Technology Solutions to the Southern California SMB Market since 1997. Their relationships with  partners such as Microsoft, Cisco, Citrix and HP have allowed them the ability to design, scale and implement effective infrastructure solutions for their diverse client base.

Intelligent Enterprise, a Microsoft Gold Certified and Business Solutions Partner and Small Business Specialist, successfully migrated to a Managed Services business model in January of 2005. Prior to this, they were operating as many other I.T. Providers have – reacting to Clients in "break-fix" mode, and dealing with the constant demand to recruit new clients and sell new solutions each and every month in order to meet their receivables goals.

Intelligent Enterprise developed an "All You Can Eat" Managed Services Approach focused on 3 Core Deliverables – Remote Help Desk, Proactive Network Monitoring, and they pioneered Vendor Management. Through the creation of a Managed Services Sales and Marketing approach unique to the Industry, Intelligent Enterprise sold over $2MM worth of

About the Author – Erick Simpson

Managed Services Agreements before being asked to share their Managed Services knowledge and expertise with hundreds of IT Service Providers, Vendors and Channel Organizations worldwide through their Managed Services University at www.mspu.us.

A recognized Author, Speaker and Trainer, and contributor to Microsoft's Small Business Channel Community Expert Column and Presenter of a continuing series of Microsoft, Intel and Cisco Workshops, Events and Webcasts on Managed Services, Erick is the author of "The Guide to a Successful Managed Services Practice - *What Every SMB IT Service Provider Should Know...*", the definitive book on Managed Services.

Erick's professional certifications include Microsoft MCP and SBSC, and affiliations include SMBTN and HTG1 Peer Group Memberships. Erick has conducted nationwide Managed Services workshops, boot camps and presentations at industry events such as the Microsoft Worldwide Partner Conference, SMBNation, SMBSummit, ITPro Conference, ITAlliance and others.

Erick also co-authored Arlin Sorensen's HTG Peer Group book *"Peer Power – Powerful Ideas for Partners from Peers "*, available at www.htgmembers.com, and his recent articles on Managed Services are available at the following web urls:

- Managed Services, your business plan and you – Author, SearchITChannel July 2007 - http://searchitchannel.techtarget.com/general/0,295582,sid9 6_gci1262243,00.html

---

The Best I.T. Sales & Marketing BOOK EVER!

About the Author – Erick Simpson

- Managed Services – What's All the Buzz About? Author, Microsoft Small Business Channel Community - https://partner.microsoft.com/us/40029753

- Managed Services – It Makes Sense – Author, ChannelPro June 2007 – http://www.channelpro-digital.com/channelpro/200706/?folio=38

- An Introduction To Managed Services – Author, Infotech Update January 2007 – http://infotech.aicpa.org/NR/rdonlyres/AC23261D-D7F4-4459-A822-DFD4FDA8F999/0/it_jan_feb07.pdf

Erick lives in Orange County, California with his wife Susan and their two sons, Connor and Riley. His prior technical experience includes overseeing the design, development and implementation of Enterprise-level Help Desks and Call Centers for Fortune 1000 organizations.

Dedication

Dedication

This book is dedicated first and foremost to my family – my wife Sue and our two boys, Connor and Riley. Without their love, tireless support and putting up with my long hours, hectic and sometimes extreme travel schedule, and general grumpiness when under a deadline (or when things just aren't going the way I wish they would)…I simply could not accomplish anything at all. I love you dearly.

Secondly, I'd like to dedicate this book to our MSPU Partners, and all of the IT Service Providers who purchased our first book, "The Guide to a Successful Managed Services Practice", and helped make it a best-selling Managed Services publication. This follow-up to that book is our response to your positive reviews, encouragement and specific requests for the content contained herein. Thank you all.

Acknowledgements

There are so many people who have influenced, encouraged and continue to inspire us to succeed, and I'd like to personally thank them here.

First, I'd like to thank my business partner, Gary Beechum. It takes a special relationship to start a business with someone, and reflect back on all of the ups and downs, highs and lows 17 years later and know that you made the right decision. Gary and I haven't always been in the I.T. business, but in each successive entrepreneurial endeavor we've attempted over the years, our mutual respect, trust and friendship for each other continued to grow and become stronger and stronger. We're a good team – each of us balances the other's weaknesses and strengths to a point where we strike a natural balance, and are much more effective together than we would ever be apart. Thanks, Gary – I can't wait to see what's next.

I'd also like to thank Arlin Sorensen, and the incredible impact that being associated with him has had in our organization and for me personally; first as a member of his HTG1 Peer Group, then on a deeper, more personal level. Arlin is one of those rare individuals that lives his faith through every aspect of his life, and uses it as his driving force in building relationships, utilizing the "servant-leader" philosophy to help those he touches realize the best in themselves and others. His dynamic HTG Peer Group concept has brought nearly 100 IT Organizations together in an open, sharing and mentoring relationship that is truly unique today. Check out www.htgmembers.com for more on Arlin's peer groups.

The Best I.T. Sales & Marketing BOOK EVER!

Acknowledgements

I'd also like to thank my peers in HTG1; Connie Arentson, Phil Kenealy, Mitch Miller, Kurt Sippel, Dave Cooksey, Don Miller, Dan Hay, Gavin Steiner, Jim Strickland, John Pritchard, Don Miller, Dan Shundoff and Jack Safrit, as well as several members in succeeding groups; Dave Siebert, Erik Thorsell, Brad Schow, Dave Sobel, Aaron Booker, Stuart Crawford, Eric Adkins and Naseem Saab. You've all been a great help and inspiration to me.

I've got a lot of folks at Microsoft to thank for their continuing support as well, including Chris Van Wesep, Ron Grattop, Tina Parkhouse, Fred Pullen, Stephen Deming, Christopher Goebel and Mike Marshall.

I owe a special thanks to Sameer Jayaker from Cisco, and Eric Townsend and John Hanna from Intel – thanks so much for being our evangelists inside your respective organizations.

Thanks go out to Harry Brelsford, Beatrice Mulzer, Nancy Williams, Jeff Middleton, Clinton Gatewood, Rajeev Laghate, Akash Saraf, Matt Makowicz, Robin Robins and Mike Iem, for your continued support.

Special recognition goes out to Vlad "ABP" Mazek and Karl Palachuk, my event posse and the kind of guys you can really feel comfortable "telling it like it is" to – and getting it right back. Also in the event posse category is Anne Stanton – the universal connector – thank you all.

Finally, I'd like to recognize our excellent staff for all the hard work they put in to keep our organizations moving forward; Flynn Bashford, Quyen Nguyen, Han Nguyen, Nilo Nogueras, David Huynh, Roger Tang, Monique Morales, Jerry Moran, Brandon Avillar, Brigitte Metzger, Jess Brandt, Vanessa

The Best I.T. Sales & Marketing BOOK EVER!

Acknowledgements

Siliezar, Jessica Cazares, and Dashmilia Guevara – we couldn't do it without you.

Foreword

This book is really the culmination of the sum total of the experiences and lessons we've learned from many different business endeavors, as well as our I.T.-specific sales & marketing knowledge and successes (and failures – who said that?). On the most fundamental level, sales & marketing is a bit like playing Blackjack – there is "basic strategy" involved in each. In Blackjack, for instance, a lot of folks mistakenly think that the goal is to get to 21, or "Blackjack", when the true goal is really to make the dealer "bust", allowing you to win no matter what's in your hand.

The "basic strategy" of marketing is to identify what you're selling, choose your target audience, create a compelling message for your product or service that your target audience will respond to, and get that message in front of a decision maker who will take action on it.

Many I.T. service providers are disappointed in their marketing results, as they either do not have a basic marketing strategy, or feel that mailing out a hundred postcards or letters every once in a while to a bad list constitutes a marketing strategy. Or their marketing strategy is much simpler - asking for referrals from their existing client base, which is spread across twenty verticals.

There are fundamental flaws with each of these approaches. The first approach is not specific or consistent enough, and fails because the success of any direct mail-driven marketing strategy lies primarily in the quality of the marketing list, secondarily on the effectiveness of the marketing message,

Foreword

and finally on the consistency of the marketing activity and follow-up.

The flaw with the second approach is the inability for the service provider to leverage the knowledge they've gained from servicing a specific vertical. If they are continually referred to new and different verticals, they never have the opportunity to recoup the lost labor hours they've spent learning how to address the last vertical client's pain, workflow, processes and software, and leverage this knowledge with new clients in the same vertical.

A smarter play would be to take the knowledge they've amassed from serving several clients in a specific vertical, create a compelling marketing message and collateral which evokes an emotional response about that vertical's clients' pain points and how they've resolved them, and deliver this message to a clean and verified vertical-specific mailing list.

These are very simple examples of the most basic of basic marketing strategies. In Blackjack, playing with a single deck and using basic strategy, the player has a 51% advantage over the dealer over time. If the player really knows the game, and has a decent bankroll, there are techniques and strategies that can increase the player's odds even higher…*but that's another book!*

So the objective of this book is to walk you through each step of selling & marketing your I.T. services – from basic sales & marketing strategy all the way through advanced techniques. Just like in Blackjack, we'll show you how to maximize your bankroll by playing like a pro.

Preface

Wow. It's hard to imagine that it's already been a year since we launched our last book "The Guide to a Successful Managed Services Practice", at the SMBNation conference in Redmond, Washington. That book was very well received, and continues to be so, because there still is no other book like it. The response to "The Guide to a Successful Managed Services Practice" really took us by surprise, as we just simply documented how we ran our thriving Managed Services business between the covers, including all of the forms, tools and collateral we had developed and were using every day to sell, implement and maintain our Managed Services deliverables.

Well, we're at it again. This book documents everything we've learned about sales & marketing, as well as techniques specific to I.T. services sales & marketing. And I've got to tell you, we've learned a tremendous amount more in the last year than we knew previously. This is due in large part to the delivery of our training services to Partners nationwide through MSP University. We have engaged more Partners, Vendor Channels and Franchise Organizations in the last year than we ever have before, and taken their best sales & marketing ideas and added them to our own. In the process we've helped hundreds of Partners improve their sales & marketing strategies, and made a positive difference to their bottom lines.

Are you ready? Buckle up and let's get started...

The Best I.T. Sales & Marketing BOOK EVER!

Section 1 - Preparation

Section 1 - Preparation

Before we can jump in and begin selling and marketing our services, there is much preparation to be done. We can't just jump into a new Jacuzzi for the first time without cleaning it, filling it with water, adding the proper mix of chemicals, heating it to the proper temperature, turning on the mood lights and music, breaking out the beverages, slipping into our

……..oops, sorry if I took that visual too far.

But you get it, right? There is preparation required for success and a good time in all endeavors.

And sitting in a dirty, chilly Jacuzzi just isn't a good time….

So the chapters comprising this section will deal with preparation – everything that must be in place before we can begin hiring, training our sales staff, and executing our sales and marketing activities.

We Can't Just Sell Managed Services

Since we're I.T. Consultants and Trusted Advisors, we have an endless selection of products and services which we sell to our clients, and one of these items is a Managed Service Agreement – but it's not the only one. We get asked by Partners all the time how to sell and integrate their Managed Services deliverable with their existing Professional Services, or Solutions deliverables. If we're talking about a new prospect, it's quite simple when we understand that we're going to sell our prospect exactly what they require in order to address their immediate need. This solution may or may not be a Managed Service Agreement, but could be a voice or data T-1 circuit, an email or spam filtering solution, a VoIP system or any of a number of other products and services that we offer.

The important thing to remember is that we want to eventually sell all of our clients all of our products and services. We discuss this concept in great detail in "The Guide to a Successful Managed Services Practice", and describe the Client Solution Roadmap (the tool we created to manage this process), and how to use it. The idea here is to list all of our clients down the left side of a spreadsheet, and all of the solutions we can possibly think of to offer them across the very top of the spreadsheet. Then we assign a red dot or a green dot in each client's corresponding cell, where their name and the solution intersect – a red dot if they don't have the solution and a green one if they do. By the time we're done with this exercise, we'll be able to determine each product or service that our clients don't have, and choose which services and solutions to start selling them in order of priority.

The Best I.T. Sales & Marketing BOOK EVER!

We Can't Just Sell Managed Services

If we've got a decent sized client list, we may never complete the roadmap, as we'll be adding new products, services and solutions to it on a pretty regular basis (for extra credit, we'll choose as many of our products and solutions from vendors and partners that pay us a commission *as well as an annuity* after a sale). Next we'll create two more rows of cells at the top of the spreadsheet above the names of the solutions, and in one row, calculate our commission for selling that solution to the entire client list, and in the other row, calculate the annuity for a year or two or three. Then at the end of our spreadsheet, we'll total up the value of all of our commissions, as well as our annuity revenue….that's how to tell what our client base is really worth from an opportunity perspective.

Pick up our last book and use this tool, if you don't already own it, or create your own – I guarantee you'll be surprised at the tremendous amount of opportunity available right in your existing client base.

Remember I said that we might never complete delivering all of the services in the Client Solution Roadmap to all of our clients? That's actually really good news! Why? Because that means that we have an almost endless stream of sales opportunities, and it's tremendously easier to sell solutions to our existing clients whom we have built relationships with, than it is to sell to new prospects.

So what types of services will we seek to add to our deliverables? Every single service that we think any of our clients will ever need. That might sound a little crazy, right? I don't mean going out and getting trained to implement and maintain a bunch of additional services – what I mean is we'll first determine what all of those services are, then find good vendor and partner relationships to help us sell, quote and deliver them. Always try to seek out vendor and partner relationships that will pay a commission as well as an annuity – this isn't always possible, but try really hard, trust me…you'll thank me later.

Let's run through a list of products and services that we've found to be a good start for our Client Solution Roadmap:

- Managed Services
- Monitoring Only Services
- Managed Firewalls
- Internet Monitoring/Content Filtering
- Disaster Recovery/Business Continuity Planning
- Website Design
- Website Hosting
- Co-Location Services
- Remote Backup/Storage
- Email and Spam Filtering
- Email Archiving
- SAN Storage Solutions
- Voice and Data T-1's
- VoIP
- Application Development
- CRM Solutions
- SharePoint Solutions
- POS/Inventory Control Solutions
- HaaS/SaaS

How many of these solutions do you currently offer your clients? As you can tell, many of these services are subscription-based, which means there is annuity to be had for as long as the client maintains the service. Did you note that I didn't say "for as long as they remain a client"? That's the beauty of annuity-based revenue – even if we sever our relationship, we'll still earn the annuity revenue month after month, year after year, as long as the client pays the vendor or partner delivering the service. How great is that?

So we expand our portfolio of solutions, and become the true I.T. Consultant and Trusted Advisor who can marshal the forces necessary to address any of our clients' needs. This is the reason we can increase our rates and charge a premium – because we'll be able to design, develop, implement, manage and maintain solutions that save our clients money, improve their efficiencies, alleviate their business pain and mitigate risk, all with the help of the right vendor and partner relationships.

Getting Vertical

Okay, we touched briefly on the concept of choosing a vertical market in our foreword. Here's where we really get into it. One of the things we've noticed in working with our Partners is that the more vertical-specific the Partner is, the more successful they are. In other words, our Partners with the highest gross revenues are verticalized, and their marketing strategy is vertical-specific.

On the other hand, our Partners with the lowest gross revenues are generally the least likely to have focused their marketing efforts on a vertical or handful of verticals, and most likely to depend upon referrals as their primary (and sometimes only) source of new client acquisition. This referral-based client acquisition strategy impedes them from leveraging their experience and success in delivering services to other clients in the same vertical.

The benefits to "getting vertical" are numerous. If you've got more than one client in a specific vertical, say Attorneys or Accountants or Non-Profits, you already understand their specific business pain points, and are intimately familiar with their business processes, workflows and the software applications that they depend on to run their organizations. Chances are you've done a good job of introducing them to solutions that have reduced their costs, increased their efficiencies and mitigated their business pain and risk. And I'll wager that they would be glad to offer up some really great testimonials that you could use in your vertical-specific marketing efforts to boot.

Getting Vertical

Why then would you not take these positive experiences and put them to work for you through vertical-specific marketing? It would be a relatively simple undertaking to list the pain points of one of your vertical-specific clients and create some powerful messaging from it.

Let's take the Attorney vertical for example, and list some common pain points:

- Heavily dependent upon email
- Require remote access to files and email when traveling or during court sessions and trials
- Use specific line of business applications such as Timeslips, Westlaw and others, which are challenging to maintain and require numerous regular updates
- Often work late and on weekends in preparation for motions and trials

These are just a few, but you can quickly see that in general, most Attorneys will readily identify with these pain points. Your "Marketing 101" task is to now take these pain points and create a compelling message from them that other Attorneys will respond to. To start, it may look something like the following:

"Frustrating email problems got you down? Having trouble getting to critical files in the office when you're at home or in court? Tired of waiting on the line for Timeslips Technical Support? Call us now to find out how we help our Legal clients reduce email downtime, provide secure remote access to critical data when out of the office, and quickly handle Timeslips and Westlaw technical support issues."

Follow this up with a choice testimonial or two from your existing Attorney clients, and you're on your way.

You can do this exercise for any of your vertical-specific clients – let's do Non-Profits next:

Pain points:

- Depend upon donations and fund-raising in order to meet operating expenses
- Often sponsor remote events or events outside of the office
- Often work late and on weekends and holidays in preparation or participation of events
- Have very tight budgets

Compelling message:

"Looking for ways to stretch dollars and meet your budget? Need a better way to track and manage fundraising activities, donors and their contributions? Call us today to find out how we help our Non-profit clients cut costs, improve efficiencies and manage their fundraising efforts easily and effectively."

Again, finish with a tasty testimonial or two, bake at 350° for ten minutes, and let cool.

Get the idea? If you're not leveraging your knowledge, experience and client testimonials across your prospects in like verticals in your marketing efforts, you're missing a tremendous opportunity. Think about it this way – if you've built your client base completely through referrals, chances are you're spread all over the place from a vertical perspective. You might have an Attorney client, a CPA client, a Non-profit client, etc. Now don't misunderstand me – we've all taken referrals, and have been mighty glad to have 'em! But as a marketing strategy, *referrals alone* are a poor choice if you want to maximize your service delivery profits.

The reason for this is quite simple. Because of the fact that generally, referrals from an existing client in a vertical seldom lead to another client in the same vertical, you lose the ability to profit from the time you've spent learning the workflow, business processes, line of business applications and troubleshooting and maintenance techniques of the original client, and apply this knowledge to the new client. In fact, what usually ends up happening is you accept the referral (and are glad to have it!), and begin learning the workflow, business processes, line of business applications and troubleshooting and maintenance techniques of the new client.

Do this over and over, and welcome to the number one drawback of referral-based marketing.

Now let's take what we've learned and apply it to the scenarios we mentioned earlier, where we take the knowledge we've gained from a specific vertical, and create compelling messaging to deliver to new prospects in the same vertical. Guess what happens? We're now profitable much sooner with a new client because we already have a good understanding of how to support their business needs. Of course, each client will vary slightly in their own individual ways, but for the most part, our time to profitability in these engagements will arrive much, much sooner.

Identifying Your Vertical Markets

Let's talk about choosing our verticals. Sometimes it may not be a good strategy to simply take all of our clients, break them down into their individual verticals, count how many are in each vertical, and go with our top two or three. Well, why not? This sounds like a perfectly acceptable way to choose our top verticals, doesn't it? And isn't this similar to the process we describe in "The Guide to a Successful Managed Services Practice" (albeit in reverse) when developing our Client Solution Roadmap; to determine what solutions to deliver to our clients? The answer to both of these questions is….yes.

But...

We might have a bunch of clients in a poor vertical – now. Take for example the Mortgage vertical. A couple of years ago this was a hot vertical. I mean, Mortgage and Refinance companies were smoking then – remember when every other advertisement in just about any medium on the planet was selling Refi's? And everybody was refinancing their homes two or three times? Man, those were good times….! But we all know what happened to that white-hot vertical, right? Many of those companies aren't even around anymore, and the ones that are have taken a significant downturn in business, with some trying their best just to stay out of bankruptcy.

What about the Manufacturing vertical? The manufacturing industry has some of the largest head counts of many verticals, so what could possibly make us think twice before attacking it? Well, for one thing, just because a vertical has a large head count of people doesn't mean there are an equal number of pc's or servers to support them. In fact, many manufacturing operations I've seen have the exact opposite in terms of users to pc's – many more users than pc's. This is exactly the type of environment that the "device cal" for Microsoft Windows Small Business Server was created to serve.

So it's important for us to choose the type of vertical market we will market to from a couple of perspectives, including the vertical's ability to pay for our services, as well as the suitability of the vertical's environment for our services. But there are other factors we should consider when determining our target verticals as well. One of these is geography – how many prospects in our target vertical are within our desired service area? This is important from the perspective of resources and dollars spent to market to our vertical; in addition to servicing it, and we'll get into these qualifiers in more detail when we cover sourcing and filtering our marketing lists later on.

Other factors to consider when choosing our verticals include gross revenue and number of desktops. All of this aggregate information will weigh heavily on the choice of verticals we will market to, in addition to our familiarity with the verticals, and our ability to deliver our marketing message to them at an equitable cost.

What do I mean by "equitable cost"? Well, this is simply the marketing costs we determine to represent a good return on our investment. For instance, we might consider it a good return on our vertical marketing investment of a couple of thousand dollars, when that investment covers the cost of purchasing a good list of a thousand names in our target vertical, the labor to create and mail a compelling series of introductory postcards to it, and the phone call follow-up to set

Identifying Your Vertical Markets

an appointment, if we could set ten appointments from this effort. Now because we are expert sales people trained in the ways of the Force, we know that all we need is to be put in front of a prospect, and we'll sell them something, right? Just channel Obi-Wan, and use the old Jedi mind-trick: "These are the services you're looking for…" works every time!

But seriously, if we can sit down in front of ten prospects, and happen to only sell one Managed Service agreement, or Solution (hey – even a blind squirrel can find a nut every once in a while, right?), the return on our marketing investment would look pretty good, especially considering that our Managed Service agreements average a couple of thousand dollars a month. Well, I know that we'll all be able to do better than that, especially after absorbing the lessons contained in this book….*but I digress.*

So if the previous example is a no-brainer when it comes to illustrating an equitable return on our vertical marketing investment, what would constitute the opposite – a non-equitable return on a vertical marketing investment? Well, pretty much any marketing activity where the cost to implement it does not meet our requirements for ROI. For example, we work with Partners who had determined in the past that a great way to market to their chosen vertical would be through a Trade Show. Sounds like a great opportunity, doesn't it? Instead of direct marketing to thousands of prospects with boring, "old school" marketing list procurement and cleaning, mailing and call-downs, how cool would it be to travel to an exciting city and become a vendor in a Trade Show geared to our target vertical market, where all of our prospects come to us? I mean, that's how the big boys do it, isn't it? It certainly is….

Identifying Your Vertical Markets

Are you waiting for the shoe to drop? Okay, here it is. The Partners we worked with in this particular scenario didn't quite receive the ROI they expected in the time they expected it – for several reasons. Remember that term "equitable"? Well, maybe we should re-label that expectation "equitable and timely". I think that would better illustrate the point here. The bottom line is that it's a very expensive proposition to participate in Trade Shows. Don't get me wrong - Trade Shows can be an excellent source of leads – this is, after all, one of the primary reasons the "big boys" do it. But the "big boys" also have big budgets. And big cash flow. And big airline miles. And big expense accounts. And someone to set up their travel and lodging. And, and, and all the things we, as SMB I.T. Service Providers….don't.

Sorry, but I can't help but think of another Blackjack analogy. Or how about Poker this time? We've all played Blackjack and Poker, whether at a party, friend's house, Vegas, etc., right? But how many of us have played in the World Series of Poker? Not many, I would guess. Well, supporting Trade Shows and Events is kind of like Poker and Blackjack – the more we play, the better some of us get, and we'll even win big once in a while. But in order to sit at the table and last through the tournament, we've got to have a big bankroll to bet.

 The bottom line is, we're going to want to choose two or three vertical markets that meet the following criteria:

- We are familiar with it
- It contains numerous prospects within our service area
- It has sufficient desktop and server counts
- It can afford our services
- We can create compelling enough messaging to establish an appointment with

---

Identifying Your Vertical Markets

- We can use strong existing client testimonials in our marketing efforts
- We can afford to maintain a long-term marketing effort to
- We receive an equitable and timely return on our marketing investment from

So sit down and choose your verticals wisely – this is an important early step in maximizing your marketing return and service profits.

Sourcing Your Marketing List

Your vertical-specific marketing efforts will either be tremendously successful, validating your marketing expertise and all that is good and right with the world (queue the nature music)

...Or

Fail miserably, spectacularly and with such a tremendous sound of sucking air that you'll mistake your office for a space station with a malfunctioning airlock.

All based heavily on the quality of your marketing list.

I'll let you in on a secret. This may be difficult to believe, but there are vendors out there that will sell you a fourth or fifth-generation marketing list that is not as effective as a first-generation list. No, this doesn't mean that list begets list, and so on and so forth, with babymomma lists running around trying to get support payments from deadbeatdaddy lists. It means that there is a hierarchy of list brokers, with a few list brokers at the top of the food chain who sell their lists; or filtered portions thereof, to list brokers below them, who do the same to list brokers below them, and so on and so on...you get the idea. So the first-generation list brokers, let's call them "Kingpins", they always have the best, freshest, most accurate lists, because they clean and verify them. Cleaning and verifying is the process whereby a contact name on a marketing list is contacted to verify that all of the information reflected about them in the marketing list is accurate and up-to-date.

As the Kingpins sell various versions of their marketing lists to the....let's call them "Runners", the Runners filter these lists further, based upon who they're selling them to. What eventually happens as these lists get more and more diluted by the Runners, and grow older, is that they become less accurate – information is not updated, and list maintenance is not performed as it is by the Kingpins. So it's vitally important to buy your marketing list from a Kingpin and not a Runner. We've included a list of good marketing list sources at the end of this chapter as a resource to get you started.

Marketing List Criteria

Now that we've determined who we'll be purchasing our marketing lists from, we need to decide on the criteria we'll use to make sure we buy the most specific list that we can. If we aren't specific in identifying our criteria, we'll receive a less than effective list that will force us to clean and re-qualify every contact in it – in most cases if this happens, it would be cheaper to buy a new list with the correct criteria specified – so we'll make certain to assign the appropriate importance to the criteria-selection phase of our marketing list procurement process.

The first criteria we will select will be our vertical market. In the world of marketing lists, verticals used to be broken down by Standard Industrial Classification, or SIC codes. An SIC Code was a numeric classification for the industry a particular company belongs to. Since companies can belong to several industries, these companies may have numerous SIC Codes.

The Best I.T. Sales & Marketing BOOK EVER!

Sourcing Your Marketing List

Here are some examples of SIC Codes for specific industries:

SIC Code	Industry
8000	Services – Health Services
8011	Services – Offices & Clinics of Doctors of Medicine
8050	Services – Nursing & Personal Care Facilities
8051	Services – Skilled Nursing Care Facilities
8060	Services – Hospitals

The above example illustrates how a company or organization can belong to several industries, and have numerous SIC Codes assigned to it. For instance, our family Doctor's practice may fall under both SIC Codes 8000 and 8011, and some more in between. So if we're marketing to a specific vertical, we've got to make certain that we choose the correct industry classification carefully.

In 1997, the Standard Industrial Classification Code system was replaced by the North American Industry Classification System, or NAICS. As you can see by the example below, the NAICS is a much more specific industry classification system than the SIC Code system was. This makes it even more important to take our time and review our industry classifications carefully when developing our marketing list criteria.

NAICS Code	Industry
621610	Home Health Care Services
621111	Offices of Physicians (except Mental Health Specialists
621399	Offices of All Other Miscellaneous Health Practitioners
623110	Nursing Care Facilities
622110	General Medical Care and Surgical Hospitals

Sourcing Your Marketing List

Now that we've determined the industry classifications for our target vertical market, we'll need to determine our geographic marketing footprint. Our service area determines our marketing list geography. Depending upon which marketing list vendor we choose, we will have the option of choosing our marketing list's geography by zip code, county, city or even area code.

The next criteria we will determine will be the number of desktops in the environment. A good marketing list vendor will have this option available as selection criteria. Since our sweet spot for delivering Managed Services is between twenty-five and a hundred desktops or so, we'll choose twenty-five as a minimum desktop count for our marketing list criteria.

Following this selection, we'll next have the opportunity to determine what size organizations we want to market to, based upon their gross yearly revenue. This criterion is important in that it can help us further hone in on our target prospect size. As we are looking for prospects that are technology dependent, or see technology investments as strategic, acceptable criteria here would be at least five million dollars a year in gross revenue, if not higher.

We'd also like to specify the length of time a prospect has been in business as selection criteria. We're not looking for start-ups, but again rather those prospects that will place the appropriate value on our services; and understand the importance in building a long lasting business partnership between our organizations, so we're going to specify a minimum term of five years in business, if not longer, for this selection criterion.

Finally, we get to choose contact criterion. We will specify who we want to contact at the organization. This will normally be the decision-maker, and options will include the President, CEO and CFO. We'll choose the CEO, and we'll want their complete name, title, phone number with extension, as well as email address, if we can get it. All contacts should come with physical addresses by default.

So let's use the Medical vertical in our example earlier to create our marketing list criterion. It would look something like this:

Medical vertical marketing list criteria:

NAICS Codes: 621610, 621111, 621399, 622110, 623110

Geography: Zip Codes 92841-92860

Number of Desktops: 25 – 100

Gross Yearly Revenue: $5MM+

Years in Business: 5+

Contact Info: CEO/President, Full Name, Phone Number/Ext., Email Address

Once submitted to our marketing list vendor, they will tell us how many unique records they have which match our selection criteria, along with the cost for each record. We can use this information to shop different marketing list vendors and decide who can give us the best deal. Remember; however, that the best deal isn't always the best deal, so we're going to ask for a guarantee with every marketing list we buy.

Sourcing Your Marketing List

Reputable vendors will provide a guarantee which covers inaccurate information in their list, and this will vary from vendor to vendor, so we'll make sure to do our research and choose our marketing list vendor wisely. In my opinion, it's much better to pay a little more for a marketing list that works as advertised, rather than pay less for a marketing list with a high "dead" count, or one which isn't cleaned and verified properly– the latter will end up costing us more money in the long run.

As marketing list vendors offer their services in varying fashions, the item that will mean the most to us is the way in which they allow us to use their lists. Some marketing list vendors will sell us their list outright, allowing us to use it at will, and as many times as we want, while others will only rent us their lists for the specific marketing campaign we will be using it for. Here again is a differentiator that will determine which marketing list vendor we will choose for our individual marketing campaigns. At the end of the day, though, if we're going to really leverage our vertical-specific knowledge and experience, and turn it to our maximum advantage, we're going to need to embrace verticalized direct marketing.

Marketing List Resources:

Harte-Hanks: (800) 456-9748

http://www.harte-hanks.com/Interior.aspx?CategoryID=1246

The Best I.T. Sales & Marketing BOOK EVER!

Sourcing Your Marketing List

Dun & Bradstreet: (800) 524-2859

http://smallbusiness.dnb.com/find-new-customers/marketing-detail.asp?cmeid=IOS200246&cm_re=find%2Dnew%2Dcusto mers%2Fbrowse%2Dproducts%2Easp*index%5F3*Marketing +Lists

InfoUSA: (800) 321-0869

http://www.infousa.com/

ZapData: (800) 590-0065

http://www.zapdata.com

Developing Compelling Vertical-Specific Collateral

Now that we've determined our vertical market and sourced our marketing list, as an SMB I.T. Service Provider, our next task ranks as possibly one of the most difficult for us to execute and get it right. Oh sure, we can fix, install, manage and maintain any I.T. product or solution – it's in our blood (*remember…we are I.T. Jedi's, after all*)! This gives us the supreme confidence to tackle any challenge head-on, doesn't it? But just like a bad Jedi mind trick, it also blinds us to the reality that no matter how good we are in all things I.T. – we are absolutely pathetic when it comes to having the inherent creativity and objectivity, not to mention the training, necessary to create compelling, visually appealing marketing material. Material that evokes emotion, and delivers its message in the most economical means, whether on paper, a postcard, direct mail – heck, even a website!

If you don't believe me, just take a look at some of your own, or your competitors' marketing materials, messaging and websites. Unless you're fortunate enough to have an in-house marketing guru, or pay a real marketing company to design and create these crucial items for you, or you're some kind of I.T. super mutant, you need some help here. And that's okay – it's better to recognize our weaknesses and find a way to balance them, than to fight an uphill battle with ourselves and come away with mediocre results that will guarantee only one thing – that we've just wasted good money purchasing a great marketing list.

And that's just what will end up happening – a waste of money on a great list, because if our message and collateral do not resonate with our target audience, and evoke emotion as we describe the pain we will remove from their businesses, or make them believe that we really can improve their efficiencies, and therefore their bottom lines, they will have a tough time buying the testimonials they'll read. Let's face it – effective marketing is an art form. I didn't really, really get it until we hired our own in-house graphic designer, and witnessed with my own eyes just how easily and amazingly he took some of the old marketing collateral that I had designed before he came aboard (you know, that I.T. Jedi marketing stuff) and blew us all away with his talent. And guess what? The results from our sending out the new collateral were like night and day from the old stuff I thought was "getting it done". Well, it's been a long time since I last stepped foot in a classroom, but I'm wise enough to know when I've been schooled, and Roger definitely took me to school.

So when I speak about the importance of getting our marketing collateral right, it's coming from a place of experience and humility – a place that demands we suck it up and admit that we've been trained and molded through thousands of hours of experience in how to design, implement, manage, maintain and troubleshoot all things I.T., and understand that that's why we're so good at it, *but also understand that this is exactly the reason why we're weak in other areas such as marketing and sales*. But I guess that's the reason you've picked up this book, am I right? Okay, moving on…

Take every piece of marketing collateral you've ever created and box it up. I mean literally – box it up so you don't refer to it while creating new marketing collateral. We want a fresh start here, a fresh perspective. We can't expect different marketing results by duplicating our past efforts. We're also not going to use our old I.T. Jedi Marketing crutch – the Internet! So just don't even think about it – as a matter of fact, make sure your browser's closed when developing your marketing message – we're not fooling anybody here!

Okay, the good news is, we've included some really great templates of Roger's work in this book for you to use. Remember Roger, our Graphic Designer who took me to school? Well, you won't need to hire your own Graphic Designer if you use our marketing templates, but you will need to come up with your own compelling vertical-specific marketing messages. So the really tough part is done for you – creating the visually appealing background upon which your message will be delivered.

The rest of the good news is, it's really not *that* tough to create your marketing message for your vertical. You've just got to keep a couple of things in mind. The first is that prospects make emotional decisions. Car salespeople know this better than anyone, and know just how to use emotion to close a car deal. Have you ever watched somebody out shopping for a new car when they know exactly the make, model and color they want? Maybe it was even you or your spouse! In fact, think back for a moment to the time when you bought your last car. After you set foot on the lot, and first sat in your future car, with the salesperson's help, you probably built up the final outcome in your mind, imagining yourself driving that new car to work and on the weekends, showing it off to your family and friends…

See what just happened here? I've just described a completely emotional experience having to do with buying a car, and you were right there with me, weren't you? You imagined the scenario right along with me, didn't you? Admit it – you know you did! Well, guess what? This is exactly how our prospects need to feel when they're reading our marketing collateral, visiting our website, and even meeting with us during our presentation – they have to have an emotional response to what they are seeing, reading and hearing. And they've got to agree with all of the above, in order for us to have a shot at scheduling an appointment.

Sounds like Voodoo or some kind of Black Magic, doesn't it? I mean, how can we evoke an emotional response powerful enough to cause a total stranger to pick up the phone and call us, or respond to one of our follow-up calls and agree to accept an appointment? Well guess what? It happens all the time, and it's called effective marketing. I know how you feel, if you haven't experienced this before from the other side of the fence (because I'm certain you've responded to a direct mail offer as the target audience – I certainly have). It sounds daunting and difficult to achieve. Well, it's like anything else, I suppose – it's easier if you've been trained to do it, and certainly gets easier the more experienced you are at it, but I'm going to walk you through a couple of exercises that will help get you started.

Our marketing message is the key here, and a great message can overcome weak visual design – I've seen this myself. I've seen a plain letter typed in Courier 10pt font sell hundreds of thousands of dollars worth of services, due specifically to its powerful marketing message. On the other hand, I've also seen some incredibly beautiful and visually appealing pieces of marketing collateral fail miserably because of confusing or ambiguous messaging, or messaging that was too technically focused to evoke an emotional response from the prospect.

The Best I.T. Sales & Marketing BOOK EVER!

Developing Compelling Vertical-Specific Collateral

So let's discuss a few key points that a compelling marketing message needs to contain. But before we do that, let's identify what needs to be *left out* of the marketing message. We're going to leave out all the technical mumbo-jumbo. You know what I'm talking about – the stuff that prospects could care less about, like how it works. Here's a news flash - Prospects and clients don't care how it works. What they do care about is if it does what you say it does. Does it improve their efficiency? Does it alleviate their business pain? Does it save them money? Does it make them money? That's what prospects and clients care about, not that it's got quad Xeon processors and bajilliabytes of RAM. Let's leave the technical specs out of our marketing message, if you please – we're not marketing to I.T. Geeks like you and me, who love that stuff, and get really turned on talking about it...

So if we're going to leave all the cool sexy technical stuff out of our marketing message, what will we put into it? The things that our prospects care about, that's what. And guess how we're going to describe it? In a way that tells a story and evokes emotion. So how does that work? Well, at a basic level, very simply. In fact, we've already done it in an earlier chapter. Remember the examples in the "Get Vertical" chapter for the Attorney and Non-profit verticals? We very easily created some compelling messaging by identifying pain points, writing an emotional message in query form, adding a few testimonials, and calling the prospect to action. So let's list these steps for clarity:

Creating a compelling marketing message:

- Identify pain points
- Create an emotional message in query form
- Add testimonials

- Call to action

Got it? Let's break down the Attorney and Non-profit marketing message creation step-by-step:

Attorney vertical

- **Identify Pain Points**

  - Heavily dependent upon email
  - Require remote access to files and email when traveling or during court sessions and trials
  - Use specific line of business applications such as Timeslips, Westlaw and others, which are challenging to maintain and require numerous regular updates
  - Often work late and on weekends in preparation for motions and trials

- **Create an emotional message in query form**

  - "Frustrating email problems got you down? Having trouble getting to critical files in the office when you're at home or in court? Call us now to find out how we help our Legal clients reduce email downtime, provide secure remote access to critical data when out of the office, and quickly handle Timeslips and Westlaw technical support issues."

- **Add Testimonials**

  - Add a client testimonial or two

The Best I.T. Sales & Marketing BOOK EVER!

Developing Compelling Vertical-Specific Collateral

- **Call to Action**

    - "Call now for a free consultation to find out how we are uniquely qualified to support your firm and improve your productivity while saving you money"

Non-profit vertical

- **Identify Pain Points**

    - Depend upon donations and fund-raising in order to meet operating expenses
    - Often sponsor remote events or events outside of the office
    - Often work late and on weekends and holidays in preparation or participation of events
    - Have very tight budgets

- **Create an emotional message in query form**

    - "Looking for ways to stretch dollars and meet your budget? Need a better way to track and manage fundraising activities, donors and their contributions? Call us today to find out how we help our Non-profit clients cut costs, improve efficiencies and manage their fundraising efforts easily and effectively."

- **Add Testimonials**

    - Add a client testimonial or two

- **Call to Action**

  - "Call now for a free consultation to find out how we can eliminate your business pain and improve your productivity while saving you money"

Pretty easy, right? Okay now let's do a compelling marketing message promoting Managed Services:

Managed Services

- **Identify Pain Points**

  - Reactive response from existing service provider
  - Fluctuating I.T. Costs
  - Trouble getting I.T. Support in a timely fashion

- **Create an emotional message in query form**

  - "Unsatisfied with your current I.T. Service Provider's response time? Tired of fluctuating I.T. costs? Is downtime affecting your staff's productivity? Call us today to find out how our Flat-Rate proactive Network Monitoring, Remote Help Desk and Vendor Management services help our clients reduce their I.T. costs, keep their systems running at peak performance and provide peace of mind"

Developing Compelling Vertical-Specific Collateral

- **Add Testimonials**

    o Add a client testimonial or two

- **Call to Action**

    o "Call now for a free consultation to find out how we can eliminate your business pain and improve your efficiencies while saving you money with our Flat-Rate I.T. Services"

Now that you've got the hang of it, you need to create a compelling marketing message for each and every one of your services. That's right – each and every one. What we're going to do after you've created all of your marketing messages is combine them with the included postcard and email marketing templates in an upcoming chapter. Once all of this is done, you'll have the basic collateral you'll need in order to execute a consistent, effective direct-mail postcard and email marketing campaign.

Extreme Website Makeover

In order to maximize our results in any successful marketing effort, it's important to carefully consider each and every method of our message delivery, and insure that the presentation and delivery of our message is consistent across all mediums. When used properly, our websites can be the most cost-effective means of marketing to our verticals, providing a vehicle to capture prospects' contact information, provide relevant marketing material to them, and promote recent newsworthy events. A well-built and easily navigable website will promote trust and confidence to its visitors.

Now more than ever prospects are becoming more accustomed to using the Internet for research as well as entertainment – from home or the office. Because of the fact that we provide Marketing Services to our Partners, including the creation of marketing collateral, messaging, website design, direct mail delivery and call-downs, we clearly see the increasingly important role that websites play in the sales and marketing process.

Prospects for whom we schedule appointments to meet with our Partners have often received a marketing postcard or email from us, and have browsed our Partners' websites by the time we initiate our first call to them, clearly supporting the importance of the Partner's web presence in the preliminary phase of the sales cycle. Here's what the process looks like:

Extreme Website Makeover

Marketing activity and prospect response

Marketing Activity	Prospect Response
• Postcard or Email delivered	• Collateral Received, if interested, prospect browses to URL in Postcard, or clicks hyperlink in Email to browse website
• Before follow-up activity	• Prospect may contact us if interested – based solely on marketing collateral received and impression of website
• Call initiated to set appointment	• If interested, and based upon preliminary website visit, prospect will be open to accepting an appointment

So we can accept the significance of the website in the marketing process, right? And we've already got a website, so we're good to go, right? Well…maybe not. It's not enough to simply "have a website" – we've got to have the "right" website. A website that speaks to our target vertical and audience, and is not technical, but focuses on the benefits of the services we provide to our clients....does this sound familiar?

All too often, we as I.T. Service Providers, fall into the same "I.T. Jedi" mindset when it comes time to put up a website, believing that because this requires technical know-how, we are qualified to create the content and message, as well as facilitate the posting and hosting duties. Creating a compelling website that delivers our marketing message effectively and is visually appealing and easy to navigate is a challenge – and much more difficult than creating the marketing collateral we discussed earlier.

The trick is getting the "visually appealing and easy to navigate" part down. We also need to create a mechanism to capture visitors' contact information, say through a newsletter subscription process, as well as by offering them a free white paper or article of interest if they register. In addition, we also need to create a mechanism to cause them to want to return to the website often – maybe through links in our newsletters that redirects the continuation of articles to a web page on our website, or a blog that we post to regularly. Lastly, we'd also like to have some great client testimonials and case studies on the site, reflecting personal client experiences to our prospects. These and many more features are used by marketing-savvy web designers, and we should be using them too!

The good news is, we've already included a great website design in this book for you to use as a basis for your own website. This design includes everything mentioned above, and we created it specifically for an I.T. Service Provider delivering Managed Services as well as Solutions. Sorry – you'll find no break-fix references here, just a cleanly designed, visually appealing website with all of the content already written, allowing your web programmer to code, brand it and make any additional changes or modifications for *Search Engine Optimization* to suit your organization's marketing efforts.

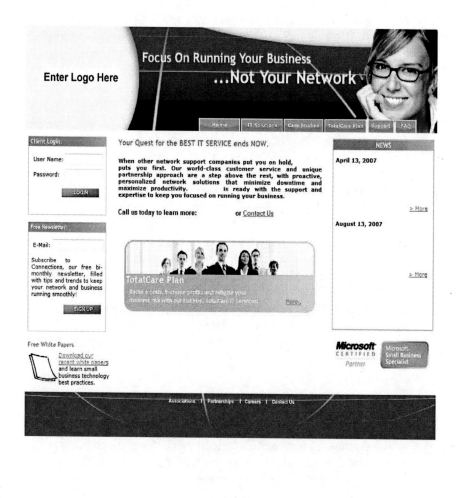

Optimize Your Website with SEO to Attract Your Vertical Market

Do you really believe that just because we've got a great-looking, visually appealing website which promotes our marketing message effectively, that prospects will just begin flocking to it, and business will begin booming? If you do, I've got a little swampland I'd like to sell you in the Everglades.....

But seriously, our job isn't complete until we have a way to drive prospects to our website. And by other means than simply sending out postcards and email to them. I'm talking about optimizing our website so that targeted traffic is directed there from search engines. When prospects search for I.T. Services or Managed Services, or specific Solutions on the Internet, we want our website to be listed in the search results of search engines like Google, Yahoo and Microsoft Live Search. These are the three top search engines in use in the United States. The higher our website appears in the rankings of these search engines, the more traffic it will receive.

Now there are two ways to achieve our desired result of appearing high in search engine rankings. One way is to pay for it, and all of the major search engines have their own services and pricing models for this option, which do not require any special modification of our website to accomplish. Another way to achieve this is to use "organic", or "natural" Search Engine Optimization in our website, which I referenced earlier. As a marketing strategy, SEO considers what search engines look for in terms of a website's coding, presentation and structure, and reduces issues that could prevent the search engines' spiders and bots from fully indexing the site.

The Best I.T. Sales & Marketing BOOK EVER!

Optimize Your Website with SEO

Because SEO is such a powerful way to increase traffic to websites, along with "white hat" SEO (techniques that search engines recommend as good design), "black hat" SEO methods have gained tremendous popularity. Black hat SEO utilizes techniques that are disapproved of by the search engines; as they are considered deceptive, and involve things such as embedding fake or hidden text in pages on the site, cloaking web pages, and using hundreds of questionable sites to build link referrals. In most cases, when search engines discover black hat SEO methods used in website design, they penalize them by reducing their search rankings, or banning them completely from their search results.

We are now going to explore using white hat SEO techniques to optimize our website, and increase its search ranking in the major search engines for our vertical-specific prospects. It's important to identify the difference between generating *more* traffic to our website, and generating *targeted* traffic to our website. Just because we drive more traffic to our website doesn't mean we'll generate more sales, but we will generate more sales if we drive *targeted* traffic to our site. The first step in our SEO process is to identify our ideal prospect. We'll do this by answering a series of questions:

Who is our ideal prospect?

- What is their title?
- What is their vertical?
- What services would they be interested in?
- What key words would they use to search for these services in a search engine?
- Where are they located in geographical relation to our service area?

Let's now answer these questions to continue the exercise:

Title:	CEO, CFO, President
Vertical:	CPA's, Accounting Firms
Services:	I.T. Services, Managed Services
Key Words:	I.T. Services, Managed Services, MSP
Location:	5 Local Cities

As you probably know, when a prospect wants to find some information on the internet, they'll type in a series of keywords or a phrase into their search engine of choice. The search engine then searches its database of indexed websites for a match of the words or phrase, then display a list of results ranked in order of relevance, based upon its particular search algorithms. So if we do a good job with SEO, our chances of achieving a high ranking when a prospect searches the term "IT Services" in our local city are good. If we do a poor job with SEO, we may not show up in the first or second page of the search engine rankings, if at all.

This is why knowing the exact words or phrases our prospects may use in their internet searches is so important. Once we determine these, we will ask our web programmer to use them in the keyword tags of all of our web pages (and the Location data – the cities we provide services in), as well as in the actual text that appears in the body of our web pages – I.T. Services, Managed Services, and MSP, in our example above. Although the relevance of keyword tags has diminished over time as search engine algorithms have grown more refined, it's still a good idea to maintain them. We'll also want to ask our web programmer to incorporate our primary keywords in our page title tags, as search engines pay special attention to page titles when assigning relevance in search results.

Text in the body of our web pages also carries a high degree of relevance for search engines, and when weighed in conjunction with text in page titles, helps increase our ranking in search results. Body content is evaluated by the number of keywords contained within it, in relation to all other words on the page. We will want to make sure that the text in the body of our web pages, in addition to containing keywords, is written in a fashion that will attract and interest our target visitors – CEO's, CFO's or Presidents of Accounting Firms or CPA practices, in our example.

We can also use the descriptive naming of links on our web pages for search algorithms to index on. The more descriptive we make the link, the higher the relevance we will receive (rather than just "click here"). Another factor that weighs heavily in most search engine's ranking systems are the number of websites that link or refer to ours. This is the reason for the black hat SEO technique that involves the creation of numerous link rings for no other purpose than to refer links back to the black hat SEO website.

Another technique we can use is simply to regularly post new content to our website. This can be a news item, a case study – even starting a Blog and posting to it regularly, or creating and maintaining a Forum will work wonders. Any of these will force search engine bots and spiders to re-index our website consistently, thereby increasing its relevance in search rankings.

Although the major search engines do not publish or disclose the proprietary methods and algorithms they use to rank pages

The Best I.T. Sales & Marketing BOOK EVER!

Optimize Your Website with SEO

they index, these are the generally accepted areas that have been shown to increase page ranking in search engines.

The last thing we're going to do after our SEO is complete, and our site is live, is submit it to Google, Yahoo and Microsoft Live Search. This is an extremely simple and self-explanatory process, and can be done online. Links to each of these search engines' submission pages, as well as their SEO information pages appear below.

Resources:

Google:

> *Add your URL to Google -*
>
> http://www.google.com/addurl/
>
> *How can I improve my site's ranking? -*
>
> http://www.google.com/support/webmasters/bin/answer.py?answer=34432&ctx=sibling

Yahoo:

> *How do I get listed in Yahoo! "Web Results", and how to increase the ranking of my site? -*
>
> http://help.yahoo.com/l/us/yahoo/search/basics/basics-14.html
>
> *Search Submit Page -*
>
> https://siteexplorer.search.yahoo.com/submit

Optimize Your Website with SEO

Windows Live Search:

Submit your website to Live Search -

http://search.msn.com/docs/submit.aspx

About website ranking -

http://help.live.com/Help.aspx?market=en-US&project=WL_Webmasters&querytype=topic&query=WL_WEBMASTERS_CONC_AboutSiteRanking.htm

Marketing with White Papers

Believe it or not, white papers are the most popular device used in the industry today to promote products and services. Not only are white papers effective tools to attract leads and close sales, but we can also use them to position ourselves as thought leaders in our specific areas of expertise. A great example of a white paper establishing an individual as a thought leader involves a situation which recently happened to my friend Karl Palachuk. Karl and I had been canoodling over a way to design and deliver Hardware as a Service (HaaS) for a while; over the phone, through email, during clandestine breakfast meetings at industry events and conferences, and after some time, Karl was finally able to put all of the pieces together in a very profitable plan that makes sense.

So I assumed Karl, being the prolific author that he is, would write a book about HaaS, but when I asked him about it, he wasn't all that warm to the idea. So my follow-up was, "Why don't you write a white paper? You could sell it for forty or fifty bucks a pop!". Can you believe that Karl didn't think that people would actually spend cold, hard cash for a white paper on how to make lots and lots of money? Well, after a little prodding and a lot of selling, Karl finally relented to my flawlessly brilliant logic. And guess what? He's now selling the definitive white paper on HaaS at www.greatlittlebook.com for less than twenty bucks – all day long!

But more important to my point is the fact that Karl has now become a "thought leader" when it comes to HaaS – now that's a little scary, if you know Karl like I do…

Anyhow, check out the webcast Karl and did on HaaS at www.mspu.us/Courses.htm.

So a white paper is an extremely versatile tool when it comes to marketing. As mentioned, it can generate leads, help close sales, and portray us as experts on the subject matter – everything we could ever want in return for a couple of hours of time to put it together. Now, although we can sell white papers, that's not the intent here. We are going to give away our white papers to prospects who visit our website in exchange for their contact information. That's all we want – a way to identify who downloaded our white paper, and how to get in touch with them.

Sounds easy, doesn't it? Well, it isn't difficult once we understand a few basics. The first thing we want to clarify is who our target prospect is. Since we're going to market free white papers on our website, we need to gear them to identify and address problems or concerns faced by our target prospects – the company CEO's CFO's and Presidents we identified previously. Then our white paper needs to illustrate the solutions to these problems offered by our organization. Since our target prospects are not technically oriented (in most cases), our white paper needs to focus on business benefits – cost reduction, improved efficiency, removing business pain and mitigating risk.

Because of the somewhat sterile nature of white papers in general, we need to be able to capture our prospects' attention in the opening paragraph, and build to keep it in successive paragraphs. This is why the opening paragraph is key, and if we lose the prospect's interest here, our efforts at attracting this prospect and the time we've taken to develop and deliver our white paper will have been completely wasted. Once we

---

lose a prospect's interest in our services, it may be very difficult to regain.

I've read all kinds of white papers, and they generally fall into two categories – the "me" white paper and the "you" white paper. The "me" white paper is all about the vendor, product or service – you know what I'm talking about, because you've seen them, right? Some of these can almost be mistaken for an overblown, technical repair manual. These are the white papers that are probably the most difficult to get through, and I highly recommend them for curing insomnia – just try to get past the third page without falling asleep. The "me" white papers are normally written for a very technical audience, and if we were attempting to convey technical information to our prospects (not likely), we would probably do it through a supplementary one-page data sheet, or product brief, but certainly not a white paper.

The "you" white paper is what it's all about. This white paper is written with the needs of the prospect firmly in mind. The "you" white paper is money. The approach to writing the "you" white paper is similar to writing a case study, which we'll cover in the next chapter.

Once our white paper is complete, we will offer it as a free download; after registration, on our website. The website design in this book includes the design and position of the white paper registration and download control.

Writing a white paper

- Identify our audience
- Determine the topic

- Create the title – 1 sentence that evokes interest and emotion
- Write the introduction – 1 paragraph that grabs the prospect's attention and describes our conclusion
- Write a high-level overview of the solution – 1 or 2 paragraphs that provide a non – technical overview of the solution. Include charts, graphs and visual aids to support this section
- Details of the solution – 1 or more paragraphs detailing a slightly more technical overview of the solution, breaking down specific components or processes. Include charts, graphs and visual aids to support this section
- Benefits to the prospect – 1 paragraph extolling the virtues of the solution. Include several client testimonials in this section for emotional impact and credibility
- Summary section – 1 short paragraph summarizing the points we'd like to impress upon our prospects.
- Contact information – how prospects can contact us for more information

Here's an example of a short white paper that conforms to many of the points above:

Proactive I.T. Services Save Small and Medium Businesses Thousands of Dollars Yearly and Improve Service Response Time

Every dollar a small business spends needs to have an immediate and quantifiable return. This is especially true for critical services such as I.T. support. If you are one of the millions of small businesses that depend upon your technology to keep your business running, proactive Managed Services will save you money, improve your efficiencies and reduce your downtime.

The Solution

With the advent of new monitoring tools and the ability to remotely deliver help desk services to small businesses all over the world, Managed I.T. Service Providers have developed proactive maintenance plans for their clients that maximize their uptime and reduce I.T. costs over time. By implementing newly available automated processes, systems can be patched and updated overnight without the need for onsite visits, or disrupting an organization's work day.

In addition, remote help desk tools and technology allow Managed I.T. Service Providers the ability to react immediately and assist users when they experience day-to-day problems, without forcing them to wait for an on-site service call.

Forward-thinking Managed I.T. Service Providers are also implementing proactive remote Network Monitoring tools and services, which evaluate the performance of systems 24 hours a day, 7 days a week, and alert these Service Providers of potential issues before they become work-stopping problems for their clients.

The Details

Implementing and receiving the benefit of these solutions is painless for the Small Business Owner, as Managed I.T. Service Providers can begin delivering these cost-saving and efficiency-improving services soon after deploying specialized software agents on all managed equipment. These agents

Marketing with White Papers

---

report device health, service pack and operating system, anti-virus and anti-spyware update information back to the Managed I.T. Service Provider's monitoring systems, allowing real-time analysis and proactive management to occur.

Specialized software applications installed at the Managed I.T. Service Provider's location also track all problems reported by their monitoring systems and end-users, and are used to document all steps initiated for resolution. These applications provide a ready knowledge-base of information which grows over time, allowing swift resolution for issues that have been previously documented.

"Our firm cannot speak highly enough about the response times and the excellent service we receive from PartnerX. We've had computer outages, bugs, surges, etc. (like any network system) and often times I'll get a call from PartnerX BEFORE I get a chance to call them and report the problem" *"The most impressive thing about our relationship with PartnerX is ... we have contracted with an IT service provider that truly cares about our business".*

- *ClientXContactName, CleintXContactTitle, ClientX*

The Benefits

Benefits from Managed I.T. Services enjoyed by Small Business Owners are many, and include increased operational efficiency, the ability to reduce and control their operating costs and gain access to Enterprise-level support. In addition, these Small Business Owners are now able to focus on running their businesses, and not their networks, and receive the peace of mind that comes with the knowledge their networks are being monitored 24 hours a day, 7 days a week.

The Best I.T. Sales & Marketing BOOK EVER!

Marketing with White Papers

For more information on how your organization can benefit from Managed I.T. Services, please contact:

Erick Simpson
MSP University
7077 Orangewood Avenue, Suite 104
Garden Grove, CA 92841
(714) 898-8195
esimpson@mspu.us

Marketing with Case Studies

One of the most compelling and effective methods of marketing a product or service is through the circulation of well-designed case studies. We create and design case studies as part of our Marketing Services to our Partners, and have seen the tangible results in increased leads and sales that good case study marketing can produce. Next to white papers, they are the second most popular device used to promote the benefits of a product or service in our industry. A case study's primary purpose is to depict an existing client's experiences and results regarding a product, solution or service that has been provided to them. In our experience, prospects tend to assign a high level of credibility to case studies, and have commented that reading case studies influenced them when deciding whether or not to engage our Partners for services.

An effective case study identifies specific problems or pain points the client experienced, what the Service Provider did to address the problems and pain points, then highlights the results and benefits to the client of the services provided to them by the Service Provider.

Creating a case study

There are three components to a case study:

- The problem or challenge
- The solution
- The results

Marketing with Case Studies

We're going to write our case studies to evoke emotion, in the same way we develop our marketing messages. An effective case study must elicit the appropriate reaction in our prospects – they need to be able to identify with the scenario documented in the case study, and relate to it. If the prospect reads the case study, but cannot relate to the scenario depicted therein, we've just lost a viable marketing opportunity, which may be difficult to regain.

Our case study also needs to be specific in nature, rather than vague - the more specific we are about the problem, solution and positive results, the more effective our case study will be. In fact, it's a better idea to focus our case study on how we solved one single problem for a client, rather than try to cover numerous issues in the case study. We also want to illustrate measurable results, if possible:

The problem: Spam

"...reduced spam by 93%, immediately improving productivity by saving 20 users an average of 2 hours per week each from manually managing spam in their email inboxes.."

The problem: High Phone Bills

"...saved the client $400 per month by transitioning all of their old-fashioned telephone and broadband services to an efficient integrated T-1 circuit..."

From a marketing perspective, fewer words and more visuals are always a plus. For instance, for an anti-spam solution case study, we could cut and paste a graphic from our spam solution's reporting database, illustrating a week's worth of statistics into our case study. For the Telco bill cost reduction case study, we could create a simple table reflecting all of the client's costs before and after the cutover to the integrated T-1 circuit.

Things to highlight in a case study

- ROI
- Cost Savings
- Productivity and efficiency improvements

In addition to all of the above, choosing an eye-catching name for our case study is critical. We want to make sure we highlight our company name and the positive results of the case study in the name:

"How MSP University saved ClientX over $30,000 a year by reducing Spam" (40 hrs per week savings x 52 x $15/hr)

"How MSP University saved ClientX nearly $5,000 per year on their telecommunications costs"

The final piece to our case study, and the icing on the cake, are the client testimonials we will add. We're going to ask our happy client to describe in their own words:

- What their situation was before the solution, and the pains they suffered
- Their impression of us during and after our meeting to discuss their needs
- Their feedback on the benefits of the solution after experiencing it for a period of time
- A glowing testimonial about our organization

The Best I.T. Sales & Marketing BOOK EVER!

Marketing with Case Studies

Our case study should be no longer than two or three pages at the very most. So let's take a look at assembling our case study:

Case study layout

- Title – 1 sentence
- Subtitle – 1 supporting sentence
- Client problem, pain or challenge – 1 or more bullet points
- Solution – 1 bullet point
- Results – 1 or more bullet points
- Client company description – short paragraph
- Client description of their situation before the solution – short statement in quotes, in client's own words
- Our company description – short paragraph selling our company with a quick elevator pitch, beginning with: ClientX soon found MSP University, an experienced I.T. Consulting Firm….etc.
- Client description of their impression of us during the discovery meeting – short statement in quotes, in client's own words
- Description of solution – short paragraph
- Client description of the benefits of the solution - short statement in quotes, in client's own words
- Short paragraph expanding on client's statement of benefits – short paragraph
- Client testimonial about our organization and service - - short statement in quotes, in client's own words

Remember to insert a visual element if appropriate - a graphic, table or chart. Here's an example case study that we created for one of our Partners that conforms to many of the points in the above layout:

Marketing with Case Studies

PartnerX Reduces IT Costs at the Law Offices of ClientX By $10,000 Per Year

IT Professionals Replace Existing IT Company and Provide Enterprise-Level Services and Solutions

Challenge:

- Needed an alternative to their existing IT Service Provider
- Wanted to reduce costs
- Required First-Class support for 75 users and a 7 server environment

Solution:

- Hired PartnerX

Results:

- Routine maintenance and support has been flawless
- Received an excellent return on investment
- Gained a broader knowledgebase of support and solutions

ClientX is a 75-person law firm specializing in personal injury. Business was good, and when their existing IT Service Provider's Primary Consultant left, the firm felt it was time to make a change.

Marketing with Case Studies

"Unfortunately, the primary person at that IT company left the business and we felt it was a good time to consider alternative solutions", recalls ClientXContactTitle ClientXContactName.

ClientX soon found PartnerX, a Microsoft Certified Partner and Small Business Specialist, who pride themselves in being much more than a reactive, "break-fix" repair shop. PartnerX's proactive, consultative approach to providing service and solutions to their Clients is focused on reducing costs, improving efficiencies and mitigating business pain and risk.

"Since employing PartnerX, we have been able to reduce our IT support payments, but we feel we have gained a broader knowledge base", says ClientXContactLastName.

PartnerX's consultative approach to reducing IT costs, improving efficiencies and mitigating business pain and risk for their clients redefined ClientX's confidence in their Service Provider.

"Our old IT company had individuals who were knowledgeable about specific subjects, whereas each of PartnerX's engineers I have met to date seem to have an all-inclusive knowledge of…. the functions of our network", states ClientXContactLastName. *"I feel that we have had an excellent return on investment"*.

PartnerX offers services including a professionally-staffed help desk to handle all daily issues that their clients' staff may experience, as well as Vendor Management services, which free staff to focus on their primary duties and responsibilities, along with round the clock Network Monitoring, to insure immediate response in addressing issues before they affect productivity.

Marketing with Case Studies

"Our firm cannot speak highly enough about the response times and the excellent service we receive from PartnerX. We've had computer outages, bugs, surges, etc. (like any network system) and often times I'll get a call from PartnerX BEFORE I get a chance to call them and report the problem", states ClientXContactLastName. *"The most impressive thing about our relationship with PartnerX is ... we have contracted with an IT service provider that truly cares about our business"*.

Marketing with Electronic Newsletters

A great way to market to both new prospects as well as existing clients is through newsletters. Newsletters are an extremely passive form of marketing, and are much less likely to be seen as spam than a standard HTML email would – especially if they contain useful information that our prospects and clients would be interested in reading. A great benefit of using newsletters for marketing is that they're visually appealing, and can include pictures, graphics, even video – along with text.

In addition to providing informational or instructional value to our prospects and clients, newsletters also serve to build trust and loyalty among them, as well as demonstrating stability through its consistent delivery. So the purpose of newsletter marketing is identical to case study and white paper marketing – to capture our prospects' contact information, and provide us the opportunity to shorten our sales cycle with them, by fostering familiarity with our services and solutions. Remember – if we're creating and delivering case study, white paper and newsletter marketing content and campaigns to our prospects properly, we're doing a good job of reinforcing our position as experts and thought leaders in our industry.

Another benefit to using newsletters is that we can grow our prospect list by allowing them to "opt-in" to our newsletter list right on our website! The website design in this book includes the design and position of the control allowing this functionality. In an upcoming section we'll discuss tying in all of our website's list-management activities directly to Constant Contact, providing an automated way to manage and maintain our contact lists for newsletters, as well as case studies and

Marketing with Electronic Newsletters

white papers, and giving us the ability to run reports on opens, clicks and click-throughs in all of the electronic messaging we create this way.

We'll always want to maximize the benefit of our newsletters by making certain to include articles that lead the reader back to our website through a hyperlink: "Continue...". This will redirect our reader to a page specifically created to continue our web-driven marketing process, and may then link off to other pages on our site highlighting the specific product or solution the article referenced.

By fine-tuning our electronic marketing efforts, we can significantly reduce our cost per lead generated, making electronic marketing our most cost-effective marketing activity. So what should we include in our newsletters? How should they be written? How often should we send them out? Here are some generally agreed-upon rules by master newsletter marketers:

Newsletter tips

- Create a consistent schedule, and keep to it
- Vary the highlighted product, service or solution – rotate through all of your products and services without duplication
- Write up some general tips or best practices about the highlighted product, service or solution
- Continue articles on your website: "Continue..."
- Call to action in the newsletter and on the web page that completes the article – ask the reader to take action: "Click here to learn more about xyz", "Click here to have one of our staff contact you to discuss xyz"

The Best I.T. Sales & Marketing BOOK EVER!

Marketing with Electronic Newsletters

- Make certain to have a link in your newsletter allowing the recipient to forward it to someone else, and inviting them to sign up to receive it

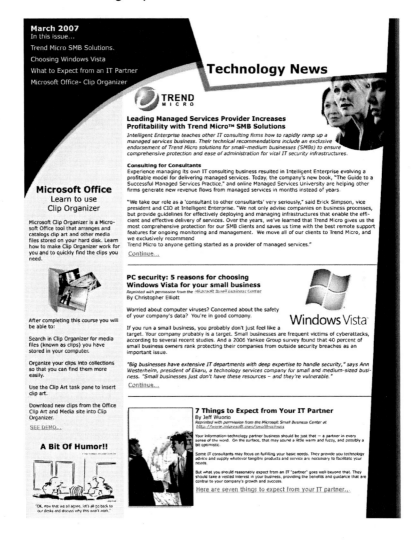

Marketing with News Releases

Press releases, also known as news releases, or media releases, are concise articles, usually no longer than a few hundred words, and highlight newsworthy events about an organization. The format for a press release follows a well-accepted standard template, with little deviation, in order to facilitate its acceptance and distribution by publicity and PR organizations to the media. While originally developed for distribution to members of the news media for print; as the name implies, with the advent of the internet and internet marketing, the term "news release" has taken on new meaning, and is now widely accepted as a vehicle for distribution over the web. News releases are very effective marketing tools that can be utilized to further deliver our marketing message to prospects and existing clients.

It's important to distinguish a news release from a news article. News articles are written by members of the press and published and broadcast in the news media – print, radio and television. In addition, news articles are based on facts and are purported to be completely unbiased. A news release, on the other hand, can be written by anyone, and is directed specifically for readers on the web. Although it is written to closely mimic a news article, the content of a news release is normally biased to favor the author's intent. What's nice about news releases is that they can be submitted to a number of online services, which then distribute them to a database of online news outlets, with the hope that they will be published on numerous websites – a great guerilla marketing tactic.

We will write news releases for each and every new client we sign to a Managed Services Agreement, as well as for every

---

solution we deliver, much akin to our case study marketing efforts. In addition to submitting our news releases to any number of free online services, which will submit them to news and search engines for us if we wish, our news releases will become the content for the "News" section of our website, as well as becoming another arrow in our marketing message quiver (the website design in this book includes the design and position of a "News" component) We will include emailing news releases to prospects and clients in our overall marketing strategy, providing us yet another vehicle through which to touch our prospects and clients.

Components of a news release

- Heading (normally "FOR IMMEDIATE RELEASE"
- Subheading (optional)
- Contact information
- Headline
- City, State, Date (begins the first paragraph)
- Content (include well-crafted quotes)
- About our organization (short elevator pitch)
- - END – (last line of the news release, letting recipients know they have received the entire release)

Sounds pretty basic, right? The only things that will change from release to release are the date and content. Let's take a look at a sample news release that conforms to many of the points in the above layout:

The Best I.T. Sales & Marketing BOOK EVER!

Marketing with News Releases

FOR IMMEDIATE RELEASE

CONTACT:
Erick Simpson
MSP University
Voice: (714) 898-8195
Fax: (714) 898-8194
esimpson@mspu.us
www.mspu.us

MSP University Publishes I.T. – Specific Sales & Marketing Book
The most comprehensive book of its kind for I.T. solution providers provides a roadmap to sales & marketing success

Garden Grove, CA 08/01/2007 - MSP University (MSPU) today announced the release of The Best I.T. Sales & Marketing BOOK EVER! The nearly 500 page book is a compendium of best marketing practices for I.T. Service Providers, and contains step-by-step instructions for transforming an I.T. practice into a well-oiled sales and marketing machine. Included in this highly-anticipated publication, a follow-up to MSPU's tremendously successful "The Guide to a Successful Managed Services Practice", is a CD filled with sales and marketing collateral and templates, tools and forms, as well as a website design valued at $5,000.

"We're excited to finally be able to release the book that our Partners all over the world have been asking for. We've taken our own best sales and marketing ideas, as well as those learned from working with our Partner base over the last several years, and removed the mystery from the sales and marketing process", said Erick Simpson, Vice President of MSPU.

The Best I.T. Sales & Marketing BOOK EVER!

Marketing with News Releases

"We've really tried to cover the creation, operation and management of an entire sales and marketing division within an I.T. organizational structure, from creating marketing messages and collateral, to hiring, training, compensating and managing sales staff, to marketing, selling and closing I.T. business", adds Simpson.

The Best I.T. Sales & Marketing BOOK EVER! can be ordered online at www.mspu.us. The website also contains more information on the specific topics covered in the book, as well as a table of contents.

About MSPU

MSP University (MSPU) is the premier authority on the development and growth of a successful I.T. Managed Services Practice. A comprehensive, vendor-neutral resource whose sole function is to collect and disseminate as much information as possible and mentor its Partners on building, operating and growing a successful Managed Services Practice, MSPU specializes in providing Managed Services training, workshops, and boot camps, as well as Sales and Marketing Services to I.T. Service Providers, Vendors and Channel Organizations worldwide. For more information, please visit www.mspu.us.

- END –

Marketing with News Releases

Free press and news release distribution services

- **Free Press Release** - http://www.free-press-release.com
- **PR FREE** - http://www.prfree.com
- **24-7 PressRelease** - http://www.24-7pressrelease.com
- **PRLog** - http://www.prlog.org
- **PR.com** - http://www.pr.com/press-releases
- **I-Newswire.com** - http://www.i-newswire.com

Marketing with Win-Wires

What in the world is a Win-Wire? That was my exact reaction when I first heard the term. If you've read our first book, "The Guide to a Successful Managed Services Practice", then you'd know what I'm talking about. But if you haven't, a Win-Wire is like a micro case study, or a micro news release, and it can take the form of a postcard or an HTML email template. A Win-Wire is a small, visually appealing announcement used as an additional marketing vehicle in our "touch" marketing campaigns, and employed interchangeably with our other forms of marketing. It's so small, and carries such a light touch, that it's very effective.

Creating content for our Win-Wires is very easy – we're just going to quickly illustrate a simple before and after scenario with a client solution, illustrating the pain before and the positive results afterwards. No client testimonials needed with a Win-Wire – minimalist is the approach here. Nice, visually appealing graphics and colors set these marketing pieces off, whether through email or by postcard.

Thanks to Dan Hay, from isoutsource.com – www.isoutsource.com, for allowing me to use his great Win-Wires as an excellent example for this chapter.

The Best I.T. Sales & Marketing BOOK EVER!

Marketing with Win-Wires

CLARK KJOS
Regional Architecture Firm

isoutsource.com®
complete information services

Laying the foundation to grow geographically
scattered architecture firm with
SQL Server 2005

BACKGROUND
Clark / Kjos Architects specializes in providing
facility design for hospitals, doctors, and other
health care providers. With offices in Seattle and
Portland and a staff of over forty, Clark / Kjos
Architects works throughout the Pacific Northwest.
The firm has plans to expand both offices, increase
the number of mobile users, and to offer
telecommuting options to help retain the best staff.

SOLUTION
isoutsource.com® installed Windows 2003 R2 and
SQL 2005 on an HP DL380 to run the Deltek Wind2
Financial Management System and a planned roll
out of SharePoint Portal Server for improved
remote access.

THE ELECTRODE STORE
Electrical Distributor

isoutsource.com®
complete information services

Electrical distributor switches from Novell to
Microsoft Windows Server 2003

BACKGROUND
The Electrode Store, a supplier of EMG and EEG electrodes,
needles, and gels, had a network that was running a Novel
server and very dated accounting software. They needed a
solution that would allow them to update their accounting
software and have a solution in place that would meet their
business critical needs. Tim Cooke, the owner, wanted to have
a solution in place that could increase work efficiency, provide
remote work capabilities, and allow them to have a new
accounting and manufacturing software solution in place.

SOLUTION
isoutsource.com® installed two servers – an HP ML350
running SBS 2003 Premium Edition and an HP ML150 running
Windows Server to support the accounting software.

isoutsource.com® also provided them with a new Watchguard
X15 firewall, Sony AIT3 tape backup, switch, anti virus
solution, tape drive, and 4 HP workstations. The SBS server
and the firewall were major points of value because of the
functionality and ability to utilize remote capabilities.

The Best I.T. Sales & Marketing BOOK EVER!

Marketing with Win-Wires

GARDNER BOND
Law Firm

isoutsource.com®
complete information services

Law firm enables growth with Exchange 2003

BACKGROUND
Gardner Bond, a 30 person law firm, was running Windows Server 2000 and Exchange 2000. The server had hit the storage capacity that Exchange2000 could handle. They had the option of deleting a lot of business critical email or to upgrade to Exchange 2003, which has a much higher storage capacity. They also needed to update their backup solution as their existing process could no longer backup their data to one tape.

SOLUTION
isoutsource.com® installed an HP ML350 server running Exchange 2003 and upgraded an existing server to Windows Server to act as a utility server. An AIT4 tape drive was installed to ensure that they had an adequate backup solution.

MAHLUM
Regional Architecture Firm

isoutsource.com®
complete information services

Multi-site architecture firm enhances client collaboration with Microsoft Windows Sharepoint Portal Server.

BACKGROUND
Mahlum Architects is a 100 person architectural firm with offices in Seattle and Portland. They had a growing need to share information and collaborate internally and with clients.

SOLUTION
isoutsource.com® installed and configured Microsoft Sharepoint Portal Server on an HP ML370 server. To support increased demands on the network infrastructure, a file and print server was also installed on an HP ML370.

PCS STRUCTURAL
Engineering Consulting Firm

isoutsource.com®

complete information services

Multi-office engineering consulting firm supports growth and mobile employees with Microsoft Exchange 2003.

 BACKGROUND

PCS Structural is a growing 55 person engineering consulting firm with offices in Seattle and Tacoma. The principals wanted to implement a messaging and calendaring solution to support their staff not only in the office but also on the road or onsite at client projects.

 SOLUTIONS

isoutsource.com® designed and implemented an Exchange Server 2003 solution running on an HP DL380 server to support the growth in PCS Structural's Seattle and Tacoma offices.

Marketing with Postcards

Ah – direct mail... the original source of the term "junk mail". Isn't that funny? Back in the day when emptying the recycle bin meant something slightly different than it does today. So I'll bet you're asking yourself "Why should we be marketing with postcards, when we've got all these cool and sexy ways to market electronically – aren't postcards way too old school?"

Well, I guess we could argue that electronic marketing is cool and sexy. And, following that logic, having a postcard printed, posted and mailed might very well be old school. But if having postcards printed, posted and mailed increased our ability to close business, would it matter whether it was old school or not? We've found through delivering marketing services to our Partners, that combining a postcard campaign with our electronic marketing efforts significantly increases our appointment-setting percentage during call-downs. In addition, a postcard stands a good chance of being saved, passed along, filed or pinned to a bulletin board. We've received calls from prospects months after they've received a postcard, who had saved them until something broke or needed attention.

There's also something that registers in a recipient's brain when they hold a postcard – the tactile feel of a crisply designed, visually appealing oversized piece of cardstock (we recommend 6"x9" postcards); that delivers an effective marketing message, is a much more personal event than scanning, reading and deleting email.

The Best I.T. Sales & Marketing BOOK EVER!

Marketing with Postcards

So we're going to include a consistent postcard marketing schedule in our overall marketing plan. This schedule will vary based upon the intent of the postcard. In our previous book, "The Guide to a Successful Managed Services Practice", we speak at length about using postcards along with HTML email templates to verify appointments, and as thank-you's after appointments, focused heavily on appointment management. We still use postcards for these events, but here we will expand the role of our postcard effort to really help attract new prospects and introduce them to our products and services.

Earlier you were asked to create a compelling marketing message for all of your products and services. Well guess where these messages will end up? That's right – on our postcards, as well as our HTML emails and throughout the rest of our marketing materials and collateral. So how many postcards will we create?

Postcards

- One for every service and solution we sell
- An appointment-verification postcard
- A thank-you postcard

As you can see, by the time we're done, we'll have created between ten or twenty postcards – or more. This is good news, as our prospects will build a perception of us as a large, trustworthy organization with expert knowledge on everything their businesses would ever need in terms of services and solutions – a real consultative, Trusted Advisor.

Now that we understand that we'll be creating our postcards by taking the marketing messages that we developed earlier and integrating them onto our postcards, how do we create the

Marketing with Postcards

visually appealing design of the postcards themselves? The good news is, we've included several different postcard designs in this book to help you along. I suggest you pick one of these templates (just one, for consistency); and use it to create the final versions of your postcards, including your appointment-verification and thank-you cards, or use these templates as a reference to create your own designs.

The next step, once we've got all of our postcards created, is to have them printed, addressed and mailed. Now there's two ways to do this, the old school way, and the new school way. The old school way, while effective, is more costly from a labor and printing perspective than the new school way. The new school way is cool and sexy, and leverages technology and the US Postal Service.

Hang on…I know what you're thinking! There must be an oxymoron in here somewhere, right? I mean, I used the terms "cool", "sexy" and "technology" with "the US Postal Service" in the same sentence – well that's my story and I'm sticking to it! Here's how it works:

The USPS Premium Postcard Service

- Go to http://www.usps.com/netpost/sendpremiumpostcards business.htm
- Sign up for the Premium Postcard Service (no fees)
- Log in to your account
- Upload your postcard graphics (front and back)
- Choose 6"x9" (these print nice and glossy on both sides)
- Upload your marketing list
- Set the date you want your campaign to run

- Submit

And that is it, my friend – you've just printed, posted and mailed an entire postcard campaign in just a few minutes, without even leaving your desk! I can't begin to express to you how amazing this is to us. We've done the math, and have concluded that we save about fifty cents per piece for every campaign we do this way, compared to the way we used to do things.

Back then, we'd have one of our staff upload our designs to one of the online printing services, pay for the printing and shipping, then wait for the postcards to arrive. Then we'd have a staff member merge our marketing list and print labels (we'd pay for those too, and the toner, of course). After this we'd have 3 staff members peel and affix labels to the postcards, then we'd drive them over to the Post Office and drop them off and pay for the postage. Bottom line: lots of costs and lots of labor.

But there are even more benefits to using this service, ready? In addition to being able to have only one person manage the entire process in just minutes, the USPS verifies each and every address in your list, increasing the odds of your postcard getting to where it's supposed to go. Furthermore, you can bring costs down even lower by purchasing these services in bulk, allowing you to submit campaigns in any quantity – down to just one thank-you postcard. Oh – and the USPS doesn't do labels – they actually print the address, zip+4 and the barcode right on the postcard – very professional.

Again, I recommend you choose the 6"x9" postcards – these really stand out among all the other mail in the pile, and the nice glossy finish on both sides, printed address and USPS logo in the corner really set your piece off. Remember to include your own

Marketing with Postcards

address in all of your mailing lists, so you know exactly when your prospects receive their postcards – the mailing goes out two days after you create the campaign, and usually takes about 5 days to arrive, based on the shipping class the USPS uses for this service. Cost per piece can be as low as $1.32 at the time of this writing, and again, by our calculations this is about fifty cents less than it cost us to do the same mailing before switching to this service, when the cost of labor, printing and shipping the collateral to us, labels, toner and postage were figured in. I just wish we could figure out how to re-sell this service!

The Best I.T. Sales & Marketing BOOK EVER!

Marketing with Postcards

IT Headaches Hurting Your Company? We have found the CURE...
AND WE'RE HERE FOR YOU!

Save $$ on all of your I.T. support costs.

Benefit from one point of contact for all of your support needs.

Your systems are continuously monitored.

Improve productivity by running your business, not your network.

Eliminate the uncertainty of fluctuating I.T. support costs.

Let us run your network, so you can run your business

CALL NOW!

The Best I.T. Sales & Marketing BOOK EVER!

Marketing with Postcards

Marketing with HTML Email

Email marketing has certainly gotten a bad rap in recent years, mainly because of the tremendous amount of spam that is being generated daily, regardless of legislation aimed at eliminating it. In fact, recent studies compiled from information provided by Google, Brightmail, Jupiter Research, eMarketer, Gartner and others indicate that in 2006, 40% of all email sent was considered spam, with 12.4 billion spam emails sent daily. But don't worry - we're certainly not going to risk violating any state or federal laws aimed at spammers, since we're not going to spam anyone. What we are going to do is collect email addresses through "opt-in" means: newsletter sign-ups, white paper downloads and during our normal telephone follow-ups after mailing out our postcards, when we ask permission to email our prospects a white paper, case study or newsletter.

So I'm going to assume that all of the email addresses we'll be mailing to will be legitimately gathered and we have the recipients' permission to send them email. Okay, so what do we send them? That's simple – to start, we're going to create HTML email templates that duplicate all of our postcards, including the appointment-setting, as well as the thank-you postcards. This is an easy task for your web programmer to accomplish, and we've made it even easier by including some HTML email designs in this book to get you started.

Now you may be wondering why we are continuing to duplicate our marketing message across so many different types of collateral. The answer is strictly "Marketing 101": the more impressions we make on our prospects, the greater their awareness and trust in our organization increases (weird but

---

true); and the more diverse our message delivery mechanisms to our prospects, the greater their impression of the size and stability of our organization becomes. These and other economic factors are why we recommend mixing up our marketing approach to our prospects. If we think about it, of all the different marketing techniques we've talked about up to this point, the only ones that are hard costs are our marketing list, which we won't count, as it's a requirement no matter how we utilize it, and our postcard mailing campaigns.

Remember our Blackjack analogy? We're always trying to preserve our stake and maximize our winnings in the game by playing basic strategy, remember? Now let's add another layer to that – in addition to playing with a set stake (budget), we're also going to try to find a one-dollar a hand Blackjack table. In the old days, when we were doing all of the postcard campaign work ourselves, and paying for it – this was our five-dollar a hand Blackjack table. Then we found and started using the USPS Premium Postcard Service, which became our two-dollar a hand Blackjack table. Now let's add all of the other "soft-cost" marketing efforts to our marketing plan; newsletters, white papers, case studies, news releases, Win-Wires, HTML emails, etc.

This means we can reduce the frequency of our postcard campaigns, as we are constantly varying our marketing message delivery system; saving more costs, and voila! - we've found our dollar-a-hand Blackjack table. This is great news, because it means we can play for a lot longer, winning more hands, and getting dealt more Blackjacks. Viva Las Vegas!

Alright, we now understand why we're creating a consistent theme with our marketing message across all of our collateral.I

Would you be able to continue business as usual in the event of a disaster?

Is your network being monitored every second of every day?

Do you *trust* your back-up?

Did you know...

- Only 6% of companies suffering from a catastrophic data loss survive,

- 43% never reopen,

- 51% close within 2 years...

WE CAN BRING YOU PEACE OF MIND!

Call now for a FREE consultation

Marketing with HTML Email

Would you be able to continue business as usual in the event of a disaster?

Is your network being monitored every second of every day?

Do you trust your back-up?

Did you know...

- Only 6% of companies suffering from a catastrophic data loss survive,

- 43% never reopen,

- 51% close within 2 years...

WE CAN BRING YOU PEACE OF MIND!

CALL NOW for a FREE consultation

The Best I.T. Sales & Marketing BOOK EVER!

Marketing with HTML Email

Would you be able to continue business as usual in the event of a **disaster**?

Is your network being monitored every second of every day?

Do you *trust* your back-up?

Did you know...

- Only 6% of companies suffering from a catastrophic data loss survive,

- 43% never reopen,

- 51% close within 2 years...

WE CAN BRING YOU PEACE OF MIND!

Call now for a FREE consultation

Microsoft

www.serenitysystems.com

A quick note regarding marketing collateral...

If you don't want to go to the trouble of creating and developing the design and all of the content for your marketing efforts yourself, sign up for our Marketing Collateral Service at MSP University. We'll design your website, and create and integrate an effective case study, white paper, news release and newsletter design and delivery service to help you increase your readers' trust and familiarity with you, while developing lead-generating opportunities. We'll also design and create your HTML email templates, postcards, line cards, and PowerPoint presentations. Visit www.mspu.us to find out more.

Marketing with Constant Contact

Embrace the idea of signing up with Constant Contact at www.constantcontact.com to manage your email marketing lists, and campaigns. No, they didn't pay me to say that. I've just found that Constant Contact makes email marketing list management simple, and provides the ability to blast out thousands and thousands of email quickly, and with only a few mouse clicks. A real benefit to using Constant Contact is the ability to have all of the unique names that prospects submit to our website automatically compiled into our email marketing list. Constant Contact will even email us when someone new joins our list.

In addition, Constant Contact provides the ability to create all of our HTML email and Newsletter content quickly and easily, and manages opt-outs and bounces automatically. In addition to inviting prospects to join our mailing list via our website, newsletters, case studies, white papers, etc., we can also place a link in our email signatures inviting prospects to sign up for our newsletters or mailing list, increasing our potential opt-in rate.

One of the best features of creating and sending email through Constant Contact is that we can view an online report of all emails that were opened, and which hyperlinks were clicked, so we can gauge the effectiveness of our email marketing campaigns.

Let's take a look at a report for an email we sent out to a list of 500 names, offering a special pre-order opportunity to purchase this book. As you can see, the email was successfully sent on 8/23/2007, and we had 12 bounces, 5

The Best I.T. Sales & Marketing BOOK EVER!

Marketing with Constant Contact

opt-outs, 145 opens and 41 click-throughs to our web page for the book.

New book pre-order announcement to 500 addresses

Now let's take a look at a report for an email campaign to 10,989 addresses sent on 8/10/2007, announcing the free HaaS webinar I did with our good friend Karl Palachuk. You'll

The Best I.T. Sales & Marketing BOOK EVER!

Marketing with Constant Contact

note that for this campaign, we had 155 bounces, 38 opt-outs, 1848 opens, and a total of 270 click-throughs, 55 to Karl's web page for his HaaS white paper, and 215 to watch our recorded webinar.

HaaS webinar announcement to 10,989 addresses

Email Details

Haas 1
(Classic Wizard)

Resend Email | Copy | Preview

Status: Sent
Template: Custom - Custom Template

List Selection: Merged List   **Delivery Date:** Friday, August 10, 2007 at 2:41 PM EDT

Email Run History

See All Email Reports

Sending Type	Sent	Run Date	Status
Original Send	10989	8/10/2007 2:51 PM EDT	Successfully Sent

Email Statistics

See All Email Reports

Sent	Bounces	Spam Reports	Opt-outs	Opens	Clicks	Forwards
10989	1.4% (155)	0	0.3% (38)	17.1% (1848)	12.7% (235)	0

Click-through Statistics

Email Link	Unique Click-throughs	Click-through Distribution
http://www.greatlittlebook.com/HaaS/	55	20.4%
http://www.mspu.us/Courses.htm	215	79.6%
Total Click-throughs	270	100%

The Best I.T. Sales & Marketing BOOK EVER!

Marketing with Constant Contact

I know you'll find Constant Contact as useful as we do. You can sign up for a 60-day free trial to get your feet wet, and I strongly encourage you to do so.

Section 2 – Hiring, Training and Managing Sales Staff

Section 2 – Hiring, Training and Managing Sales Staff

If you're like most of our Partners – I.T. Service Providers for whom the very thought of managing sales staff (and all that comes with it) is like Kryptonite to Superman, don't feel too badly. Remember – we're trained and experienced in handling technical issues – and sales & marketing falls way outside of most of our comfort zones. This next section will delve deep into each and every area you'll need to know about in order to really maximize your sales & marketing efforts through other people – your sales staff. We'll cover resume reviews, the interview and hiring process, compensation strategies, training, tracking sales performance and managing sales cycles, among other things. Yep - this is where the real fun begins…

Writing Effective Employment Ads for Sales Staff

Writing an employment ad for sales staff may be the first act we undertake in building our sales force. Let's take a moment to understand the differences between writing employment ads for sales staff and for technical staff. Our technical staff's ideal work environment may include challenging technical work, ongoing training opportunities and a team approach to problem solving and solution design and delivery, along with appreciation and respect for their contributions to the team; with high monetary incentives ranking lower on the list of needs when seeking employment, or in their decision to remain with their current employer. Technicians' behavior normally falls into the Coordinator/ Supporter/ Relater areas of a DISC (behavioral) Profile. A DISC Profile is a psychometric testing technique that uses a simple questionnaire as a basis for revealing insights into a person's normal, adapted and work behaviors, and we will explore utilizing DISC Profiles to our advantage during the hiring process in the next chapter.

Sales staff's motivations differ markedly from our technicians'. Being primarily motivated by money, secondarily by utilizing their own special sales abilities, and thirdly by being of service to others, effective employment ads for sales staff highlight these specific areas in the body of the employment ad. Our job is to effectively promote our employment opportunity to the best sales candidates available. We're not looking for anybody that can fog a mirror – we want seasoned sales professionals, whose past performance is an indicator of their future potential.

Writing Effective Employment Ads for Sales Staff

The best sales staff we've ever hired didn't worry about learning every last detail about all of our products and services, and weren't afraid to admit to prospects that they weren't subject matter experts on everything. But they were excellent at marshaling our own internal resources (sales engineers, technicians, etc.) in order to help them set appointments or close sales. These are the type of folks that jumped right in to their positions soon after they were hired, and weren't afraid of the phone.

Where technicians and engineers see things as black and white problems to solve without a lot of emotion, good sales staff are quite the opposite – they are relationship monsters. They understand that their job is to build rapport and relationships with our prospects and clients, establishing the trust necessary to allow them the ability to ask for their business – and they'll play in the grey area in order to get things done. This can sometimes wreak havoc with engineering – whose job it is to implement what's been sold (and make it do what the sales staff said it would!). This is why the sales engineer role is so important – to keep things in check, and make certain that the appropriate expectations are set and met with prospects and clients for all services and solutions sold. We'll get into the sales engineer's critical function in the sales process in an upcoming chapter.

So we need to structure our employment ad to cover the basics, plus highlight the nuances that will attract the sales professionals we seek. In the old days (pre-Internet), we used to have to excel at "classified ad shorthand". This is the process where we would try to condense full words enough to save on the cost of the ad, while still conveying the gist of our message. Nowadays, we have the luxury of posting just about any size ad we like through online job sites such as Monster, Careerbuilder, Dice, Hotjobs and the like for a reasonable fee,

The Best I.T. Sales & Marketing BOOK EVER!

Writing Effective Employment Ads for Sales Staff

---

in addition to having it run for months at a time, if we wish. Let's look at the basic components of an employment posting for a sales position:

- Our company name and location
- Job status – Full Time, Employee
- Relevant Work Experience – 5 years minimum
- Job Category – Sales
- Career Level – Experienced
- Job Description – Several short paragraphs documenting our desired candidate's qualities, the position's responsibilities and job duties (emphasis on generating income, leveraging special sales talent and being of service to others)
- Minimum Skills Required – A short bulleted list of required skills and experience
- Benefits – A short paragraph detailing salary range, commissions and bonuses and other benefits
- A method of contacting us

Okay, now let's take a look at a representative employment ad that conforms to many of the points in the above layout:

Company: MSP University
Location: Garden Grove, CA 92841
Status: Full-Time, Employee
Job Category: Sales
Relevant Work Experience: 5-7 Years
Career Level: Experienced (Non-Manager)

We are currently seeking a highly skilled IT Sales Representative with the drive and determination to help us expand our client base. This position reports to our Director of Sales and Marketing. We are looking for an individual who is a

---

Writing Effective Employment Ads for Sales Staff

---

closer and has a proven track record of generating sales, and is accustomed to earnings commensurate with their sales skills, experience and effort. If you have the experience and the fire, we'd like to talk to you.

Our Sales Representatives are responsible for establishing a new corporate client base through effective prospecting, as well as growing and developing opportunities with existing clients through exceptional relationship building. Candidates must be energetic and focused with an unstoppable motivation to sell and strong desire to succeed. Maintaining accounts requires dedication, persistence, follow-up, effective utilization of provided resources and unbeatable customer service.

This position will include defining client needs through product knowledge and positioning, and involves working with our Sales Engineers in the architecting of solutions. Responsibilities include identifying, forecasting and attaining sales objectives by providing technology based solutions to accounts in Southern California.

Job duties include prospecting, qualifying and closing sales. Overall relationship management and the ability to coordinate required resources to respond to complex IT requirements is a necessity. Other requirements include ongoing training and manufacturer certifications, developing and maintaining relationships with client and vendor contacts, and preparing and presenting detailed quotes and proposals.

Minimum Skills Required:

- Minimum five years direct selling experience
- Excellent knowledge of Microsoft software technologies and programs

---

Writing Effective Employment Ads for Sales Staff

- Strong interpersonal skills required to effectively communicate with clients and vendors
- Experience with HP, Cisco and Citrix offerings a plus
- Valid California Driver's License and Proof of Insurance
- Background check and drug screen required

This Position Entails:

- Building client relationships over the phone and in person
- The ability to sell our IT Products and Services
- Sales Lead Follow-up
- Assessing Client Needs
- The ability to learn quickly and adapt to changing requirements

The Successful Candidate must be:

- Professional and articulate
- Interpersonally adept
- Technically proficient
- A relationship builder
- A problem solver

Benefits include group medical/dental insurance, paid vacation, holidays, personal & sick time. Our generous Salary, Commissions and Bonus compensation plans are structured as Base plus Commission, with initial compensation commensurate with relevant experience.

Writing Effective Employment Ads for Sales Staff

Qualified candidates please submit a current resume, along with salary history to: hr@mspu.us.

Resources

- Careerbuilder.com
  www.careerbuilder.com
- Dice.com
  www.dice.com
- Hotjobs.com
  www.hotjobs.com
- Monster.com
  www.monster.com

Using DISC Behavioral Profiles before Interviewing Candidates

---

Using DISC Behavioral Profiles before Interviewing Candidates

I remember clearly how hit-and-miss our success at hiring the right staff used to be before we discovered the value of utilizing DISC Behavioral Profiling in our hiring process. Based upon the groundbreaking work of William Moulton Marston Ph.D. (1893 - 1947) in the (then) emerging field of psychology, DISC measures four dimensions of normal human behavior:

- Dominance - relating to control, power and assertiveness (how we respond to problems or challenges)
- Influence - relating to social situations and communication (how we influence others to our point of view)
- Steadiness (submission in Marston's time) - relating to patience, persistence, and thoughtfulness (how we respond to the pace of our environment)
- Conscientiousness (or caution, compliance in Marston's time) - relating to structure and organization (how we respond to rules and procedures set by others)

We have not only been able to significantly improve our success rate at hiring the right staff since implementing DISC Profiling, but we have used DISC Profiles to help in team-building efforts. If you haven't read Jim Collins' excellent book "Good to Great", do yourself a favor and pick up a copy. One of the key concepts in "Good to Great" is that of not only "getting the right people on the bus", but "getting the right

---

The Best I.T. Sales & Marketing BOOK EVER!

Using DISC Behavioral Profiles before Interviewing Candidates

people in the right seats on the bus". DISC Behavioral Profiles help us achieve both of these objectives.

Based upon answering a series of twenty-four questions, each with the directive to choose what a candidate is "most like" and "least like", the DISC Profile will generate a voluminous report describing the subject's behavior with incredible accuracy. Here is a representative example of the types of questions a subject is asked to answer in a DISC Profile:

Each question has two answers – choose one answer that indicates which you are Most Like, and one answer that indicates which you are Least Like. Each question requires two choices:

Most Like   Least Like

Most Like	Least Like	
		Gentle, kindly
		Persuasive, convincing
	X	Humble, reserved, modest
X		Original, inventive, individualistic

Most Like	Least Like	
		Attractive, Charming, attracts others
X		Cooperative, agreeable
		Stubborn, unyielding
	X	Sweet, pleasing

Most Like	Least Like	
	X	Easily led, follower
X		Bold, daring
		Loyal, faithful, devoted
		Charming, delightful

The Best I.T. Sales & Marketing BOOK EVER!

Using DISC Behavioral Profiles before Interviewing Candidates

---

It seems almost unbelievable that merely completing twenty-four questions like this can create a comprehensive behavioral profile that we have come to rely on in each and every one of our hiring decisions. And I've got to admit that when we have gone ahead and made a hiring decision in spite of some red flags uncovered by a DISC Profile, we've always come to regret it.

Here's a sample portion of an actual summary from a DISC Profile of one of our sales people:

Brandon prefers being a team player, and wants each player to contribute along with him. Many people see him as a self-starter dedicated to achieving results. He can be blunt and critical of people who do not meet his standards. He may have difficulty dealing with others who are slower in thought and action. Brandon has the ability to question people's basic assumptions about things. He prides himself on his creativity, incisiveness and cleverness. He can be incisive, analytical and argumentative at times. He is aggressive and confident. He tends to have a "short fuse" and can display anger or displeasure when he feels that people are taking advantage of him. Brandon is forward-looking, aggressive and competitive. His vision for results is one of his positive strengths. He is comfortable in an environment that may be characterized by high pressure and is variety-oriented.

Brandon will work long hours until a tough problem is solved. After it is solved, Brandon may become bored with any routine work that follows. He is logical, incisive and critical in his problem-solving activities. He sometimes gets so involved in a project that he tends to take charge. He usually takes time when confronted with a major decision; that is, he takes an unemotional approach to analyzing the data and facts. Others

---

---

may see this as vacillating; however he is just thinking through all the ramifications of his decision. Brandon finds it easy to share his opinions on solving work-related problems. Sometimes he may be so opinionated about a particular problem that he has difficulty letting others participate in the process. He sometimes requires assistance in bringing major projects to completion. He may have so many projects underway that he needs help from others. He likes the freedom to explore and the authority to re-examine and retest his findings.

Brandon tends to be intolerant of people who seem ambiguous or think too slowly. He usually communicates in a cool and direct manner. Some may see him as being aloof and blunt. When communicating with others, Brandon must carefully avoid being excessively critical or pushy. He tries to get on with the subject, while others may be trying to work through the details. He is skilled at asking informed questions and extracting information, but for some people he may need to phrase his questions more tactfully. His creative and active mind may hinder his ability to communicate to others effectively. He may present the information in a form that cannot be easily understood by some people. Others often misunderstand his great ability as a creative thinker. He is not influenced by people who are overly enthusiastic. They rarely get his attention. He may display a lack of empathy for others who cannot achieve his standards.

Here are some other excerpts from Brandon's DISC Profile:

Value to the Organization:

This section of the report identifies the specific talents and behavior Brandon brings to the job. By looking at these

---

Using DISC Behavioral Profiles before Interviewing Candidates

---

statements, one can identify his role in the organization. The organization can then develop a system to capitalize on his particular value and make him an integral part of the team.

- Thinks big
- Forward-looking and future-oriented
- Presents the facts without emotion
- Places high value on time
- Usually makes decisions with the bottom line in mind
- Innovative
- Always looking for logical solutions
- Initiates activity
- Challenge-oriented

Ideal Environment:

This section identifies the ideal work environment based on Brandon's basic style. People with limited flexibility will find themselves uncomfortable working in any job not described in this section. People with flexibility use intelligence to modify their behavior and can be comfortable in many environments. Use this section to identify specific duties and responsibilities that Brandon enjoys and also those that create frustration.

- Evaluation based on results, not the process
- Non-routine work with challenge and opportunity
- An innovative and futuristic-oriented environment
- Projects that produce tangible results
- Data to analyze
- Private office or work area
- Environment where he can be a part of the team, but removed from office politics
- Forum to express ideas and viewpoints

The Best I.T. Sales & Marketing BOOK EVER!

Using DISC Behavioral Profiles before Interviewing Candidates

Perceptions:

A person's behavior and feelings may be quickly telegraphed to others. This section provides additional information on Brandon's self-perception and how, under certain conditions, others may perceive his behavior. Understanding this section will empower Brandon to project the image that will allow him to control the situation.

Self-Perception:

Brandon usually sees himself as being:

- Pioneering
- Assertive
- Competitive
- Confident
- Positive
- Winner

Other's Perception:

Under moderate pressure, tension, stress or fatigue, others may see him as being:

- Demanding
- Nervy
- Egotistical
- Aggressive

And, under extreme pressure, stress or fatigue, others may see him as being:

The Best I.T. Sales & Marketing BOOK EVER!

Using DISC Behavioral Profiles before Interviewing Candidates

---

- Abrasive
- Controlling
- Arbitrary
- Opinionated

Descriptors:

Based on Brandon's responses, the report has marked those words that describe his personal behavior. They describe how he solves problems and meets challenges, influences people, responds to the pace of the environment and how he responds to rules and procedures set by others.

Dominance	Influencing	Steadiness	Compliance
Demanding	Effusive	Phlegmatic	Evasive
Egocentric	Inspiring	Relaxed	Worrisome
		Resistant to Change	Careful
Driving	Magnetic	Nondemonstrative	Dependent
Ambitious	Political		Cautious
Pioneering	Enthusiastic	Passive	Conventional
Strong-Willed	Demonstrative		Exacting
Forceful	Persuasive	Patient	Neat
Determined	Warm		
Aggressive	Convincing	Possessive	Systematic
Competitive	Polished		Diplomatic
Decisive	Poised	Predictable	Accurate
Venturesome	Optimistic	Consistent	Tactful
		Deliberate	
Inquisitive	Trusting	Steady	Open-Minded
Responsible	Sociable	Stable	Balanced Judgment
Conservative	Reflective	Mobile	Firm
Calculating	Factual	Active	Independent
Cooperative	Calculating	Restless	Self-Willed
Hesitant	Skeptical	Alert	Stubborn
Low-Keyed		Variety-Oriented	
Unsure	Logical	Demonstrative	Obstinate
Undemanding	Undemonstrative		
Cautious	Suspicious	Impatient	Opinionated
	Matter-of-Fact	Pressure-Oriented	Unsystematic
Mild	Incisive	Eager	Self-Righteous
Agreeable		Flexible	Uninhibited
Modest	Pessimistic	Impulsive	Arbitrary
Peaceful	Moody	Impetuous	Unbending
Unobtrusive	Critical	Hypertense	Careless with Details

Using DISC Behavioral Profiles before Interviewing Candidates

---

Adapted Style:

Brandon sees his present work environment requiring him to exhibit the behavior listed on this page. If the following statements DO NOT sound job related, explore the reasons why he is adapting this behavior.

- Precise, analytical approach to work tasks
- Acting without precedent, and able to respond to change in daily work
- Sensitivity to existing rules and regulations
- Limited contact with people
- Disciplined, meticulous attention to order
- Having the ability to see the "big picture" as well as the small pieces of the puzzle
- Careful, thoughtful approach to decision making
- Quickly responding to crisis and change, with a strong desire for immediate results
- Anticipating and solving problems
- Persistence in job completion
- Dealing with a wide variety of work activities
- Calculation of risks before taking action
- Accurate adherence to high quality standards

Keys To Motivating:

Brandon wants:

- Evaluation on not only the results achieved, but the quality of the work and the price he paid for performance
- Sincere appreciation for achievements--may interpret as manipulation if overdone

---

The Best I.T. Sales & Marketing BOOK EVER!

Using DISC Behavioral Profiles before Interviewing Candidates

---

- To explore new ideas and authority to test his findings
- To be part of a quality-oriented work group
- Support staff to do detail work
- To know the agenda for the meeting
- New challenges and problems to solve
- Freedom from controls that restrict his creativity
- To be seen as a leader
- Prestige, position and titles so he can control the destiny of others
- Meetings that stay on the agenda, or reasons for changing the agenda

Keys To Managing:

Brandon needs:

- To know results expected and to be evaluated on the results
- To adjust his intensity to match the situation
- To be more cooperative with other team members
- A program for pacing work and relaxing
- To analyze constructive criticism to see if it's true and how it may be impacting his career
- To display empathy for people who approach life differently than he does
- To understand that his tendency to tell it like it is may reduce performance rather than raise it with some people
- To understand his role on the team--either a team player or the leader
- To negotiate commitment face-to-face
- Appreciation of the feelings of others

Using DISC Behavioral Profiles before Interviewing Candidates

---

- To be objective and listen when others volunteer constructive criticism
- The opportunity to ask questions to clarify or determine why

Areas For Improvement:

In this area is a listing of possible limitations without regard to a specific job. Review with Brandon and cross out those limitations that do not apply. Highlight 1 to 3 limitations that are hindering his performance and develop an action plan to eliminate or reduce this hindrance.

Brandon has a tendency to:

- Have no concept of the problems that slower-moving people may have with his style
- Be inconsistent because of many stops, starts and ever-changing direction
- Set standards for himself and others so high that impossibility of the situation is common place
- Have difficulty finding balance between family and work
- Have trouble delegating--can't wait, so does it himself

I hope by now you can see how extremely valuable this tool is, and why we choose to include it as a requirement during our hiring process.

So how exactly do we use the DISC Profile? Well, we will review all of the resumes that come in for a particular job posting, and then determine who our top candidates are. After this, we will conduct a quick phone interview with each

Using DISC Behavioral Profiles before Interviewing Candidates

---

candidate, and the ones that make it to the next cut will be emailed a link to take our DISC Behavioral Profile online. We then review the resultant report, and decide who to call in for in-person interviews.

For sales staff candidates, in addition to the standard DISC Behavioral Profile, we will also have them take a specialized version of the DISC Profile, called the Sales Strategy Index. The Sales Strategy Index is an objective analysis of the candidate's understanding of the strategies necessary to sell successfully. Understanding effective sales strategy, and the ability to implement it to close business, is how we define a successful sales person. We utilize the Sales Strategy Index to identify a candidate's sales strengths and weaknesses. The Sales Strategy Index presents a candidate with a series of sales scenarios, and asks that they choose the most correct response for each situation. It then calculates the percentage of times the candidate chose the most effective, and second-most effective strategy for the given situation. The following is a sample of the results from an actual Sales Strategy Index for one of our sales people:

Name: **Brandon**

PROSPECTING / QUALIFY: The first step of any sales system. It is the phase of the sale where prospects are identified, detailed background information is gathered, the physical activity of traditional prospecting is coordinated and an overall strategy for face-to-face selling is developed.

- (5/9) 56% of the time you chose the most effective strategy

---

Using DISC Behavioral Profiles before Interviewing Candidates

- (2/9) 22% of the time you ranked the second most effective strategy as your first choice

FIRST IMPRESSION / GREETING: The first face-to-face interaction between a prospect and the salesperson, this step is designed to enable the salesperson to display his or her sincere interest in the prospect...to gain positive acceptance and to develop a sense of mutual respect and rapport. It is the first phase of face-to-face trust building and sets the face-to-face selling process in motion.

- (6/8) 75% of the time you chose the most effective strategy
- (2/8) 25% of the time you ranked the second most effective strategy as your first choice

QUALIFYING / QUESTIONS: The questioning and detailed needs analysis phase of the face-to-face sale, this step of selling enables the salesperson to discover what the prospect will buy, when they will buy and under what conditions they will buy. It is allowing the prospect to identify and verbalize their level of interest and specific detailed needs in the product or service the salesperson is offering.

- (4/6) 67% of the time you chose the most effective strategy
- (0/6) 0% of the time you ranked the second most effective strategy as your first choice

DEMONSTRATION: The ability of the salesperson to present his or her product in such a way that it fulfills the stated or

Using DISC Behavioral Profiles before Interviewing Candidates

---

implied needs or intentions of the prospect as identified and verbalized.

- (6/8) 75% of the time you chose the most effective strategy
- (2/8) 25% of the time you ranked the second most effective strategy as your first choice

INFLUENCE: What people believe enough, they act upon. This step is designed to enable the salesperson to build value and overcome the tendency that many prospects have to place little belief or trust in what is told to them. It is this phase of the sale that solidifies the prospect's belief in the supplier, product or service and salesperson.

- (3/6) 50% of the time you chose the most effective strategy
- (2/6) 33% of the time you ranked the second most effective strategy as your first choice

CLOSE: The final phase of any selling system. This step is asking the prospect to buy, dealing with objections, handling any necessary negotiation and completing the transaction to mutual satisfaction.

- (6/8) 75% of the time you chose the most effective strategy
- (1/8) 13% of the time you ranked the second most effective strategy as your first choice

GENERAL: This area represents an overall understanding of the sales process. Knowledge of the process can lead to a

---

Using DISC Behavioral Profiles before Interviewing Candidates

---

positive attitude toward sales and a commitment to the individual sales steps.

- (5/9) 56% of the time you chose the most effective strategy
- (3/9) 33% of the time you ranked the second most effective strategy as your first choice

QUESTION ANALYSIS

- 35 times chose the MOST effective strategy
- 12 times chose the SECOND most effective strategy as #1
- 6 times chose the THIRD most effective strategy as #1
- 1 times chose the LEAST effective strategy as #1

As you can tell, this portion of the Sales Strategy Index reveals just about everything we need to know to not only determine the candidate's effectiveness as a sales person, but it can also be utilized as a tool to improve existing sales staff's skills. The following section illustrates the Sales Strategy Index's findings in a more visually appealing manner, and ranks the candidate's responses against top sales performers:

The Best I.T. Sales & Marketing BOOK EVER!

Using DISC Behavioral Profiles before Interviewing Candidates

---

The following graph illustrates YOUR understanding of the most effective sales strategy in a series of sales situations. Research validates that understanding and applying an effective sales strategy is directly related to sales success. The higher the score in any particular area the stronger your specific understanding of what is required to be successful in the sales process.

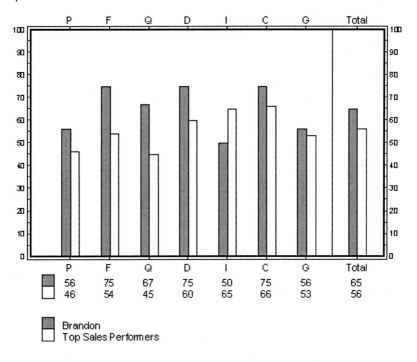

	P	F	Q	D	I	C	G	Total
Brandon	56	75	67	75	50	75	56	65
Top Sales Performers	46	54	45	60	65	66	53	56

P=Prospecting   F=First Impression   Q=Qualifying   D=Demonstration   I=Influence   C=Close   G=General

---

The Best I.T. Sales & Marketing BOOK EVER!

Using DISC Behavioral Profiles before Interviewing Candidates

This graph illustrates your overall knowledge of the most and second most effective sales strategies. The higher your score in any segment, the better your broad understanding of the overall sales strategy required in that step of a successful sale.

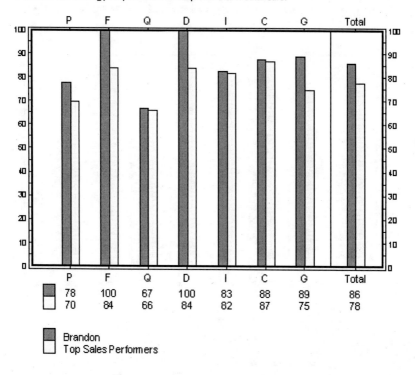

	P	F	Q	D	I	C	G	Total
Brandon	78	100	67	100	83	88	89	86
Top Sales Performers	70	84	66	84	82	87	75	78

Brandon
Top Sales Performers

P=Prospecting   F=First Impression   Q=Qualifying   D=Demonstration   I=Influence   C=Close   G=General

The Best I.T. Sales & Marketing BOOK EVER!

Using DISC Behavioral Profiles before Interviewing Candidates

Knowing what NOT to do in a given sales situation can be just as important as knowing what to do. Your understanding of what NOT to do will keep you from building barriers to a successful presentation. A HIGH SCORE indicates that you have a strong understanding of what strategies to avoid when selling.

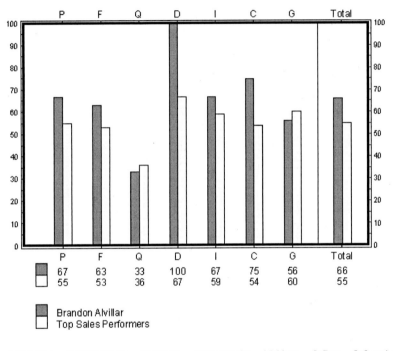

	P	F	Q	D	I	C	G	Total
Brandon Alvillar	67	63	33	100	67	75	56	66
Top Sales Performers	55	53	36	67	59	54	60	55

P= Prospecting   F=First impression   Q=Qualifying   D=Demonstration   I=Influence   C=Close   G=General

As you can see from these graphical representations, Brandon consistently scored highly in every area of the Sales Strategy Index, and beat the scores of Top Sales Performers in every single category save two. Based upon the information reflected in this Sales Strategy Index, along with an evaluation of Brandon's DISC Behavioral Profile, it's immediately apparent that he would make an extremely strong candidate for a position on our sales team.

Using DISC Behavioral Profiles before Interviewing Candidates

---

There is also a Technical version of this Index available for evaluating technicians and engineers prior to making a hiring decision for technical staff.

Because we realize the tremendous value these DISC Behavioral Profiles and Sales and Technical Strategy Indexes offer to any employer, we have created a DISC Profile service for our Partners which not only allows them to run online DISC Profiles for their own staffing requirements, but also affords them the opportunity to re-sell this service to their clients, and earn additional revenue for providing this valuable online service. Contact us at partnersupport@mspu.us for more information, and to order a complimentary DISC Profile of your own.

The Interview Process for Hiring Sales Staff

Now that we've reviewed the DISC Behavioral Profile and Sales Strategy Index results of our top candidates, we can decide which of these merit an in-person interview. Note that we have minimized much of the effort we used to expend when hiring staff in the old days. Those were the days when candidates would show up to our offices after sending in a resume that looked promising, and we'd take lots and lots of time out of our busy schedules to interview them. And guess what? Most of the interviews for sales positions went really well – making it difficult for us to choose the right candidate. If you think about it, a sales person is always selling, or as Alec Baldwin's character states in the movie *Glengarry Glenn Ross*: "A, B, C - always be closing". And that's what sales people do – they're always closing. They'll close us right during the interview, and have us believing that our sales problems will be over the minute they're hired. Their tales of past successes will read like a veritable I.T. business owner's dream. And the really savvy ones will negotiate the best deal possible for themselves, *no matter if they sell or not*.

This is one of many reasons many of our partners have soured on the idea of having sales staff in general – they don't know how to choose the right candidate, negotiate their compensation plan and hold them accountable to sales goals. In many cases, they get closed during the interview, hire a less than competent candidate, then end up compensating them way more than they're worth. And to make matters worse, they keep believing the imaginary sales opportunities that are "just about to close" month after month, until they finally have to embrace the reality and let the sales person go.

The Best I.T. Sales & Marketing BOOK EVER!

The Interview Process for Hiring Sales Staff

Always remember to keep in mind the sales person's current employment situation during the interview and hiring process, and ask pointed questions regarding their prior and current employment history. A great sales person should not currently be out of work, unless there is a very compelling reason for it. It's simple logic to assume that successful, aggressive and motivated sales people worth their salt should currently be employed. And if they are successful, they should look and act the part. A good sales person realizes the value of first impressions and follow-up. If they're not dressed to impress, and speak confidently and articulately during interviews, that's strike one. If they don't initiate good follow-up after interviews, that's strike two. If they are not responsive to your attempts at contact after interviews, that's strike three.

Successful sales candidates will have a firm knowledge of their compensation history at previous employers, and be able to communicate their past commission and bonus plans, as well as their monthly and yearly income for the past 5 years. We're also going to ask them specific questions about their sales quotas, and how often they exceeded them (and by how much), and how often they failed to achieve them. If they stutter or stammer, or begin tap-dancing during this line of questioning, that's a red flag. And as with any potential hire, spotty or short tenure at previous employers is always a matter for concern. Read between the lines of the candidate's resume, and don't be afraid to ask the tough questions – be direct and look for the same in return. If you're not good at confrontation, for Pete's sake, please have someone else perform these initial interviews for you. The success or failure of your marketing effort lies entirely with the decisions you make during the hiring process.

Let's take a look at areas to evaluate when interviewing a sales staff candidate (an experienced sales person will qualify themselves by answering the following questions successfully):

- CRM and Sales Tracking Process Knowledge
    - Is the candidate experienced and trained in methods for tracking sales funnel activity, prospects and suspects?
- Sales Tracking Execution
    - Does the candidate track gross touches and follow-ups, and are their follow-up calls scheduled at their current employer?
- Outbound Cold Calls
    - Can the candidate make at least 100 outbound call attempts daily?
- Awareness of Peak Calling Windows
    - Does the candidate understand the increase in hit ratio of cold calls made Monday through Wednesday, as opposed to Thursday and Friday?
- Call Statistics
    - Does the candidate know the average hit ratio of Gross Calls to Net Calls when setting appointments for their current employer?
- Sales Funnel Reporting
    - Can the candidate easily create a basic sales funnel report in excel or any other CRM application?
- Getting Past The Gatekeeper
    - Can the candidate illustrate successful methods they've used to get past gatekeepers and reach the decision-maker?
- 30-Second Elevator Pitch

- o Can the candidate present a convincing elevator pitch of their current product or service to the interviewer?
- Product Knowledge
  - o Is the candidate more focused on product specifications, or features and benefits?
- Likeability
  - o Does the candidate understand that prospects buy from people they like?
  - o Do people tend to like the candidate easily over the phone, or in person?
  - o Does the candidate make friends easily, and do they have a lot of friends?
- Role Play
  - o Is the candidate effective in qualifying the interviewer during a mock role-play phone call and live appointment?
- Prospects And Suspects
  - o Can the candidate accurately describe the difference between a prospect and a suspect?
- Understanding Sales Cycles
  - o Can the candidate accurately verbalize the sales cycle of the product or service they are currently selling, with timelines from initial call to closing a sale?
- Live Presentation Skills
  - o Based upon review of the Sales Strategy Index and candidate's performance during the initial interview, can the candidate present a product or service effectively?
  - o Has the candidate ever attended speaking or sales training (Toastmasters, Sandler Sales Institute, etc.)?
- PowerPoint Presentation Skills

- o Can the candidate conduct a PowerPoint Presentation effectively (ask them to conduct one for the interviewer)
- Closing Technique
  - o Based upon review of the Sales Strategy Index and candidate's performance during the initial interview, can the candidate close business (role play with the candidate, once they understand your product or service)?

These are the sales-specific areas we will cover during the initial live interview with all candidates, as well as the sales-specific activities they will be asked to perform during the interview. The best sales candidates will rise to the top of the list naturally. But let me throw out a cautionary note here – we don't want to make the mistake of hiring the best candidate of the bunch just because they are the best candidate of the bunch. We've got to hire the best candidate for our organization. This means we must be prepared to see many candidates before making the commitment to hire and train one.

Some general questions we would also like to have answered include:

- What do you know about our company?
  - o What we are gauging here is their preparation for the interview – a good candidate would have researched our website, at the very least
- Tell me a little bit about yourself and your previous employment history
  - o What we are looking for is a brief description of their work history & skills, a narrative of their personal and professional experiences

The Best I.T. Sales & Marketing BOOK EVER!

The Interview Process for Hiring Sales Staff

- What are some of your strengths?
  - This question should not be difficult for the candidate to answer
- What are some of your weaknesses?
  - A good candidate should not have any trouble naming 3 weaknesses – give them plenty of time to answer
- What do you see yourself doing in 3 years? .... how about in 5 years?
  - Is the candidate a goal-setter?
- Tell me about a time when you made a mistake with a client and what steps you took to resolve the issue
  - Look for awareness of fallibility, and gauge the candidate's problem-resolution technique
- What do you get excited about? .... What upsets you?
- What situations make you lose your temper?
  - These last two questions are more personal in nature, and will be explored in more detail when discussing the candidate's DISC Profile with them
- What was one of your greatest successes?
- What are 3 things you do extremely well?
  - A solid candidate will have no trouble answering this question
- What are 3 things that you need to improve on?
  - A good candidate should not have any trouble naming all 3 things – give them plenty of time to answer
- In a group or team what position do you take on – leader, coordinator or support?
  - We're looking for natural leaders here
- Tell us about a team you have worked in

- o What we are looking for is what their role was, again to determine if they are a leader, facilitator, or socializer
- What are three positive things your last boss would say about you?
  - o A good candidate should have no problem answering this question
- How much guidance and management do you like?
  - o We are trying to determine how independent the candidate is
- How much do you feel you need?
  - o A good candidate will be able to verbalize when they need direction
- What type of people do you work best with?
  - o This may elicit a canned response, but we may also get a nugget of insight if the person replies, "People who aren't idiots."
- If budgets were of no concern at the your current or previous employer, what would be the first thing you would spend money on and why?
  - o The answer to this question gives an insight as to how involved the person was at their previous job. How quickly candidates respond lets us know how much thought they've put into this subject in the past.
- Can you send us an example of something you've written – a quote or proposal?
  - o We need to gauge the candidate's ability to write quotes and proposals, if required
- Is there anything that would interfere with your regular attendance?
  - o A boilerplate question which may reveal any personal conflicts
- What is would your perfect job look like?

The Interview Process for Hiring Sales Staff

- This is the candidate's opportunity to push the envelope, and test our response – the more descriptive, the better
- Why should we hire you? .... What makes you more qualified than the other applicants?
    - This is the candidate's opportunity to sell us and try to close the deal
- What skills do you possess that you think would benefit our company? ....How do you see yourself fitting in?
    - A follow-up on the previous line of questioning
- Rate yourself on a scale of 1-10 on Word, Excel, PowerPoint, Outlook, XP...
    - We're looking for the candidate's proficiency with our basic office applications
- How do you respond to pressure & deadlines?
    - There isn't a specifically wrong answer here, but we're looking for the candidate's coping mechanism – we might hear: "It stresses me out when...", to which our follow-up would be: "How do you deal with it"?, to which they might answer: "I just get out of the office for a few minutes, and take a walk to clear my head"
- If you could start your career again, what would you do differently?
    - We're looking for an honest appraisal
- How would you describe your personality?
    - Easy going, problem solver, director, like talking to people, make friends easily, etc.
- What is your favorite movie of all time? Why?
    - Just a question to loosen up the mood, we might find a common interest and chat for a bit
- Describe a time when you made a customer/client extremely happy?
    - A positive, reinforcing question

- Do you mind if we call your former employer?
  - A good reason for a negative answer here must be offered
- Why are you considering a career change at this time, or leaving your current position?
- What do you like and dislike about your current position?
  - A couple of basic interview questions meant to provide insight into the candidate's current state of mind and desires
- What about this position do you find the most appealing? .... Least appealing?
  - We're looking for something in addition to the compensation
- In your present position, what problems have you identified and taken action to fix?
  - We're gauging how deeply the candidate cares to involve themselves as a change agent for the benefit of others besides themselves
- What kind of feedback have you received from past clients?
  - Expect positive reviews here
- How have you handled negative feedback from clients, or team members?
  - We're looking for a truthful response here – ask for a specific incident
- Give an example of a time where there was a conflict in a team/group that you were involved in and how it was resolved.
  - What did they do, how did they handle it? What we are looking for is the ability to go straight to the source. Telling the boss right away, without telling the person concerned or ignoring the

---

        situation and hoping it will go away are not
        good signs.
- Do you have any questions for us?
  - A good candidate will always have questions

These are all excellent questions to pose to potential candidates for our sales position. I'm certain you can now see why we don't just interview anyone that can fog a mirror – the interview and hiring process is lengthy, and deservedly so – we need to be absolutely certain that we do everything in our power to minimize the possibility of hiring the wrong person. If we're going to spend the considerable time and money to hire and train a new sales person, we want an excellent return on our investment.

So let's say we've found one or two candidates that we feel have the "right stuff", and would be a positive addition to our team. Our next step is to schedule an interview with *another member* of our organization. At MSPU, all job candidates for key roles are interviewed by either me or my business partner. If they are a technical candidate, I perform the first live interview, and if they are a sales and marketing candidate, Gary performs the first live interview. Then we swap roles, so Gary gets to perform the second live interview with all technical candidates, and I do the same for the sales and marketing candidates. This second interview will either validate or solidify the decision to hire a candidate, or not. Like it or not, unless we're a seasoned HR or hiring professional, sometimes it's difficult to be completely objective during the interview and hiring process. This is where having another trusted individual available to compare notes with can be invaluable – especially in situations when there needs to be a "tie-breaker" – two equally qualified candidates that we may find challenging to choose between.

The Interview Process for Hiring Sales Staff

In addition, when I'm the second interviewer, I know that the candidate has already passed muster in order to get to me, so I begin exploring other areas that the first interviewer may not have covered – to answer questions about compatibility (will the candidate be able to fit into our culture), and I try to gauge from a gut feeling (I know, the DISC Profile doesn't lie!) and comfort level my impression of how easy it will be to work with and integrate the candidate into our organization. I'll ask questions specifically intended to reveal the more personal side of the candidate, like what their taste in movies or T.V. shows is, what they do for recreation, and ask them about their immediate family, as well as their parents and their backgrounds; to get an idea of their stability and support system, and attempt to uncover any stressors that may affect performance on the job. This is all carried out in a friendly, conversational, "get to know me" manner, where I will share personal information with the candidate myself, a la Hannibal Lecter in *Silence of the Lambs* "...quid pro quo, Clarisse...."

If the candidate stands a good chance of joining the team, it's important to begin building a relationship early on. If we really want to win over a candidate, we need to show them the human side of our organization, as well as the career opportunity. Assuming the second interview goes well, we now have a green light to formalize an offer to the successful candidate. During the first interview, items such as compensation, duties and responsibilities and quotas would naturally have been discussed, as well as a projected start date of employment, should the candidate be awarded the position.

It's now time to formalize our offer to the successful candidate by means of an offer letter.

The Offer Letter

The offer letter will detail our intent to hire the candidate, what their roles and responsibilities will be, as well as their compensation, bonus and benefits plan. As with any and all forms used in your business practice, please consult with your legal advisor before relying on them.

Let's take a look at a standard offer letter:

Offer of Employment and Employment Contract

Saturday, March 17, 2007

(Employee's Name)

(Employee's Address)

Dear (Employee Name);

We are pleased to offer you a position with MSP University ("Company"). Your start date, manager, compensation, benefits, and other terms of employment will be as set forth below and on EXHIBIT A.

TERMS OF EMPLOYMENT

---

1. **Position and Duties.** Company shall employ you, and you agree to competently and professionally perform such duties as are customarily the responsibility of the position as set forth in the job description attached as EXHIBIT A and as reasonably assigned to you from time to time by your Manager as set forth in EXHIBIT A.

2. **Outside Business Activities.** During your employment with Company, you shall devote competent energies, interests, and abilities to the performance of your duties under this Agreement. During the term of this Agreement, you shall not, without Company's prior written consent, render any services to others for compensation or engage or participate, actively or passively, in any other business activities that would interfere with the performance of your duties hereunder or compete with Company's business.

3. **Employment Classification.** You shall be a Full-Time Employee and shall not be entitled to benefits except as specifically outlined herein.

4. **Compensation/Benefits.**

> 4.1 **Wage.** Company shall pay you the wage as set forth in the job description attached as EXHIBIT A.

> 4.2 **Reimbursement of Expenses**. You shall be reimbursed for all reasonable and necessary expenses paid or incurred by you in the performance of your duties. You shall provide Company with original receipts for such expenses.

> 4.3 **Withholdings**. All compensation paid to you under this Agreement, including payment of salary and

taxable benefits, shall be subject to such withholdings as may be required by law or Company's general practices.

4.4 **Benefits.** You will also receive Company's standard employee benefits package (including health insurance), and will be subject to Company's vacation policy as such package and policy are in effect from time to time.

5. **At-Will Employment.** Either party may terminate this Agreement by written notice at any time for any reason or for no reason. This Agreement is intended to be and shall be deemed to be an at-will employment Agreement and does not constitute a guarantee of continuing employment for any term.

6. **Nondisclosure Agreement.** You agree to sign Company's standard Employee Nondisclosure Agreement, Non-Compete and Proprietary Rights Assignment as a condition of your employment. We wish to impress upon you that we do not wish you to bring with you any confidential or proprietary material of any former employer or to violate any other obligation to your former employers.

7. **Authorization to Work.** Because of federal regulations adopted in the Immigration Reform and Control Act of 1986, you will need to present documentation demonstrating that you have authorization to work in the United States.

8. **Further Assurances.** Each party shall perform any and all further acts and execute and deliver any documents that are reasonably necessary to carry out the intent of this Agreement.

9. Notices. All notices or other communications required or permitted by this Agreement or by law shall be in writing and shall be deemed duly served and given when delivered personally or by facsimile, air courier, certified mail (return receipt requested), postage and fees prepaid, to the party at the address indicated in the signature block or at such other address as a party may request in writing.

10. Governing Law. This Agreement shall be governed and interpreted in accordance with the laws of the State of California, as such laws are applied to agreements between residents of California to be performed entirely within the State of California.

11. Entire Agreement. This Agreement sets forth the entire Agreement between the parties pertaining to the subject matter hereof and supersedes all prior written agreements and all prior or contemporaneous oral Agreements and understandings, expressed or implied.

12. Written Modification and Waiver. No modification to this Agreement, nor any waiver of any rights, shall be effective unless assented to in writing by the party to be charged, and the waiver of any breach or default shall not constitute a waiver of any other right or any subsequent breach or default.

13. Assignment. This Agreement is personal in nature, and neither of the parties shall, without the consent of the other, assign or transfer this Agreement or any rights or obligations under this Agreement, except that Company may assign or transfer this Agreement to a successor of Company's business, in the event of the transfer or sale of all or substantially all of the assets of Company's business, or to a subsidiary, provided that in the case of any assignment or

The Best I.T. Sales & Marketing BOOK EVER!

The Offer Letter

transfer under the terms of this Section, this Agreement shall be binding on and inure to the benefit of the successor of Company's business, and the successor of Company's business shall discharge and perform all of the obligations of Company under this Agreement.

14. **Severability.** If any of the provisions of this Agreement are determined to be invalid, illegal, or unenforceable, such provisions shall be modified to the minimum extent necessary to make such provisions enforceable, and the remaining provisions shall continue in full force and effect to the extent the economic benefits conferred upon the parties by this Agreement remain substantially unimpaired.

15. **Arbitration of Disputes.** Any controversy or claim arising out of or relating to this contract, or the breach thereof, shall be settled by arbitration administered by the American Arbitration Association under its National Rules for the Resolution of Employment Disputes, and judgment upon the award rendered by the arbitrator(s) may be entered by any court having jurisdiction thereof.

We look forward to your arrival and what we hope will be the start of a mutually satisfying work relationship.

Sincerely,

MSP University

By: _____
     MSPU Authorized Representative

The Offer Letter

Acknowledged, Accepted, and Agreed

Date: _____

By: _____
    Employee

Once the employee signs the Offer Letter, they will have formally agreed to the terms and conditions of our employment as described. An EXHIBIT A would follow this agreement, stipulating the employee's job description, duties and compensation. Let's review an example EXHIBIT A:

Exhibit "A"

Job Description – Account Manager

Start Date Is Monday, March 19, 2007

This position will require, but not be limited to the following Essential Responsibilities:

The Best I.T. Sales & Marketing BOOK EVER!

The Offer Letter

- Contact (#) prospects weekly and present MSPU Products and Services
- Conduct Weekly webinars for MSPU Services as required
- Close (#) prospects for MSPU Boot Camps Monthly
- Close (#) prospects for MSPU Marketing Services Monthly
- Generate ($) monthly of new revenue to qualify for residual commissions
- Close (#) MSPU Subscriptions per month
- (%) Residual commissions will be paid monthly on MSPU subscriptions sold
- (%) Residual commissions will be paid monthly on Marketing Services sold
- (%) Residual commissions will be paid monthly on Help Desk Services sold
- (%) commission will be paid monthly on all Boot camp Services sold
- All commissions and residuals will be applied against base salary.

Base Salary for this position will be ($) per year.

Of course, your particular business model, products, services job requirements and compensation schedules will dictate how you structure EXHIBIT A.

The Employment Agreement

As part of the HR and hiring process, we are going to require our new sales person to sign an Employment Agreement. The Employment Agreement will detail the sales person's job title and duties and responsibilities, and will contain Non-Disclosure and Non-Compete language in order to protect ourselves from the potential for one of our competitors to hire our sales person away at some later date, and leverage our business plans, processes or other intellectual property against us. Depending upon your local or state laws, NDA and Non-Compete language and/or Agreements will need to be tailored specifically to protect your rights in a court of law. As with any and all forms used in your business practice, please consult with your legal advisor before relying on them.

Let's take a look at a standard Employment Agreement:

EMPLOYMENT AGREEMENT

This Employment Agreement (this "Agreement") is made effective by and between MSP University ("MSPU"), of 7077 Orangewood Avenue, Suite 104, Garden Grove, California, 92841 and (employee's name) ("Employee"), of (employee's address).

A. MSPU is engaged in the business of Providing Information Technology Services. Employee will primarily perform the job duties at the following location: 7077 Orangewood Avenue, Suite 104,

The Employment Agreement

Garden Grove, California.

B. MSPU desires to have the services of Employee.

C. Employee is willing to be employed by MSPU.

Therefore, the parties agree as follows:

1. EMPLOYMENT. MSPU shall employ Employee as a (job title). Employee shall provide to MSPU the following services: duties as needed. Employee accepts and agrees to such employment, and agrees to be subject to the general supervision, advice and direction of MSPU and MSPU's supervisory personnel. Employee shall also perform (i) such other duties as are customarily performed by an employee in a similar position, and (ii) such other and unrelated services and duties as may be assigned to Employee from time to time by MSPU.

2. BEST EFFORTS OF EMPLOYEE. Employee agrees to perform faithfully, industriously, and to the best of Employee's ability, experience, and talents, all of the duties that may be required by the express and implicit terms of this Agreement, to the reasonable satisfaction of MSPU. Such duties shall be provided at such place(s) as the needs, business, or opportunities of MSPU may require from time to time.

The Employment Agreement

---

3. EXPENSE REIMBURSEMENT. MSPU will reimburse Employee for "out-of-pocket" expenses incurred by Employee in accordance with MSPU policies in effect from time to time.

4. RECOMMENDATIONS FOR IMPROVING OPERATIONS. Employee shall provide MSPU with all information, suggestions, and recommendations regarding MSPU's business, of which Employee has knowledge, which will be of benefit to MSPU.

5. CONFIDENTIALITY. Employee recognizes that MSPU has and will have information regarding the following:

- inventions

- products

- product design

- processes

- technical matters

- trade secrets

- copyrights

- customer lists

- prices

- costs

The Employment Agreement

- discounts

- business affairs

- future plans

- marketing plans and methods

- communications

- meetings

- conversations

- training

- emails

- faxes

- documents

- wage and compensation information

- disciplinary actions

- policies

and other vital information items (collectively, "Information") which are valuable, special and unique assets of MSPU. Employee agrees that Employee will not at any time or in any manner, either directly or indirectly, divulge, disclose, or communicate any Information to any third party without the

---

The Employment Agreement

---

prior written consent of MSPU. Employee will protect the Information and treat it as strictly confidential. A violation by Employee of this paragraph shall be a material violation of this Agreement and will justify legal and/or equitable relief.

6. UNAUTHORIZED DISCLOSURE OF INFORMATION. If it appears that Employee has disclosed (or has threatened to disclose) Information in violation of this Agreement, MSPU shall be entitled to an injunction to restrain Employee from disclosing, in whole or in part, such Information, or from providing any services to any party to whom such Information has been disclosed or may be disclosed. MSPU shall not be prohibited by this provision from pursuing other remedies, including a claim for losses and damages.

7. CONFIDENTIALITY AFTER TERMINATION OF EMPLOYMENT. The confidentiality provisions of this Agreement shall remain in full force and effect for a 1 year period after the termination of Employee's employment.

8. NON-COMPETE AGREEMENT. Employee recognizes that the various items of Information are special and unique assets of the company and need to be protected from improper disclosure. In consideration of the disclosure of the Information to Employee, Employee agrees and covenants that for a period of 1 year following the termination of this Agreement, whether such termination is voluntary or involuntary, Employee will not compete directly or indirectly with MSPU. The term "not compete" shall mean that the Employee shall not, on Employee's behalf or on behalf of any other party, solicit or seek the business of any customer or account of the Company existing during the term of employment and wherein said solicitation involves a product and/or service substantially similar to or competitive with any

---

The Employment Agreement

present or future product and/or service of the Company. This covenant shall apply to the geographical area that includes all of the State of California. Directly or indirectly engaging in any competitive business includes, but is not limited to: (i) engaging in a business as owner, partner, or agent, (ii) becoming an employee of any third party that is engaged in such business, (iii) becoming interested directly or indirectly in any such business, or (iv) soliciting any customer of MSPU for the benefit of a third party that is engaged in such business. Employee agrees that this non-compete provision will not adversely affect Employee's livelihood.

9. EMPLOYEE'S INABILITY TO CONTRACT FOR EMPLOYER. Employee shall not have the right to make any contracts or commitments for or on behalf of MSPU without first obtaining the express written consent of MSPU.

10. BENEFITS. Employee shall be entitled to employment benefits, including holidays, sick leave, and vacation as provided by MSPU's policies in effect from time to time.

11. TERM/TERMINATION. Employee's employment under this Agreement shall be for an unspecified term on an "at will" basis. This Agreement may be terminated by MSPU at will, and by Employee upon 2 Week's written notice. If Employee is in violation of any part of this Agreement, MSPU may terminate employment without notice and with compensation to Employee only to the date of such termination. The compensation paid under this Agreement shall be Employee's exclusive remedy.

12. COMPLIANCE WITH EMPLOYER'S RULES. Employee agrees to comply with all of the rules and regulations of MSPU.

13. RETURN OF PROPERTY. Upon termination of this Agreement, Employee shall deliver to MSPU all property which is MSPU's property or related to MSPU's business (including keys, records, notes, data, memoranda, models, and equipment) that is in Employee's possession or under Employee's control. Such obligation shall be governed by any separate confidentiality or proprietary rights agreement signed by Employee.

14. NOTICES. All notices required or permitted under this Agreement shall be in writing and shall be deemed delivered when delivered in person or on the third day after being deposited in the United States mail, postage paid, addressed as follows:

Employer:

MSPU

(MSPU Representative)

(MSPU Representative's title)

7077 Orangewood Avenue, Suite 104

Garden Grove, California 92841

The Employment Agreement

Employee:

(Employee Name)

(Employee Street Address)

(Employee City, State ZIP)

Such addresses may be changed from time to time by either party by providing written notice in the manner set forth above.

15. ENTIRE AGREEMENT. This Agreement contains the entire agreement of the parties and there are no other promises or conditions in any other agreement whether oral or written. This Agreement supersedes any prior written or oral agreements between the parties.

16. AMENDMENT. This Agreement may be modified or amended, if the amendment is made in writing and is signed by both parties.

17. SEVERABILITY. If any provisions of this Agreement shall be held to be invalid or unenforceable for any reason, the remaining provisions shall continue to be valid and enforceable. If a court finds that any provision of this Agreement is invalid or unenforceable, but that by limiting such provision it would become valid or enforceable, then such provision shall be deemed to be written, construed, and enforced as so limited.

18. WAIVER OF CONTRACTUAL RIGHT. The failure of either party to enforce any provision of this Agreement shall not be construed as a waiver or limitation of that party's right to subsequently enforce and compel strict compliance with every provision of this Agreement.

19. APPLICABLE LAW. This Agreement shall be governed by the laws of the State of California.

EMPLOYER:

MSP University

By: _____

Date: _____

     (Authorized MSPU Representative Name)

     (Authorized MSPU Representative's Title)

AGREED TO AND ACCEPTED.

The Best I.T. Sales & Marketing BOOK EVER!

The Employment Agreement

EMPLOYEE:

By: _____

Date: _____

Compensation Plans

Throughout the years we've had the opportunity to work with our Partners, one of the topics that seems to be the most challenging for them is creating an equitable compensation plan for sales staff. Now, as I.T. Service Providers, our perception of an equitable compensation plan and our sales staff's perception of an equitable compensation plan may not always match. A generally accepted industry statistic regarding compensation is that a sales person should generate four to four and a half times their compensation in gross profit. This means that a sales person earning $100,000 a year should be generating anywhere from $400,000 to $450,000 in gross profit per year. Please note that we are not speaking of gross sales here, but rather the product of gross sales minus the cost to deliver the solutions sold (normally the cost of labor and hardware/software). So if our organization realizes a blended gross profit across all services of 35%, a sales compensation plan based upon a sales person generating 4x gross profit would look similar to this:

Monthly Sales	GM per Month	Yearly Sales	GM per Yr	Comp
$35,000.00	$12,250.00	$420,000.00	$147,000.00	$44,100.00
$45,000.00	$15,750.00	$540,000.00	$189,000.00	$56,700.00
$55,000.00	$19,250.00	$660,000.00	$231,000.00	$69,300.00
$65,000.00	$22,750.00	$780,000.00	$273,000.00	$81,900.00
$75,000.00	$26,250.00	$900,000.00	$315,000.00	$94,500.00
$85,000.00	$29,750.00	$1,020,000.00	$357,000.00	$107,100.00
$95,000.00	$33,250.00	$1,140,000.00	$399,000.00	$119,700.00

The Best I.T. Sales & Marketing BOOK EVER!

Compensation Plans

Here's how to read the table:

- **Monthly Sales**
  - Illustrates the sales person's gross monthly sales
- **GM Per Month**
  - Illustrates the gross margin, or gross profit (35%) of the Monthly sales column
- **Yearly sales**
  - Illustrates Monthly Sales multiplied by 12
- **GM Per Year**
  - Illustrates the GM Per Month column multiplied by 12
- **Comp**
  - Illustrates a commission-only based yearly compensation calculated at a blended 30% commission across GM Per Year (the sales person's compensation is equal to a commission of 30% of their gross margin sales in this example)

This simple compensation plan assumes the sales person has surpassed their base, and is being compensated by commission only of 30% of GM (base against commission). For this example I've assumed a 20% commission on labor sales and a 10% commission on hardware/software sales blended to reflect a 30% commission on GM. A more detailed compensation plan would break out separate columns for labor sales, hardware/software sales, and any other services the sales person would be compensated for, such as Managed Services Agreement sales.

A compensation plan for a new sales person will normally be structured as either base plus commission, or base against commission. A base is a guaranteed amount of compensation the sales person will receive each month, regardless of whether they sell or not – but if they do sell, additional commissions can be realized. In a base plus commission compensation plan, we generally see lower commission percentages structured in to offset the guaranteed base. In a base against commission plan, once the sales person's commission has exceeded their base, their compensation plan pays them their commissions only. Good base plus commission compensation plans will require the sales person to exceed their base for two or three consecutive months before triggering a commission-only transition in their compensation plan. This insures that the sales person can consistently exceed their base before taking it away from them.

In base against commission plans, we generally see higher commission percentages being offered, in consideration of the sales person's losing their guaranteed base after exceeding it through commissions earned. We've also seen commission-only compensation plans, but have found that it's much more difficult to attract top talent with this type of compensation plan, as a seasoned sales person will know that it takes time to ramp up in a new sales position, and gain product and sales-specific knowledge in any new opportunity, and will not want to risk the possibility of receiving no income until they've made their first sale.

Current trends reflect that a base salary in our industry should fall somewhere between 15% and 40% of a sales person's total compensation, with the balance of 60% to 85% being made up in commissions. Following this logic, a well-balanced compensation plan would then be structured so that 35% of a new sales person's total compensation would be realized by a base salary, and the remaining 65% earned in commissions in a base plus commission compensation plan. So in our example in the previous table, a base of roughly $3,500 per month would be assigned to a new sales person. As they gain experience and become more successful at closing sales, their additional commissions would increase their total compensation. In a base against commission plan, we would still assign a base monthly amount of roughly $3,500 per month, but as soon as the sales person's commissions exceeds this base for an established period of time, their compensation would revert to a commission-only structure. As mentioned earlier, we would likely modify both our base and commission percentages based upon whether our compensation plan is based upon base plus commission, base against commission, or commission only.

We feel that sales staff should be compensated for all services they sell or influence, and like the idea of providing them an additional residual commission for annuity-based sales for products such as Managed Services Agreements. One strategy to compensate for these types of sales is to commission the sales person an amount equal to one month of the service agreement's value, paid out over a period of time, or all at once. For example, if a Managed Services Agreement worth $1,000 a month is sold, we have some Partners who will compensate their sales staff $1,000 as a commission for the sale. Some do it all at once, and some break it up over a period of months. This commission would be in addition to any other annuity-based residuals which might be included in their compensation plan. Not all of our Partners offer annuity-based commissions for these sales after the fact, but for the ones that do, they generally vary from 1% to 5%, and are sometimes governed by a sliding scale based upon the monthly value of the agreement, as well as other factors, such as the length of the agreement. Take a look at the following example of a Managed Services Agreement residual commission strategy:

Monthly	GM	Commission	Monthly Annuity
$0-$500	50%	5%	$0-$12.50
$501-$1500	50%	4%	$13.00-$30.00
$1501-$3500	50%	3%	$31.00-$52.50
$3501-$7500	50%	2%	$53.00-$75.00
$7501+	50%	1%	$76.00-$?

Here's how to read the table:

- **Monthly**
    - Illustrates the value of the monthly invoice for the Managed Services Agreement
- **GM**
    - Illustrates the gross margin of the Monthly column
- **Commission**
    - Illustrates the sliding commission scale based upon the value in the Monthly column
- **Monthly Annuity**
    - Illustrates the monthly annuity amount commissionable to the sales person for each Managed Services Agreement sold

Compensation Plans

We've also seen compensation plans that commission on the aggregate value of all Managed Services Agreements sold by the sales person, rather than a commission amount based upon each individual agreement's monthly value, per the previous table. In any case, the idea here is to provide an additional incentive for the sales person to remain in the company's employ. We recommend there be an established minimum new sales quota that the sales person must meet each month in order to qualify to receive their residual commissions. We don't want to create a situation where the sales person can take a month off and continue to receive their residuals – we commission on performance only.

Many of our Partners also commission a percentage of the first month's agreement value upon renewal. So if a client renews a Managed Service Agreement worth $1,000 per month, a 50% commission would net the sales person a $500 commission. Again, the percentage of commission on renewals varies among our Partners; if it's offered at all, as well as it's method of distribution.

It's completely up to you what your staff's sales compensation, bonus and commission structure will be. Just remember to make certain to determine what your actual gross margins are for each product or service you deliver, and commission only on this number – as it's a key to insuring profitability. Also keep in mind that you have the ability to modify your compensation and commission plan at any time – unless you specifically stipulate in writing to the opposite (which I would strongly advise against). Although it's never popular among sales staff when compensation plans are re-written, sometimes we have no choice, due to any number of factors, including the cost of service delivery, new services and solutions, or just to maintain or increase profitability!

Compensation Plans

A common belief among our Partners is that a sales person should have some sort of cap on their compensation. We don't share that belief. Remember, a sales person is driven first and foremost by their compensation, and if they're consistently producing anywhere near four and a half times their compensation in gross margin sales, why would we ever think of stifling their drive to excel? Keep in mind that a good compensation plan is one that is crafted to take into account individual hardware and project sales, as well as service agreement sales, and all other revenue-generating solutions. What about renewals on service agreements and license renewals (such as Antivirus or other yearly renewal fees – think firewall services) – should we compensate for these as well? We think so, but at a smaller percentage. In general terms, a sales person should be compensated for each and every revenue-generating sale they influence. And when selling annuity-based products and services, we believe they should earn an annuity as well. Talk about an awesome plan for keeping great sales staff – the greater their annuity revenue grows, the more difficult it is for them to walk away from it.

Again, they'll need to qualify to receive their annuity and other bonuses each and every month by reaching minimum sales goals, and remember - because we're paying them a base against commissions, as soon as their commissions surpass their base, their compensation becomes based solely on commissions.

Let's break down the commission to a sales person for a new project they've sold. Let's say we've got an infrastructure project valued at $60,000, with labor comprising $25,000, and the hardware/software portion comprising $35,000 of the total invoice. Let's also assume that our margin on the labor is 40% of the total billable cost, and the margin on hardware and

The Best I.T. Sales & Marketing BOOK EVER!

Compensation Plans

software is 15%. In this example, our sales person's commission will be based upon these gross margin numbers. So what is our sales person's commission? Let's choose a 20% commission on labor sales, and a 10% commission for hardware/software sales for this particular scenario. Now let's calculate our gross margin on this project sale:

Labor Cost	GM	Commissionable Labor
$25,000	40%	$10,000

HW/SW Cost	GM	Commissionable HW/SW
$25,000	15%	$5,250

Now that we've figured out our gross margins, let's calculate the sales person's commission on this sale:

Commissionable Labor	Commission Rate	Commission
$10,000	20%	$2,000

Commissionable HW/SW	Commission Rate	Commission
$5,250	10%	$525

Total Commission		$2,525

The Best I.T. Sales & Marketing BOOK EVER!

Compensation Plans

So our sales person's total commission for this $60,000 project sale is $2,525. Let's now take a look at a very simple commission plan displayed in the following table:

Project Sales Commission Plan

GM Labor	Labor Commission	GM HW/SW	HW/SW Commission
$1-$5,000	10%	$1-$5,000	5%
$5,001-$15,000	15%	$5,001-$15,000	7%
$15,001+	20%	$15,001+	10%

Here's how to read the table:

- **GM Labor**
  - Illustrates the gross margin value of the invoiced amount of project labor
- **Labor Commission**
  - Illustrates the commission percentage paid on the GM Labor column
- **GM HW/SW**
  - Illustrates the gross margin value of the invoiced amount of project hardware and software
- **HW/SW Commission**
  - Illustrates the commission percentage paid on the GM HW/SW column

Are you getting the idea? Once you've determined what your own gross margins are for project labor and hardware/software sales, Managed Services deliverables, and all of your other products and services, you'll be able to create a compensation

---

plan that rewards performance, while guaranteeing profitability. Remember to include monthly and quarterly sales goals that the sales person will need to achieve, and bonus on their attainment as you see appropriate. A yearly bonus for achieving a stretch goal is always a great motivator for keeping sales people selling through the fourth quarter, where it becomes more difficult to close business due to the holiday season, when decision-maker availability is at a premium.

So let's review some key points to think about when developing our compensation plan for sales staff:

- Calculate our gross margin for every single product or service we sell
  - This is critical in determining our base salary and commission plans
  - Forecast how much of each product and service you offer a trained, aggressive sales person could sell monthly and yearly in aggregate
- Decide on what our base salary and commission structure will be
  - Remember – a well-balanced compensation plan suggests that a sales person's base salary should be 35% of their total compensation
  - The balance of our sales person's salary should be attained through commissions earned
  - Use your forecasted sales potential as a guide here
- Decide on an equitable commission percentage for each of your products and services based upon gross profit, or margin

---

- o Use your base salary and commission structuring exercise as a guide, and standardize upon it
- Decide on whether or not to include annuity, or residuals as commission for annuity-based services
  - o This decision will affect your calculations in terms of exponential residuals paid to sales people – forecast out residual payments based upon sales potential for ten years – this will significantly affect the residual percentage you're willing to offer them
- Decide on whether or not to commission on renewals of licensing, services, warranties and service agreements
  - o Again, factor in your commission percentages based upon sales potential, and calculate commissions accordingly

Wow – it's a lot to consider, isn't it? But when your compensation plan is complete, you'll be much better prepared to negotiate with potential new sales staff hires – secure in the fact that your compensation plan is fair, and insures your profitability through their success. It will be much more difficult for a savvy sales person to convince you to let them write their own meal ticket, once you've hammered out the numbers and have them documented as a standard.

Okay, so let's put it all together in a very basic table for analysis:

The Best I.T. Sales & Marketing BOOK EVER!

Compensation Plans

Hardware/Software Commissions

GM HW/SW	HW/SW Commission
$1-$5,000	5%
$5,001-$15,000	7%
$15,001+	10%

Project Commissions

GM Labor	Labor Commission	GM HW/SW	HW/SW Commission
$1-$5,000	10%	$1-$5,000	5%
$5,001-$15,000	15%	$5,001-$15,000	7%
$15,001+	20%	$15,001+	10%

Managed Services Agreements Commissions

Monthly	GM	Commission	Monthly Annuity
$0-$500	50%	5%	$0-$12.50
$501-$1500	50%	4%	$13.00-$30.00
$1501-$3500	50%	3%	$31.00-$52.50
$3501-$7500	50%	2%	$53.00-$75.00
$7501+	50%	1%	$76.00-$?

Managed Services, Software License and Product Warranty Renewal Commissions

Renewal Fee	GM	Commission
Any	10%	10%
Any	20%	20%
Any	30%	30%
Any	40%	40%
Any	50%	50%

Keep in mind that all commissions are paid on GM, so in the *Managed Services, Software License and Product Warranty Renewal Commissions* table, the values in the Commission column are calculated as a percentage of the corresponding GM column. For example, if a Cisco SmartNet renewal is invoiced at $450, and our GM is $90, or 20%, then our sales person's commission is 20% of our GM, or $18, for facilitating that renewal.

Now I hope I've done a decent job of taking some of the confusion out of this nebulous topic for you – or scrambled your brain beyond all hope of repair! Please do not take any of the figures in this chapter as gospel – I've gratuitously borrowed some from I.T. think-tank organizations, others from Partners, and the rest from our own experience to illustrate the concept. Don't think that by reading this chapter you will be able to save yourself some homework and come away with a ready-made compensation plan that you can simply slap your company's name on, implement and be successful.

You've got to do your own legwork and investigation into what your true margins and profitability are for each of your services, products and solutions. From there, you've got to dig down deep into your gut and come up with a realistic expectation of how much of each of the above a trained sales person can sell in a year's time. Then you've got to take all that, shake it up (not stirred, if you please) and create an attractive compensation plan that allows your sales staff to earn 65%+ of their salary through commissions and bonuses.

Sound challenging? It gets better - you're going to review your compensation plan every six months; if not quarterly in the beginning, and make necessary adjustments – just like a disaster recovery plan, a good compensation plan requires regular review and updating, if necessary. But I guarantee that if you follow the basic strategy (there's that Blackjack reference again) laid out in this chapter, you'll be much more successful in your efforts at creating an equitable compensation plan that focuses on maintaining profitability, while motivating and incenting your sales staff.

Training Sales Staff

The function of training sales staff is obviously much different than training technical staff, when job-specific areas of training are delivered. In addition to training sales staff in our overall day-to-day operations and functions, we've got to make certain we spend the time necessary, and deliver the training required to make our sales staff successful, in order to receive the maximum return on our hiring investment. One major difference in the training process for sales staff versus technical staff is the amount of role-playing we will be conducting. We will require our sales staff to role-play each function of their job description that involves contact with suspects, prospects and clients. This includes cold calling, appointment setting, and each type of prospect and client meeting, covering every aspect of the sales cycle. Like the old adage says, practice makes perfect. A sales person has a much better chance at success once they've been drilled in each of these components – to the point that they can train others in them.

Let's identify the common training that we'll deliver to all staff, regardless of their job description, before we get into sales-specific training topics:

- Company Overview Training
  - Vision, mission, values, philosophy, goals
- HR Process Training
  - Overview of compensation, benefits, conduct, sick day and vacation policy, Employee handbook, acceptable use policy
- Administrative Setup and Training

- o User and email account creation, telco account, extension and voicemail creation,
- o Use of company equipment (cell phone, PC, laptop, etc.)
- o Use of company software, Instant Messaging, remote access and remote email
- Formal introduction to management and staff
  - o Tour of facility
  - o Introduction to all management and staff

The above points cover in broad strokes some of the tasks associated with any new employee's basic training and indoctrination to an organization – of course, your policies and procedures may differ from those illustrated.

So what <u>sales staff-specific</u> training do we need to deliver to insure our sales person's success? Let's highlight some of the obvious areas for our sales manager to address:

- Product and Service Training
  - o We need to make certain we spend the time needed in order to bring our sales person up to speed on every one of the products and services they will be selling. This training includes GM and retail pricing, along with features and benefits for the client. We may also avail ourselves of vendor-delivered training; if available, through webcasts or live events.
  - o It's a good idea to select two or three products or services to train the sales person on initially, and create a sixty or ninety-day training calendar to cover the rest, so as not to overwhelm them, and allow them the

opportunity to begin selling in a shorter period of time. We'll prioritize the products and services on our training schedule based upon those items in the sales person's compensation plan that they can experience early success in closing with, as well as earning additional commissions – early success is a great confidence builder and motivator for a new sales person.

- Lead Generation Training
    - We will train our sales person on all of the ways we generate leads for our products and services, and which activities it will be the sales person's responsibility to perform.
        - Direct mail
        - E-mail, E-newsletters, case studies, news releases, win-wires, website
        - Events
        - Networking groups
        - Cold calls and call-downs
- Sales Tracking Training
    - We'll want to train our sales person in the proper operation and navigation of our CRM or Sales Management solution. We'll spend as much time here as necessary – the sales person must understand the value of working the system properly, tracking all marketing and sales activity – mailings, calls, appointments and follow-ups, and documenting each interaction, assigning the appropriate status for suspects and prospects, along with the potential value of all opportunities in their sales funnel.

- Sales Process Training
  - We'll need to guide our sales person through the entire sales cycle for each and every solution they will eventually be selling, identifying each action, followed by a timeline to trigger the next action in the sales cycle. For example:
    - Marketing campaign begins with postcard
    - 3 days later, follow-up call made, postcard receipt verified, contact information verified, 1st attempt at appointment setting
    - Appointment scheduled
    - 1st appointment completed, needs analysis performed
    - 1 day later, meet with sales engineer to discuss, approve solution
    - 2 days later, quote completed, call initiated to schedule follow-up appointment
    - Follow-up appointment completed
    - Project approved, initial payment made
    - Project handed off to sales engineer and project manager for ordering and scheduling
    - Project completed, balance of payment made
- Sales Expectations
  - It's important to clearly define our expectations of our sales person. We need to set clear, attainable sales goals for them, and continually review them, adjusting them as the sales person becomes more experienced and successful.

- Self-study
  - We will require our sales person to continue to educate themselves on their own time, and assign resources for them to explore, and books and articles for them to complete on a continuing basis.
    - Good to Great by Jim Collins
    - Execution – The Discipline Of Getting Things Done by Larry Bossidy and Ram Charan
    - The E-Myth, E-Myth Mastery by Michael Gerber
    - Who Moved My Cheese? by Spencer Johnson
    - The Accidental Sales Person by Chris Lytle
    - Solution Selling by Michael T. Bosworth
- Sales Meetings and Reporting
  - It's important that our sales manager enforces attendance to regular sales meetings, and defines the reporting mechanisms we will use to monitor performance of our sales staff during these meetings, as well as opportunity status.
- Listen-ins and Ride-alongs
  - One of the best ways to bring a new sales person up to speed is to have them listen in on every type of phone engagement made by another member of the sales team (or ourselves, if this is our first sales hire)
    - Cold calls and call-downs
    - Appointment setting
    - Conference calls
  - We'll also want to make certain the new sales person goes on as many field engagements as

possible with another member of the sales team or ourselves

- All appointments
  - Needs analysis
  - Cost-savings analysis
  - Network analysis
  - Client presentations
  - Closing the deal
  - Etc.
- Role-play, role-play, role-play
  - It is imperative that we require our sales staff to role-play each type of engagement they will conduct with suspects, prospects and clients with our sales manager, other sales staff or ourselves. This point can't be stressed enough. In the sales boot camps we conduct for our Partners, the experience attendees receive the most value from is the intense role-playing we put them through, where their performance is judged by our instructors, as well as their peers. Our sales staff's initial confidence and success will in large part be derived from the amount and quality of the role-playing that we require them to conduct.

The Sales Manager

When is it a good time to hire a sales manager, what is their function, and how do we compensate them? Basic management 101 teaches us that one person can manage four or five people effectively, so how do we apply this concept to ourselves as I.T. Service Providers? If the Partners we train who are five to ten-person shops are any indication, we're probably close to being maxed out in the numbers of staff we manage already, especially if we haven't hired (and are performing the functions of) a service manager. Here's what I mean – let's say we're a seven-person shop, and our staff is broken down as one admin, four techs and an HR/AR/AP person, along with ourselves. In most cases, we are managing all six of these folks directly, along with performing all of the sales & marketing activities, and being the highest point of technical escalation as well. We're already one person over our basic management 101 rule, and now we're going to hire our first real sales person, who we'll need to train on top of our other duties and responsibilities.

Sounds pretty challenging, doesn't it? Well, let's first make a couple of changes that will give us some relief. We're going to choose one of our technical staff to become the service manager, and highest point of escalation (I know, I know, we're still going to get called, but we're trying to buffer these incidents as much as we can). Now we're directly managing three staff – much better. So we go ahead and hire our first sales person, train and tutor them to be successful, and in the process are managing four staff. After a bit, we decide to hire another sales person (maybe an appointment-setter, or full-fledged sales person), and are now managing five staff. If we've got our processes and procedures in place, and are holding our staff accountable to executing their duties and responsibilities, we can hire an additional sales person when the time is right, and lean on our current sales staff's knowledge and experience to train them. But once we get past this point, we've again exceeded our basic management 101 rule, and will need to start looking to either promote a sales manager from within and hire a new sales person, or hire a sales manager from outside the organization to help us continue to grow and manage our sales efforts.

The sales manager's duties and responsibilities will include:

- Developing, tracking and managing all internal and external marketing activities
  - Direct mail
  - E-mail, E-newsletters, case studies, news releases, win-wires, website
  - Events
  - Networking groups
  - Cold calls and call-downs
- Training and motivating sales staff
- Developing and executing new marketing ideas and activities
- Building and solidifying close relationships with distributors, vendors and fulfillment partners
  - Participating in events
  - Identifying where vendor MDF (marketing and distribution funds) can be petitioned to help defray sales & marketing costs
  - Gaining exposure with vendors through case studies and win-wires featuring their solutions
- Setting sales goals for the sales department and creating incentives to reach those goals

- Tracking all sales activity, opportunity and sales funnel activity
  - Insuring product, service and solution sales flow smoothly through their sales cycles
- Assist sales staff in closing business

We're looking for a seasoned sales manager that can do all of these jobs much better than we can. Remember – if we're a mediocre sales manager, let's embrace the reality that we're sitting in the wrong seat on the bus, and get up and make room for the right person. If we're serious about affecting true change in our organization in the areas of growth and profitability, we need to do things differently. We can't expect different results next quarter by doing the exact same things we've done in previous quarters.

So how do we compensate our sales manager? Well, we're going to need to come up with a compensation plan that takes into account the time the sales manager will not be able to directly make sales, but manage the team, create new marketing opportunities and build strong vendor and fulfillment-partner relationships. And we'll do this by offering our sales manager an override on the overall sales of the department. We're also going to bonus the sales manager when the sales team makes their bonuses.

Now, we're again going to commission on gross margin, or gross profit for the sales manager, and because they should actually have a smaller direct role in end-client sales, they will be commissioned at a much smaller percentage than each individual sales person. But since their commissions will be calculated across the sales of the entire sales team, they will have the opportunity to receive compensation commensurate with their success at growing sales.

The Sales Manager

We might believe that a management position would receive higher compensation than a sales person would, but this is only possible in scenarios where the sales manager has the opportunity to sell and close business directly to end-user clients, along with executing their management responsibilities, and lands some pretty serious deals. In fact, a sales person is generally always the highest-paid employee in the organization.

So let's say our sales manager does have the ability to bring in the occasional direct sale – in these scenarios our standard sales compensation plan could apply. But how do we determine their salary and commissions for managing the sales department? Since we expect the sales manager to spend the majority of their time on non-direct sales activities, we would need to modify our aforementioned formula of 35% of total compensation realized as salary, and 65% of total compensation realized as commissions. In fact, we might simply flip those numbers, so that 65% of total compensation is realized as salary, and 35% is realized as commissions. Let's take a look at a couple of scenarios where the sales manager is managing a staff of 3 sales people, supported by an appointment setter, for a total of 4 people under management.

We are going to commission the sales manager on the aggregate GM sales of the 3 sales people:

The Sales Manager

Monthly Sales	GM per Month	Yearly Sales	GM per Yr	Comp
$105,000.00	$36,750.00	$1,260,000.00	$441,000.00	$13,230.00
$135,000.00	$47,250.00	$1,620,000.00	$567,000.00	$17,010.00
$165,000.00	$57,750.00	$1,980,000.00	$693,000.00	$20,790.00
$195,000.00	$68,250.00	$2,340,000.00	$819,000.00	$24,570.00
$225,000.00	$78,750.00	$2,700,000.00	$945,000.00	$28,350.00
$255,000.00	$89,250.00	$3,060,000.00	$1,071,000.00	$32,130.00
$285,000.00	$99,750.00	$3,420,000.00	$1,197,000.00	$35,910.00

Here's how to read the table:

- **Monthly Sales**
  - o Illustrates the 3 sales people's gross monthly sales
- **GM Per Month**
  - o Illustrates the gross margin, or gross profit (35%) of the Monthly sales column
- **Yearly sales**
  - o Illustrates Monthly Sales column multiplied by 12
- **GM Per Year**
  - o Illustrates GM Per Month column multiplied by 12
- **Comp**
  - o Illustrates a commission of 3% across GM for the year

So if 35% of our sales manager's compensation is derived from commissions, or overrides on the sales people they manage, and this commission equals roughly $36,000 per year, their base salary would need to be around $60,000 (I left some room for the sales manager's direct sales commissions to round out their compensation). Now that you have a good understanding of the different commissioning structures we've discussed, tweak and tune your compensation plans for sales people and sales managers in order to come up with a formula that works for you in reaching your profitability goals.

The Function of the Sales Engineer

The importance of the sales engineer's role in building, growing and supporting our sales and marketing efforts cannot be overstated. The sales engineer is the buffer between sales and deployment, and is one of the keys to project profitability. Let's face it – we all know that a good sales person is going to do everything in their power in order to close a deal. While this is great news (as we all want more sales), sometimes a sales person's eagerness can create a client expectation that is difficult to meet. I'm certain that you know exactly what I'm talking about. A sales engineer not only helps train sales staff in what is and is not possible; and at what cost, but is also instrumental in working with vendors and partners in order to flush out a solution, put together a parts list and develop a project plan.

All of these functions are critical in insuring smooth project delivery. Let's take a look at a typical scenario where a sales person has made the initial contact with a new prospect for an infrastructure upgrade. The sales person has performed a needs analysis, and a technician has completed a network analysis. The result is that the prospect will need to migrate from Microsoft Windows Small Business Server 2000 to Small Business Server 2003, and replace all 10 of the users' desktops with new ones running Microsoft Windows Vista. Because the prospect has an aging analog phone system, the sales person would like to quote a VoIP solution to them as well. The sales person and technician have done a good job at gathering all of the necessary information the sales engineer will need to review for the proposed solution: network documentation, license information, existing DSL and

The Function of the Sales Engineer

Telco bills for the last ninety days, and contact and physical location information for the prospect.

The reason we gather the DSL and Telco bills for the last ninety days is so that we can determine whether or not the prospect will experience a cost savings by switching to a Flex or Integrated T-1, and we need the physical location information in order to quote these services.

The sales engineer will discuss the proposed solution with the sales person and technician in order to get a clear understanding of the "lay of the land" at the prospect's location, and ask specific clarifying questions in order to shape the final solution and proposal. In many cases, our sales staff will put together standard proposals for say, Managed Services Agreements or simple services and solutions, but the sales engineer will always review <u>any and all quotes and proposals</u> for approval before they are presented to a prospect or client. This process has saved us countless thousands of dollars over the years, as it reduces the chance of quoting the wrong service, solution, equipment and/or price, which always affects client satisfaction. In addition, it sets appropriate prospect and client expectations in terms of provisioning, implementation and turn-up schedules.

Based upon the complexity of the proposed solution or other factors, the sales engineer may meet with the prospect or client themselves; always with the sales person, whose job it is to build and maintain the client relationship. It is the sales person's responsibility to marshal the support necessary to meet the prospect's or client's needs, and they must constantly be operating in this fashion – we always want the sales person to be the client contact in the relationship,

The Function of the Sales Engineer

---

deepening their bond in order to build the trust needed to continue to sell solutions deep into their environment (becoming the Trusted Advisor).

Once the sales engineer feels that they understand the prospect's or client's needs completely, and has all of the information required in order to scope the solution, they can move from the discovery phase to the design phase of the project. This is where the value of a good sales engineer really shines. An effective sales engineer also has the responsibility to build close relationships, but where the sales person builds these relationships with clients, the sales engineer builds them with vendors and fulfillment partners. The reason for this is simple, and reflects the basic tenets of human nature – people respond best to those with whom they have a relationship; and the closer the relationship, the better and faster they respond. We've all seen this in our daily lives, haven't we?

So the sales engineer will leverage the relationships they've built with their distributors, vendors and fulfillment partners in order to price, quote and deliver this infrastructure upgrade. Their distributor will provide the best quotes they can on server and desktop hardware, as well as licensing. Since the solution requires a VoIP quote, the sales engineer will engage their VoIP vendor, as well as their T-1 vendor, who will be upgrading the bandwidth at the location in order to support the prospect's new voice and data requirements.

Once the sales engineer has received several different quotes from the distributor, VoIP and broadband vendor, they will determine whether or not to present the prospect with different options, or present a single quote in their proposal reflecting their preferred solution. This decision will be based upon

---

current company policy, as well as our overall profit goal for the solution.

We've found that our closing percentage for solutions is directly related to the quality of our proposals. This is why we always include a Microsoft Visio drawing of the proposed solution from a "before" and "after" perspective, as well as a breakdown of the phases of the project, along with an estimated timeline of the proposed work scope. We have included a sample I.T. Solution Proposal in this book for your review and use, if you do not already have a solution template.

Once the proposal has been created, the sales engineer briefs the sales person on the solution and goes over the proposal with them in detail. The last part of the proposal to be finalized will be the quoted price and payment details. In our proposals, we always ask for the equipment to be paid for in advance, as well as any lab labor we will initiate at our offices to prep the solution before landing it at the client's location. We then bill the client the actual onsite labor that it takes us to complete the installation, which is due upon completion.

We've found that billing in this manner keeps us from going out of pocket in the initial phases of our projects, and also insures that we're paid for every hour we're onsite delivering our solutions. I'm sure you've experienced all kinds of surprises and "gotcha's" at client locations when performing the onsite phases of project delivery. Since many of our solutions sometimes involve numerous vendors or fulfillment partners; where we are not in direct physical control of each aspect of project delivery, we feel that it's safer to build an understanding with the client beforehand that the onsite work will be billed per actual hours spent, instead of quoting a fee, then trying to renegotiate that fee when we encounter exceptions to our expected completion time.

We do work with many Partners; however, that have perfected (for the most part) their onsite project quoting process to the point where they quote and guarantee their final solution price. This can be achieved when they are in physical control of each phase of project delivery, and only then through a very detailed and thorough project planning process, which includes meticulous onsite prep work to identify every single item that needs to be addressed in specific detail during project rollout and implementation. But even the best laid plans can go awry, so they make certain to include enough "cushion" in their quotes to absorb any unforeseen variables that can impact the profitability of the project.

Once the sales person has been briefed on and agrees with the proposal; based upon the complexity of the solution, the sales engineer may become involved in the final presentation of the proposed solution to the prospect. Their intimate understanding of all facets of any solution they've designed makes them an invaluable asset in many client presentations.

Let's take a look at the process the sales engineer will go through in this scenario:

- Receives information/documentation from the sales person and technician for the proposed solution
- Meets with the sales person and technician in order to understand the basic needs and spell out the preliminary scope of the proposed solution
- May meet with the prospect along with the sales person in order to clarify specifics of the prospect's needs

The Function of the Sales Engineer

- Meets with the sales person to finalize the solution before the design phase of the project
- Contacts distributors, vendors and fulfillment partners for price quotes
- Receives quotes back from distributors, vendors and fulfillment partners and determines the best method of creating the proposal with input from the sales person
- Creates the proposal with network drawings, phases of the project and an estimated timeline
- Briefs sales person on the completed solution and proposal
- Becomes a resource to be called upon during future client presentations

As you can easily see, a good sales engineer not only helps close client business; increasing revenues, but also saves money by insuring that solutions are scoped properly and quotes and proposals are priced correctly. And finally, a good sales engineer helps to increase client satisfaction through all of the above, as well as by helping shape appropriate client expectations.

The Appointment Setter

In order to really maximize our sales and marketing efforts, we have found it a necessity to employ an appointment setter. Having an appointment setter on staff allows the sales people the ability to spend their attention on closing sales. Our appointment setter's responsibilities include cold calls and call-downs to follow up on direct, indirect and email marketing efforts, as well as to schedule appointments. We've found that the success of our appointment setters lies in their training and the quality of the scripts they utilize to interest prospects in our products and services, paving the way for an appointment to be scheduled.

We're only going to hire experienced candidates for this position – they need to be able to make 100 calls per day, and not be fazed when prospects say "no" to them. An appointment setter's training will be nowhere near as extensive as the training our sales people undergo – they simply need the basics:

- Company Overview Training
  - Vision, mission, values, philosophy, goals
- HR Process Training
  - Overview of compensation, benefits, conduct, sick day and vacation policy, Employee handbook, acceptable use policy
- Administrative Setup and Training
  - User and email account creation, telco account, extension and voicemail creation,
  - Use of company equipment (cell phone, PC, laptop, etc.)

- - Use of company software, Instant Messaging, remote access and remote email
- Formal introduction to management and staff
  - Tour of facility
  - Introduction to all management and staff

Along with some <u>appointment setter-specific training</u>:

- Appointment Setting Script Training
  - We need to make certain we spend the time needed to train our appointment setter in all of our phone scripts – we will have several we use for different purposes:
    - Outbound cold-call script
    - Outbound collateral follow-up script
    - Appointment setting script
    - Appointment confirmation script
    - Appointment re-schedule script

    (some of these aren't really "scripts" in the literal sense, but a standard, duplicable set of points to make during the call)

- Lead Generation Training
  - We will train our appointment setter on all of the ways we generate leads for our products and services, and which activities will be theirs to perform.
    - Direct mail
    - E-mail, E-newsletters, case studies, news releases, win-wires, website
    - Events
    - Networking groups
    - Cold calls and call-downs

The Appointment Setter

- Call Tracking Training
    - We'll want to train our appointment setter in the proper operation and navigation of our CRM or Sales Management solution. We'll spend as much time here as necessary – the appointment setter must understand the value of working the system properly, tracking all of their marketing activity – calls, appointments and follow-ups, and documenting each interaction, assigning the appropriate status for suspects and prospects, along with the call status for all "hits" (speaking with a decision-maker)
    - We'll need to train our appointment setter on our daily and weekly reporting requirements – calls made, voicemails left, "hits", appointments set, and potential appointments.
- Sales Process Training
    - We'll need to guide our appointment setter through a generic sales process, so they understand their position in the cycle. For example:
        - Marketing campaign begins with postcard
        - 3 days later, follow-up call made, postcard receipt verified, contact information verified, 1st attempt at appointment setting
        - Appointment scheduled
        - 1st appointment completed, needs analysis performed
        - 1 day later, meet with sales engineer to discuss, approve solution

---

- 2 days later, quote completed, call initiated to schedule follow-up appointment
- Follow-up appointment completed
- Project approved, initial payment made
- Project handed off to sales engineer and project manager for ordering and scheduling
- Project completed, balance of payment made
- Appointment Setting Expectations
  - It's important to clearly define our expectations of our appointment setter. We need to set clear, attainable dial and appointment setting goals for them.
- Sales Meetings and Reporting
  - It's important that our sales manager enforces attendance to regular sales meetings for the appointment setter, and defines the reporting mechanisms we will use to call and appointment setting statistics during these meetings.
- Listen-ins
  - One of the best ways to train a new appointment setter is to listen in on all of their calls, and provide constructive criticism to help them get past stumbling blocks and overcome objections
    - Cold calls and call-downs
    - Appointment setting
- Role-play, role-play, role-play
  - Just as with our sales people, we will require our appointment setter to role-play each type of engagement they will conduct with suspects, prospects and clients with our sales manager,

other sales staff or ourselves. This critical training exercise cannot be overlooked.

Let's take a look at a couple of sample phone scripts:

Cold Call

Lead call:

Hello,

My name is _____ and I'm calling from _____. Is _____ available?

We are calling on behalf of (your company name), a Microsoft (Gold, Certified, Registered) Partner, and have been assigned to conduct a free Network Security Evaluation for your company if you qualify. I will need to speak with (the decision maker) to ensure you do qualify.

Decision maker:

Hello,

My name is _____ and I'm calling from ___(your company name)___. The reason I'm calling is that we are your Microsoft (Gold, Certified, Registered) Partner, and I have been assigned to find out if you qualify for a Microsoft Network Security Evaluation. We are conducting these evaluations free of charge, and you will be provided with a printed security risk analysis when our evaluation is complete. Again, this is a no obligation offer to receive a Free Microsoft Network Security Analysis. I just need to make certain you qualify by asking you a few questions, would that be alright?

The Best I.T. Sales & Marketing BOOK EVER!

The Appointment Setter

How many computer work stations you have at your facility?

Do you currently have a disaster recovery plan in place?

Do you have an onsite IT department or do you outsource that work?

When is the best time for you, your IT department, or any other relevant personnel to schedule time for this analysis – it usually takes about an hour or so?

As you can see, we are leveraging our status as a Microsoft Partner, along with the hot topic of Network Security in order to secure an appointment. Modify this script as you see fit to match your services and offerings. <u>We have had the best success with Network Security and Disaster Recovery scripts as a lead-in script topic.</u>

Call-Down

Hi,

My name is _____ from _____.

Recently we sent (insert contact name) some information in the mail and I just want to confirm that he/she received it. We sent a giant post card regarding a free Microsoft Network Security Analysis. Do you know if (insert contact name) would be the person we should have sent that type of information to? (If not, get new contact info and title)

Maybe you can help me really quickly to make sure your company qualifies for the Analysis. Do you have at least (number of required workstations) computers in your office? Do you have an IT department or do you outsource that work?

Vertical-Specific

Is your company using (insert software platform or hardware device)? Is anyone there having issues with that?

Disaster Recovery

Do you currently have a disaster recovery plan in place?

If they qualify:

Great, your company does qualify. Is (insert contact name) available to speak to me about the Microsoft Network Security Analysis?

If they do not qualify:

I'm sorry. Only organizations with (number of required workstations) workstations qualify for the free Microsoft Network Security Analysis. Thank you for your time though, and have a great day.

If available:

Hello,

My name is _____ and I'm calling from (your company name). The reason I'm calling is that we are your Microsoft (Gold, Certified, Registered) Partner and have been assigned to conduct Free Microsoft Network Security Analyses for companies that qualify – and while speaking with your assistant, I realized that you do qualify. We are conducting these analyses free of charge, and you will be provided with a printed security risk analysis when our analysis is complete. Again, this is a no obligation offer to receive a Free Microsoft Network Security Analysis.

Vertical-Specific

From what I understand your company is using (insert software platform) correct? Is anyone in your company having issues with that?

Disaster Recovery

From what I understand your company does not currently have a disaster recovery plan in place – is that correct?

When is the best time to schedule this analysis – it usually takes about an hour or so?

If they have questions:

That's a great question. If you don't mind holding just a second I can get my client-support manager to join us on this call, who will be happy to answer that for you.

Similar to our cold-call script, I'm sure you noticed it's just slightly different in the opening, allowing this script to be customized to leverage vertical-specific pain points.

Section 3 – Selling Services and Solutions

If we're now ready to sell our services and solutions, we are to be congratulated, as this means that we have successfully prepared our organization to actually implement an effective marketing and sales effort, close business and earn revenue. Let's review some of the key things we've accomplished in order to get to this point:

- Identified our vertical
- Created vertical-specific messaging
- Sourced our marketing list
- Created all of our marketing collateral
- Redesigned our website
- Advertised for sales staff
- Created our compensation plans
- Interviewed and hired sales staff
- Trained sales staff
- Created appointment setting scripts

How different is the process we've illustrated so far from the way you currently sell and market your products and services today? I'm certain there are at least a few items in the list above that you could either modify or implement in your own process that would increase your success in marketing and sales – I know from our own experience, as well as working with many of our Partners, that as we accomplish each and every one of the activities documented in this book, our sales opportunities increase, it becomes easier to sell our products and solutions, we achieve higher closing rates, and the value of our average sale has grown. In this next section, we will now focus on the execution of marketing activity designed to put us in front of a prospect to sell our products and services to, and the process of pitching our prospects during each phase of the sales closing process.

Tracking Sales and Marketing Activity

Our efforts at sales and marketing must be tracked, quantified and analyzed if we're going to realize success. The only way to accurately measure how good our sales team, marketing plan and even products, services and pricing structure are, is to create a sales management process. This process will track and quantify the efforts of every sales staff member and every marketing activity that is executed. Simply put, every action that is initiated in our sales and marketing effort is scheduled, documented and managed. Think of it as the equivalent of problem resolution at the help desk – we document each action that we take to resolve a service request, then run regular reports to gauge our effectiveness and client satisfaction, which we evaluate in order to tune and improve our process and results. We're going to do the same thing with our sales and marketing process, it's just called sales & marketing management, and it can be complex, certainly tedious, but lays the groundwork for our ability to trend and evaluate our marketing efforts, providing us the raw data needed to gauge our effectiveness in order improve our results.

At the help desk, we utilize PSA software as our tool to manage our service delivery and problem management process. Some PSA software such as ConnectWise (www.connectwise.com) also allows us the ability to manage our sales and marketing processes as well. The sales and marketing tracking and management concepts we discuss in this book can easily be managed in ConnectWise; however, configuration of specific software solutions falls outside of the scope of this particular book in our series, and we will illustrate basic tracking and statistical analysis of sales and marketing

---

activity in simple Microsoft Excel worksheets, providing you the opportunity to begin learning and working with these basic concepts immediately.

In our first book in this series, *The Guide to a Successful Managed Services Practice*, we discuss the topic of "reverse projection", whereby we calculate how much, and what type of sales and marketing effort it takes in order to create a managed services sale. The sales and marketing tracking process we will discuss here will provide us the information over time that will reveal to us exactly how much and what type(s) of effort is needed in order for us to sell each and every one of the products and services we offer. The concept is really quite simple – we design a marketing campaign behind a particular product or service – let's take managed services (since we've segued quite nicely to it). Let's say that our average Managed Services Agreement is worth $1,000, and we've set a goal for our sales team to increase our managed services revenue by $5,000 per quarter for the next 3 quarters, and by $10,000 per quarter by the end of the 4th quarter. What would we do, and in what order; to insure that we reach our goal the first quarter, and how do we repeat that achievement over the next two quarters, and then double our previous successes in the last quarter?

Well, we're first going to need to develop our marketing strategy, or plan. Our marketing plan will include a specific number of activities, which may encompass direct mail, email and newsletter marketing, as well as presentations at a couple of networking events a month, followed by some call-downs to schedule appointments with prospects. In our initial marketing plan, we will decide how much of each of these activities we are going to execute. Since our goal basically boils down to selling 5 new Managed Services Agreements in the existing quarter, we need to carefully track the results of each activity

The Best I.T. Sales & Marketing BOOK EVER!

Tracking Sales and Marketing Activity

in our marketing campaign. Let's say that we know from past experience that we close about 50% of the prospects that we present a managed services solution to. This means that we'll need to present our solution to at least 10 prospects. So our charge is to figure out what it takes for us to sit down in front of 10 prospects. We're going to need to experiment with our marketing plan in order to guarantee a repeatable outcome based upon the activity generated.

So our first stab at a marketing campaign designed to garner 10 appointments might include 100 HTML email messages sent to a targeted list of prospects, followed closely by 100 postcards. Our appointment setter will then follow up with 100 call-downs to attempt to gauge interest at that point and set some appointments. A few days later, our monthly newsletter will go out, further reinforcing our featured solution and message. While this activity is in motion, our sales person will conduct presentations at 2 networking functions, feeding leads back to our appointment setter for follow up, and adding them to our email, newsletter and postcard campaign. If necessary, our appointment setter will then make a second call-down the following week to prospects that have not yet responded, to attempt to secure an appointment. With any luck, we'll set our 10 appointments. If not, we'll modify our marketing plan in any number of ways, including increasing the size of the initial prospect list. We continue tweaking and tuning the plan until we achieve our desired result.

During this entire process, we are documenting, quantifying and tracking each and every activity, so when we do achieve our goal of setting 10 appointments and closing 5 new managed services deals, we will have a blueprint on how we did it. Then we test the process the next quarter, and if we've done our job correctly, we will be able to duplicate our results with minimal modification. So how do we double our results in

---

the last quarter? That's easy – we simply double our activity! While no marketing plan is absolutely perfect, and will not always yield the exact same results, at least we'll be "in the ballpark", and be more successful than not, by tracking and quantifying our results through each and every marketing campaign.

We are going to duplicate this process with each and every product and solution we deliver, so that we can build a "playbook" of marketing strategies that we can go back to again and again. In fact, this is the only way we will be able to successfully market several different solutions concurrently with measurable success, and be able to forecast with surprising accuracy the resources and cost each individual campaign will require – as well as its return on our investment. This then is the first step in our ability to calculate our cost of sales, as we'll know exactly what it will cost to design each piece of our marketing collateral, print and mail our postcards, and the labor to make our call-downs, follow-ups and set appointments, as well as the cost of participation in any networking events. Now that's what I call smart marketing!

Let's break down the steps required for our marketing campaign:

Goal – 5 new Managed Services Agreements

- **Phase 1: Preparation**

- o Identify target market, source/filter list for 100 names
- o Create/select HTML email template to use
- o Create/select website landing page that all urls in email, newsletter and postcard marketing collateral point to
- o Create/select postcard template to use
- o Create/select telemarketing/appointment setting script to use
- o Create Newsletter highlighting/reinforcing benefits of featured service or solution
- o Identify 2 local networking events and schedule attendance/presentation
- o Create/select presentation for local networking event

- **Phase 2: Execution**
  - o Schedule and send email to targeted list
  - o Schedule and send newsletter to targeted list
  - o Schedule and send postcard to targeted list
  - o Schedule and execute call-downs/set appointments
  - o Schedule, attend and present at 2 local networking events
  - o Add networking event leads to marketing campaign, and schedule and send email, newsletter and postcards to new leads and execute call-downs/set appointments
  - o If necessary, schedule and execute 2nd call-down/set appointments

The Best I.T. Sales & Marketing BOOK EVER!

Tracking Sales and Marketing Activity

- **Ongoing: Tracking**
  - Track date all email sent
  - Track date all newsletters sent
  - Track date all postcards sent
  - Track date all call-downs made
  - Track date all outbound follow-up phone calls made
  - Track all "hits" with a decision-maker
  - Track all appointments set
  - Track value of all potential opportunities

Let's take a look at the following Microsoft Excel we've created in order to track our activity and results for this particular marketing campaign:

Marketing Stats Campaign 1											
Vertical	Gross Calls	Gross Conv	Hit Rate	Vmails	F/U Calls	Conv D/M	Emails	News	Cards	Appt Set	Close Ratio	Oppty
CPA, Finance	100	76	76.00%	32	133	28	100	100	100	20	71.43%	$20,000

Here's how to read the table:

- **Vertical**
  - Illustrates the vertical market we are targeting
- **Gross Calls**
  - Illustrates the number of initial outbound call-downs made
- **Gross Conv**
  - Illustrates the number of conversations had with anyone other than the decision-maker in the prospect's office

- **Hit Rate**
  - Illustrates the percentage of calls where a conversation was had with anyone other than a decision-maker at the prospect's office
- **Vmails**
  - Illustrates the number of Voicemail messages left
- **F/U Calls**
  - Illustrates the number of follow-up calls made
- **Conv D/M**
  - Illustrates the number of calls where a conversation was had with a decision-maker
- **Emails**
  - Illustrates the number of emails sent
- **News**
  - Illustrates the number of newsletters sent
- **Cards**
  - Illustrates the number of postcards sent
- **Closing Ratio**
  - Illustrates the percentage of appointments set against the value in the Conv D/M column
- **Oppty**
  - Illustrates the potential value should each appointment yield a sale for the product or service marketed through this campaign

Our efforts, as tracked in the above simple table, look pretty good, don't they? Now if we can repeat this activity with a new list of prospects, and come close the same results, we can have confidence in our formula, and use it as a basis for forecasting revenue. More sophisticated sales and marketing tracking systems provide us more granular reporting, and display our opportunities in a visual sales funnel. A sales funnel is basically a representation of our sales pipeline, and allows us to track in which phase of the sales cycle all of our opportunities are. Some of the more sophisticated sales and marketing systems also help to keep opportunities moving through the sales funnel, by prompting us to perform scheduled activities in order to prevent sales cycles from slipping. ConnectWise, mentioned earlier, has a very powerful marketing engine providing this capability, along with a graphical display of the sales funnel. We're going to want to graduate to a more sophisticated system for tracking our sales and marketing activities, as well as our sales funnel, once we have mapped out each and every sales and marketing activity we will execute for all of our products and services, and especially after we hire our first sales person. We'll need an automated means of tracking and reporting on our overall sales activity and status of all potential sales, quotes and proposals in our sales pipeline in order to manage our sales efforts.

The Solution Selling Sales Process

As with any endeavor, our chances of success, along with the degree of success we attain are both affected by; and can be increased dramatically through, the application of an effective, repeatable process. If we are to achieve the highest degree of success in our marketing and sales efforts, we must have a documented process for marketing and selling each and every service and solution we support, and this process needs to include every potential activity or action necessary in order for us to close a deal. This discipline should reflect our process for documenting each phase of the delivery, implementation and maintenance of every product and solution we support.

Let's take a look at a documented process for selling and implementing an Integrated T-1:

- Establish appointment with the prospect
    - o May obtain telco bills before appointment
- Send appointment confirmation postcard to prospect
- Send appointment confirmation HTML email to prospect the day before the appointment
- Conduct sales appointment with prospect
    - o Pick up 3 month's previous telco bills, if not received previously
        - Local service bills
        - Long distance bills
        - Broadband bills
        - Equipment bills
    - o Note make and model of existing phone system, as well as type and number of handsets and voicemail type and capacity

The Solution Selling Sales Process

- Deliver all bills to office for document scanning and review
- Prepare and send prospect follow-up email summarizing meeting, detailing next steps and setting appropriate expectation
- Update status of opportunity in sales & marketing (CRM) system and upload scanned documents
- Create and assign tasks and timeline for telco bill audit, Integrated T-1 vendor quote and application, and proposal creation
- Create and submit proposal and all supporting documents to sales engineer for review and approval
- Schedule 2nd appointment with prospect to review proposal
- Send prospect appointment confirmation postcard
- Send prospect appointment confirmation HTML email the day before the appointment
- Conduct 2nd appointment with prospect, review proposal, obtain signed T-1 vendor contract and approval for project implementation

Scheduling, Implementation and Cutover

- Develop 60 day project plan
  - Assign a project manager
  - Integrated T-1 order placement
  - Integrated T-1 provisioning from vendor
  - Scheduling of service delivery
  - Phone and Fax number/800 number audit
  - Number Port
  - T-1 installation from LEC
  - Inside wiring modification
  - Router modification
  - MX/A/DNS record modification

The Solution Selling Sales Process

- o Hunt group/Extension configuration
- o Cutover
- o Testing
- o Disconnection from old telco services
- Schedule project planning meeting with client
- Send appointment confirmation postcard to prospect
- Send appointment confirmation HTML email to prospect the day before the appointment
- Project manager conducts project planning meeting with client
  - o Present project plan and tentative scheduling with client
  - o Set appropriate expectations with client
  - o Gather any additional required information for project
- Project manager prepares and delivers weekly email updates to client regarding project status
- Project manager conducts weekly conference calls with client to review and update status of project
- Final cut sheets for phone number/800 number porting are developed and delivered to client
- Project manager conducts conference call with client to review number port
- Client approves number port with signature
- T-1 installation and port dates are verified with client and service cutover process is reviewed
- Client is sent follow-up email summarizing conference call, and documenting installation, port and cutover dates, as well as the cutover process

Note – each and every activity is updated in our sales and marketing or CRM system as it occurs.

The Solution Selling Sales Process

- Conduct project review with client's existing phone system vendor
  - Schedule re-programming of phone system if needed
  - Obtain passwords to phone system
  - Obtain passwords to router, or cpe
- Schedule port date with LEC/CLEC
- Obtain new IP address range from LEC/CLEC
- Provide Professional Services team with all required information needed to implement cutover
  - Hardware documentation
  - Passwords
  - IP addresses
  - Scheduling information
- Reconfirm cutover/port date and time with client
  - Afternoon ports only
  - No ports on Fridays
- Conduct cutover and port
  - Meet phone vendor on-site
  - Coordinate port with LEC/CLEC project coordinator
  - Supervise cross-connects
  - Test all lines
    - DID's
    - Handsets
    - Hunt goups
    - Modems
    - Fax machines
    - Call forwarding
    - Voicemail
- Have client sign completed work order for implementation.
- Schedule dedicated internet cutover with client
  - Verify IP addresses and router/cpe passwords

The Solution Selling Sales Process

- Conduct data cutover
    - Modify A/MX/DNS records
    - Test Internet access
    - Test email operation
    - Test locally hosted websites
- Have client sign completed work order for implementation.
- Email client telco disconnect schedule of old service for approval
- Receive telco disconnect approval from client via email
- Initiate telco disconnect process of old services with vendor
- Meet with client to perform satisfaction survey and deliver final Invoice
- Send client handwritten thank-you card

Remember – each and every step we undertake to sell, market and deliver our solution is documented in our sales and marketing, or CRM system. This process of documentation and activity tracking is exactly what is required in order to improve our efficiencies, shorten sales cycles and meet client expectations – thereby increasing client satisfaction, which results in timely payments and improved opportunities to sell the client additional solutions and services in the future. In addition to these benefits, the documentation and tracking of the solution implementation/delivery process keeps our staff and vendors informed of critical information and dates for each phase of implementation, allowing us much greater control in holding everyone accountable during the entire process, smoothing solution delivery and allowing identification of any hiccups in the process in time to remediate them before they have a chance to derail the project.

The Best I.T. Sales & Marketing BOOK EVER!

The Solution Selling Sales Process

I'd also like to take a moment here to reinforce the concept of the Trusted Advisor. We've alluded to it before, and if you've listened to any of our webcasts, or been to one of our workshops, boot camps or other live presentations, you've seen and heard us bang that gong repeatedly. If we're only reactive, break-fix firefighters, it's simply not possible to be perceived as a Trusted Advisor by our clients – and if we're not Trusted Advisors, we're a commodity. This means that the only relationship we have with our clients is a service relationship – something breaks and they need service, we take care of it – instead of a business partnership. If this is the case, our clients place a much lower value on our services, and are more sensitive to pricing – always looking for a better price, and/or nickel-and-diming us on Invoices.

If we are to evolve to the level of the Trusted Advisor, our value needs to be perceived as such by our clients, where the relationship is worth more than the sum of our Invoices. In *The Guide to a Successful Managed Services Practice*, I go into considerable detail on this topic, and how we need to first overcome our internal perception of ourselves and the value of our services to our clients, becoming a Trusted Advisor in our own perception and ego. Only then can our internal perception become our outward reality, allowing us to reflect that to our clients. It's timely that I happen to be writing this part of the book now, as I just returned from a conference where one of our Partners picked me out of the crowd and asked for a few moments of my time to discuss some issues they were having in their transition to Managed Services.

During our conversation, it became immediately apparent to me that this Partner had not made the internal transition within his own perception to the role of Trusted Advisor. He made a comment that blew me away – he told me that he didn't think that delivering Managed Services to clients in the 20 to 50 pc

---

range was of value to them. After taking a moment to recover from this comment, and make certain that I heard him correctly, I spent quite a bit of time in hallway conversation attempting to determine how he could sell a product or service to his clients that he did not believe was valuable to them, why he thought this was true, and then tried to illustrate the flaws in his opinion. I shared with him that I could state to any prospect or client with complete confidence that through the delivery of Managed Services, their networks would be better maintained than they ever had been in the past.

I mean – think about it for a second. In the old break-fix days, we would react to a problem at a client's location by physically driving there. Then we would spend the next hour or longer applying patches and updates (since it had been a while since we'd been there), hoping that this activity would resolve some issues – all the while trying to avoid getting jumped in the hallway ("the I.T. guy's here!") – you know exactly what I'm talking about. So a potential 2 hour visit would predictably become a 4 hour visit, plus drive-time both ways. In contrast nowadays, we schedule patching and updating proactively and deliver it remotely, and monitor and alert on thousands of network, device and service issues when they occur. This type of proactive maintenance is bound to increase our clients' uptime and efficiencies, so the value of these services to clients should be immediately obvious to anyone that understands these basic concepts. In addition, we are quieting the noise in these networks through our proactive management and immediate remote response – no longer does the client need to suffer until we can schedule an onsite service call and free up a technician to drive over to resolve their issues.

Well, I suppose like many other things in life, not everyone gets it. But in order for us to achieve the Trusted Advisor role, our clients certainly need to get it. If we can illustrate to our clients that we are not interested in a service relationship with them, but rather a business partnership, we would be taking an important step towards the Trusted Advisor ideal – whether we deliver Managed Services or not. But I believe the delivery of Managed Services helps us achieve Trusted Advisor status more quickly and easily. Think about this for a second. In a reactive, transaction or project-based service delivery model, the client bears all of the risk in the relationship. What I mean is that if a non-Managed Services client's server goes down hard, and it takes us 12 hours to bring the server back up, the client is on the hook to pay us for 12 hours of our labor. On the other hand, if they are a Managed Services client, we're billing them on a flat-fee basis, and now if it takes us 12 hours to remediate the problem, not only does it hurt the client from an availability perspective, but it also hurts us as well from a profitability perspective. As an MSP, the quicker we can resolve our clients' issues, the more profitable we become. So if we can impress upon our clients the reality that the better we care for their networks, and continue to bring them solutions that improve their efficiencies, save them money and mitigate their business pain and risk, the more profitable they become – and so do we. Hence we wish to move our clients away from these "service relationships" and over to "business partnerships", as we now share in our clients' IT risks – as we've got a lot of skin in the game.

So our goal is to become the Trusted Advisor. Let's take a look at some of the benefits we can realize once we have attained this status with our clients:

- Increase client satisfaction
- Build client loyalty
- Experience easier solution selling

The Solution Selling Sales Process

- Direct our client's technology roadmap
- Command premium rates
- Increase our referral potential
- Enjoy direct access to decision makers

As we can see, the road to increased and easier solution sales is facilitated by becoming the Trusted Advisor.

Let's now take a look at the sales, implementation and delivery process for another solution – a website:

- Establish appointment with the prospect
- Send appointment confirmation postcard to prospect
- Send appointment confirmation HTML email to prospect
    - Cc email to web developer
- Review competitive websites to prospect's business prior to appointment
- Send work order to web developer for a site comp
- Review prospect website comp with web developer 2 days prior to client appointment
- Send appointment confirmation HTML email to prospect the day before the appointment
- Conduct sales appointment with prospect
    - Discuss site comp, likes/dislikes, note changes
    - Gather all required information for next phase of project
        - Website functional requirements
        - Back-end database integration/shopping cart integration
        - Other design requirements
- Prepare and send prospect follow-up email summarizing meeting, detailing next steps and setting appropriate expectation

---

The Solution Selling Sales Process

- Update status of opportunity in sales & marketing (CRM) system
- Create draft website sitemap with web developer from client feedback on initial site comp
- Finalize website sitemap with web developer
- Schedule 2nd appointment with prospect to review sitemap
- Send prospect appointment confirmation postcard
- Send prospect appointment confirmation HTML email the day before the appointment
  - Cc email to web developer
- Conduct 2nd appointment with prospect, review sitemap and new comp for changes and modifications
- Create and submit proposal and all supporting documents to sales engineer for review and approval
- Schedule 3rd appointment with prospect to review proposal
- Send prospect appointment confirmation postcard
- Send prospect appointment confirmation HTML email the day before the appointment
- Conduct 3rd appointment with prospect, review proposal, obtain signed authorization and approval for project implementation from client
  - Collect any additional content from client in order to begin development
- Establish projected timeline for phased deliverables based upon receipt of all required content from client

Scheduling, Implementation and Go Live

- Develop project plan
  - Assign a project manager
  - Determine milestones and projected completion dates

The Solution Selling Sales Process

- o Create content responsibility document for client
- o Create requirements document for client
- Schedule project planning meeting with client
- Send appointment confirmation postcard to client
- Send appointment confirmation HTML email to client the day before the appointment
- Project manager conducts project planning meeting with client
  - o Present new comp, receive feedback
  - o Present project plan, projected milestones and completion dates with client
  - o Set appropriate expectations with client
  - o Gather any additional required information for project
  - o Present content responsibility and client requirements document to client for signature
- Send thank you card to client
- Project manager prepares and delivers weekly email updates to client regarding project status
- Project manager conducts weekly conference calls with client to review and update status of project
- Once all website content is received from client, email is sent acknowledging receipt of same to client and web developer
- Scan all content as needed (photos, etc.) and upload to sales management/CRM system
  - o Website project cannot begin until all content is received
- Web developer codes initial beta of website from approved comp
- Project manager reviews site with web developer 2 days prior to client presentation and review
- Schedule conference call with client to review site

- Conduct client conference call and review site with client for feedback/changes
- Prepare and send client follow-up email summarizing conference call and requested modifications, detailing next steps and setting appropriate expectation
    - Cc web developer

Note – each and every activity is updated in our sales and marketing or CRM system as it occurs.

- Review modifications with web developer 2 days prior to client conference call
- Conduct conference call with client to review modifications for final approval
- Client approves site
- Schedule go-live date
- Host/upload site
    - Modify A/MX/DNS records as needed
- Test site functionality
- Meet with client to perform satisfaction survey and deliver final Invoice
- Send client handwritten thank-you card

These example solution sales and implementation workflows provide a high-level overview of the activities necessary to track the sale and delivery of a solution to a client in a sales and marketing or CRM system. They are not a project plan for these solutions by any stretch of the imagination.

The Managed Services Sales Process

Believe it or not, we have a process for conducting Managed Services sales appointments in addition to all of our other solutions and services sales processes. Although our book *The Guide to a Successful Managed Services Practice* does an excellent job of providing a step-by-step process to sell Managed Services, we're going to deep-dive into each individual appointment required to close a Managed Services deal; what we say and do, and how we overcome objections, all culminating in a Managed Services sale. And we're going to try not to duplicate the great information contained in our previous book in this series, so if you haven't read it, please pick up a copy, as it really is the only book on Managed Services that provides a comprehensive viewpoint on its subject matter, and contains information you can use to increase your annuity-based revenues immediately.

Our sales process for selling Managed Services is built around 3 appointments. Although we can sell Managed Services in 2 appointments using our methodology, we have built it around 3 appointments, with a visit to the prospect's location between the first and second appointment in order to conduct a network analysis and gather the information needed to deliver a cost savings analysis. In our first appointment with a prospect, we conduct a needs analysis, using a template we've created. Alternatively, we could also use Microsoft's Business and Technology Assessment Toolkit: https://partner.microsoft.com/40025740.

During the first appointment, our primary goal is to determine whether or not we want to do business with the prospect. Does that sound odd? I say this because of the fact that we want to work with only "A" clients, and need to choose which clients we do business with carefully as an MSP, or risk profitability. Remember we are looking for business partnerships, not service relationships, so we only want to do business with clients that "get it", and will allow us the opportunity to sell them additional products, services and solutions over the term of our relationship – and we want that relationship to be a long one. Wouldn't you rather have less clients paying you more money, than the other way around? Well, here is our opportunity to begin that process.

During our first appointment with a prospect, we're going to look for any signs, or red flags which indicate that this might not be a good relationship to enter in to. What do I mean by red flags, and how can we possibly know during a first appointment whether or not we should do business with a prospect? Well, I'm certain you've met with enough prospects to have developed a "spidey sense" about these things by now, but a couple of my favorites include:

- During the appointment, the prospect continually answers the phone or cell phone, interrupting your presentation or conversation
- During the appointment, the prospect's staff repeatedly interrupts your meeting at the doorway, and the prospect continues to wave them in
- During the appointment, the prospect checks their email
- During the appointment, the prospect replies to Instant Messages

And my all-time winner of the red-flag during a first appointment award is:

- During the appointment, the prospect begins text-messaging on their cell phone

Believe it or not, I have experienced every one of these scenarios. Guess what? If the prospect does not value your time during your very first appointment, what makes you think that they'll value your relationship? In each situation where I have felt that my time didn't mean anything to the prospect, I have ended the appointment early, and politely excused myself. There are simply more important things for me to be doing, and people to be seeing, than these prospects. Now of course, these are obvious indications of a bad appointment, and a bad prospect for our services, but there are more subtle ones which you'll need to be watching out for – trust your instincts, it's always better to pass on a questionable prospect than to take their business blindly.

So let's say everything feels right, and we want to go to the next step with this prospect after performing our needs analysis or Business and Technology Assessment. We'll next schedule some time to have one of our technicians come out and do a thorough network analysis (we want to know what we're getting ourselves into, and what will be required in order to bring the client's environment up to our "certified network" standard), and we'll also use the information gathered in order to create our Managed Services Proposal. In addition, we'll need to collect the information necessary to create our Cost Savings Analysis. This means that we'll need to speak with 3 of the prospect's staff – the person who deals with all issues involving vendors who service their network, the person who does "lightweight" I.T. work and "keeps things running" until they run into a problem that requires them to call in their existing reactive, break-fix I.T. service provider, and the person that handles payroll. The reason we need to speak with these folks is that they can tell us how much time they spend dealing with vendor issues, performing maintenance to devices on the network, and provide us with staff salary information. I bet you're wondering why we need all of this data – because we're going to show the prospect how much money they're losing by not signing our Managed Services Agreement. Don't worry – it'll all become clearer as we move forward.

Once we've gathered all of this data, we can create a quote to bring the environment up to "certified network" status, a Managed Services Proposal and Agreement, and a Cost Savings Analysis. I've mentioned "certified network" a couple of times, and by this I mean an environment that is running current, licensed, updated and patched software and equipment that we maintain, and where all critical device and software warranties are in place, among other things. Basically, a "certified network" is whatever we say it is, based upon best practices, our experience, skill set and comfort level.

Once we've gathered the required information and created these documents, we can close the prospect at any time, but normally wait until the third appointment, unless the prospect is ready to go in the second appointment. This is due to the fact that we have a very granular process of closing the sale with three appointments, where we perform activity specific to each of these appointments designed to reinforce the prospect's decision to do business with us. During the second appointment, we're going to talk about the services and benefits our company can provide the prospect, which we purposely do not do in the first appointment. Remember, in addition to determining whether or not we want to build a business partnership with the prospect, we conduct the first appointment simply to understand the prospect's pain points and current situation, and to listen carefully. We do not sell ourselves or our services during this appointment – it's all about the prospect. So in the second appointment we get to pitch the prospect on ourselves, and use a short Microsoft PowerPoint printed slide presentation to keep us on point. We'll also present the findings from our Cost Savings Analysis to the prospect, and discuss the requirements that need to be met in order for us to deliver our services.

The prospect's response at this point will determine whether or not we move forward with the close on our Managed Services Agreement, disclosing the cost of remediating their network in order for us to deliver our services, in addition to the monthly fee we'll charge for these services. If we can close at this point, we will, but if not, we'll schedule another appointment, to "crunch the numbers", even though we already have them.

So during the third appointment, we're going for the close. As you can tell, our process for closing a Managed Services deal is pretty straightforward. We'll break it down piece by piece in the next few chapters.

Oh yes, before I forget – we track each phase of our Managed Services sales process in our sales and marketing, or CRM system, just as we do for all of our other solutions and services.

Selling Managed Services – 1st Appointment

We have several goals we're trying to reach during the 1st appointment to sell Managed Services:

- Build rapport with the prospect
- Determine the viability of a business partnership
- Gather preliminary data

Before we meet with the prospect, we're going to do some homework and perform a web search on the principal's name and the company. We want to get some background on the organization we're preparing to visit. Prospects are very proud of the businesses they've built, or the organizations they work for, and appreciate it when they learn that we have taken the time to learn something about them. I remember one prospect that is a CPA, and became a client, who had won a prestigious CPA award, and had it prominently announced on their website. All we had to do was mention it, and they were so proud, they went on and on about it. That single topic broke the ice during our first appointment, and they subsequently went on to become a great "A" client.

So we're going to sit down with the prospect, and "warm-up" – find a common point to build a discussion around. Sometimes it will be about something we discovered during our web search, and sometimes it will be something that we notice in the prospect's office. If we walk in to a prospect's office, and see several pictures of the prospect on a boat, guess what we'll be talking about for the first ten minutes? Have you ever played one of those memory games where you look at a picture for a minute, then try to remember what objects are in

---

it, or the color of things? That's how we're going to operate during the first few seconds of our meeting with the prospect – we're going to observe very carefully the surroundings to find an object or topic that we can build a discussion around. Sometimes it's simply family photos – then we're talking about our kids, etc. – you get it. So the topic can be anything really; hobbies, sports, family, business, you name it. The warm-up is probably the most critical point in the first appointment, and so many of our Partners get it wrong by rushing headlong into discussing how great and wonderful they and their company are, their client list, and how they can help the prospect, yada yada yada…

That's exactly what we don't want to do during the first appointment, and specifically why we save some of that for the second appointment only. You've heard this before, but it bears repeating – courting a new prospect is like dating – if you understand the dynamics of a series of dates, you know that we're being judged every minute of every date for flaws, and a decision on whether we'll get to go on another one. This is why we're always on our best behavior when we're dating a new person; opening doors for them, bringing them gifts, sending them cards and cutesy notes, etc. Prospect appointments are the same way – it's all about the prospect, not us – we want a second and third date, in most cases, so let's not blow it during the first date.

Okay, we're on our best first-date behavior, and we now begin to learn about the prospect's business by means of our needs analysis, or Business and Technology Assessment. This is conducted in a conversational manner – not as an interrogation. We're going to learn all about the prospect's business, network, equipment, vendors and pain points. And I'll remind you to maintain your keen observational skills working throughout the entire appointment, we're closely watching for any comments or behavior that would cause us to second-guess building a partnership with the prospect.

So when the appointment ends, we're going to politely thank the prospect for their time, and if it makes sense to move to the next step, we're going to ask the prospect's permission to schedule an onsite network analysis, and the ability to speak with the people on their staff that manage the vendors, perform lightweight I.T. functions, and handle the payroll. We're going to explain to the prospect that we'll need to gather data from these folks in order to perform a cost savings analysis and find out if we can save the prospect on their I.T. costs with our services. I've very seldom had a prospect say no to this request, and for the ones that did, we simply did not do business with them. If they will not provide us the information we need in order to determine whether we can help them or not, then there's no point in going any further, as they don't "get it", and we only spend our time with prospects and clients that do.

Alright, let's break down the talking points for the first client appointment:

Talking Points:

- Warm-up
- Let Client know you've researched their organization
- Find a common point to build a discussion around
    - Hobbies
    - Sports
    - Family
    - Business
- Learn about Client's business

- o Time in business
- o Type of business
- o Number of Employees
- Learn about Client's Network
  - o Infrastructure
  - o Number of Servers
  - o Number of Desktops
  - o Other Network Devices
  - o Line of Business Applications
- Learn about Client's Vendors
  - o Number of Hardware Vendors
  - o Number of Software Vendors
  - o Number of Service Vendors
  - o Products/Services provided
- Walk through Needs Analysis
  - o Collect all necessary data
- Learn about Client's pain points
  - o Uptime
  - o Security
  - o Viruses/Spam
  - o Productivity
  - o LOB's
  - o Equipment
  - o Mobility
  - o Business Continuity
  - o Website
  - o Phone System
  - o T1 Service/Costs
  - o CRM System

The Best I.T. Sales & Marketing BOOK EVER!

Selling Managed Services – 1st Appointment

Next let's walk through a 1st prospect appointment role-playing session we conducted with one of our Partners; Marco Alcala from Alcala Consulting, during a Managed Services Sales Training boot camp.

1st Prospect Appointment Role-Play Transcript:

Warm Up:

Gary: Marco, good morning, I'm Gary from Intelligent Enterprise.

Marco: *It's nice to meet you, Marco Alcala.*

Gary: I'm glad you let us come in and talk with you today. How are you doing today?

Marco: Good and you?

Gary: I'm doing great. I did a little research on your company on my way over here, and I'm quite impressed with what you guys have done. I was on your website.

Marco: *Oh thank you.*

Gary: Looks like you've done some really successful things I notice that you're the #1 accounting firm in this area, you talk about that on your website, how'd you guys become the number one accounting firm?

Marco: *Through lots of hard work, we make sure we that we take good care of our customers and we exceed their expectations every time. We have people that specialize in doing quality control so we do follow up with our clients and* make sure that they're totally satisfied with our work, and we've been growing our business based on referrals, we don't have to do any marketing.

Gary: Nice, so obviously customer service is a big part of your business.

Marco: *It is.*

Gary: Can you tell me how you started your business?

Marco: *Yeah, well, I was a finance major in college and right out of college I took the CPA exam, I passed it on the first try and then opened up my office and borrowed a whole bunch of money on credit cards and here we are 20 years later. I have 15 employees.*

Gary: Wow so I guess you're the prototypical entrepreneur.

Marco: *Yes.*

Gary: Oh I like that because you know I'm an entrepreneur myself, so I love to see entrepreneurs because you know, some guys get into the business, have inherited the business, they bought into the business, but somebody who built it from the ground floor up, that says a lot to me about your character and what kind of person you are, because I started my business the same way, and it's always nice to see somebody else that, you know, is a serious entrepreneur, I respect that.

Marco: *Thank You.*

Gary: I also looked at your company from the D&B perspective, because they do these profiles on companies, and I always like to check companies out, and see how they're doing, and see how the D&B thinks they're doing, and you guys look very good financially, I mean you guys did what, 3 or 4 million dollars last year?

Marco: *Yes we did.*

Gary: Wow that's very successful. So the reason I say that is part of our relationship is looking to work with successful companies that we can add value to, because part of my reason for being here is to take a look at your entire IT operation and give you some feedback and analysis on where you are with respect to best practices in our industry. But at the same time part of our reason for being here is to look for a fit between my company and your company, because there has to be a fit for us to work for you. I've got to be able to show you that we can reduce your costs or increase your efficiencies, and mitigate your business pain with respect to I.T., or there's not a good fit. We are not in the business of giving you fast PC's or fast servers; you can get that from Dell, you don't need to get that from us. So there has to be a relationship that works. So part of my questioning today is going to be based on me trying to discover what things, if any, we can do for your company, that reduces cost and or increases efficiency, and removes your business pain - that's a big part of it. So I appreciate your story about how you got started. Now are you in entwined in your network, do you know a lot of stuff about your PC's and servers?

Marco: *No I don't. One of our CPA's here, he loves computers and he's the one who sets them up.*

Gary: Okay, and what's his name?

Marco: *His name is Joe Smith.*

Gary: Okay, got to love Joe Smith, he's got a very common name. How long has he been doing that?

Marco: *He's been doing that for about 4 years.*

Gary: Okay, so then he really does know the network. Okay so I'm going to skip some of the technical questions because It'll be easier, probably, for me to talk to Joe about it, and maybe you can give me his email address or contact information, or maybe I can go see him after we're done and talk to him and let him know we're doing an evaluation of what you have right now and he can share that information with me.

Marco: *Okay*

Gary: So are you a football fan?

Marco: *Yeah my kid wants to go to USC. He watches most of the games so I like to sit down with him and watch the games.*

Gary: So you're an SC fan?

Marco: *Yes.*

Gary: That's unfortunate.

Marco: *Why is that?*

Gary: I'm a UCLA fan.

Marco: *You are?*

Gary: Yeah, I've been watching you guys for a while and I respect the team and all that, but UCLA had a pretty good upset this year.

Marco: *Yeah you got us this time.*

Gary: But we caught you sleeping.

Marco: Most of the time we beat you.

Gary: Yeah, you guys got the record on us, no question, but we caught you guys sleeping and kicked you out of that national championship run, which was quite nice for us. It's a good rivalry. I guess we've been at it for a long time between basketball and football. You guys have dominated on the football side for quite a while now, but anything we can do that helps us to have one notch up on you, whenever we can upset you, is always a good thing. But I just wanted to tease you about that a little.

Gary: What about pro football?

Marco: *Pro football? Yeah, I used to watch the Steelers in the 70's when I was a kid. So I got to watch them win four super bowls, so…*

Gary: I'm unhappy with them right now because I'm a Cowboys fan.

Marco: *You are?*

Gary: And we've had the 5 Superbowl rings that we used to dominate forever, until you guys moved into that circle along with us and the 49ers and I'm still trying to get over that. I mean I like Howard, you know he's a good guy and all, but you know, I didn't want to see them win, because my Steelers buddies, that's been the only thing I can say to them for the last 10 years is that until you get 5 rings, you can't even sit at the table with us. Now they have 5 rings, which is good for them, but not so good for us. I always like to talk the football talk, because we are going to spend a lot of time together down the line I hope and it gives me some kind of insight into things we might have in common. I appreciate a good football fan anyway.

Gary: Now let me ask you some quick, brief questions, I know you don't know the technical stuff but do you know how many servers you have here? I mean a total of servers?

Marco: *I think we have a couple of computers in the back that are functioning as servers.*

Gary: Okay.

Marco: *but we'll have to talk to Joe and see what he says.*

Gary: How about desktops? How many users are there?

Marco: *Well I have 20 CPA's here and they all have a desktop computer. Some of them have laptops because they have to go out and see clients.*

Gary: Okay do you know, do you have any idea of what that breakout is? Or do I have to get that from Joe as well?

Marco: *Check with Joe, but I think it's about 5 guys that have laptops, who go out to see clients.*

Gary: Okay, and do they have remote access to the network when they go offsite?

Marco: *They do.*

Gary: Okay, what about Spyware? A lot of clients have that kind of problem do you have a lot of problems with Spyware?

Marco: *No, not recently we used to have problems when we were running old computers but Joe has handled that situations for us and we don't seem to have a problem with that anymore.*

Gary: Okay, so there are no problems there. How about viruses, when was the last time you had a virus problem?

Marco: *I get pop-ups on my computer once in a while saying that there's some kind of virus has been detected, but I get an option there to remove it. So it seems to be working fine.*

Gary: Okay. What about Internet filtering, do you care about that? What I mean by that is some owners want to filter their internet traffic or be able to monitor their traffic to find out where the users go and when.

Marco: *As far as I know we don't have anything in place; you can go anywhere you want to if you open the web browser.*

Gary: Okay so you don't have filtering and you don't need any, is what you're saying? Sometimes owners want to measure and or track that and sometimes limit that.

Marco: *I see, well I'm interested in exploring that, but I don't know how you would use it. So if you could tell me how it would work for me.*

Gary: Okay I'll put something together for you. What about backups? I'm assuming that Joe is responsible for your backups.

Marco: *I think so, yes he is.*

Gary: Okay so do you have a backup strategy that he has put together for you in respect to what would happen if a disaster were to occur to your servers so that you can recover them?

Marco: *I don't know.*

Gary: You don't know that? We are very serious about backups with our clients, because no matter what happens to your hardware, as long as we have the data, as long as we have control of it and you have it, then we can always bring you back up at some point in time. Do you have any backup tapes yourself at home that Joe gives you?

Marco: *No*

Gary: Do you happen to know if he has anything at home?

Marco: *No, I have no idea.*

Gary: Okay, that's a huge point there. We create Disaster Recovery plans that deal with what to do if you walked in tomorrow and your building was on fire and you couldn't get in and the server was destroyed. Do you have a plan for how to deal with that?

Marco: *No I don't*

Gary: Are you interested in a plan on how to deal with that?

Marco: *Yes let's explore that.*

Gary: Because that doesn't happen often but I have a client where a simple thing like the awning on the front of his building fell off and the building and safety folks came over and condemned the building for two weeks until they could get the construction folks to show up, remove the debris and check the structure to proclaim it was safe. So for two weeks they couldn't enter their building and they had no way of remotely accessing their server. They were a financial services company and it really hurt their business for two weeks, so you never know how a simple thing like that can affect you. What about your website, I looked at it, and it looks very, very nice, when was the last time you updated it?

Marco: *I don't know my cousin Harry is a web developer so he assists the company with the website development. I don't know when the last time he worked on it.*

Gary: Now are you using your website to drive revenue? Or is it just an information page?

Marco: *It's an information page. It's like a brochure.*

Gary: How you ever thought of using it that way?

Marco: *I have thought about it but I really need to get some assistance with that. I'm not technically savvy so if there are any ideas that you might have in that area to help me increase revenue I am definitely willing to explore that.*

Gary: Okay, because we do have some thoughts, we work with a number of CPA's and there are some nice clean ways of doing that. And since your cousin is doing it he's probably hosting it for you I would assume?

Marco: *We use a hosting company that I know called Crystal Tech. We pay 20 bucks a month. You mentioned that you are doing some things for other CPA's in terms of their websites - what kinds of things are you doing for them to help them drive revenue??*

Gary: Well what they've done, through their website, is host QuickBooks for their clients – an ASP QuickBooks program.

Marco: *I see.*

Gary: So their smaller clients, they charge them a monthly recurring fee for that. And it's simple; they don't have to go to the site or have them email files, it's a nice exchange for them and their small clients and they can give them whatever reports they need, or make adjustments to their QuickBooks file or whatever they're using, and that site puts both of them together. And it's got a database backend so they can run reports and stats against it so it's very, very clean. It has changed their business.

Marco: *How much are they charging per user for that?*

Gary: It varies, you know they sort of customize that based on the market they're going with, so when we sit down and talk that through, I'll give you some options of what works there, the numbers that they use that actually drive revenue, what people can afford to pay, what the prices are.

Marco: *That's very interesting I would like to explore that.*

Gary: Okay, great. So firewall, this is a semi technical question, but I imagine that Joe knows the firewall you use, but I want to ask you a different question, how serious is security in the network to you?

Marco: *Very serious. There are many regulations that apply to accountants. We are held responsible if files are accessed by the wrong people. We are in charge of keeping those files secure. It's very important to us that nobody has access to those files.*

Gary: I don't know what your firewall situation but we have a top Microsoft certified security guy working for us, so we do a great job of making sure clients are protected in terms of security proactively. Now, I'm going to talk about that on my next visit in great detail. I am aware of your security requirements as well because I'm in your space, and I'm going to talk to Joe more specifically about that. I have had clients tell me that they cannot be hacked, and maybe they can, but you want to at least make sure that if you ever get into a legal situation, you can say I have done everything I can do as a business owner to make sure we are meeting best security practices.

Marco: *Are your technicians bonded if they come in and do work for us and there is a problem, do you guys have some kind of insurance?*

Gary: Yes and I can show you all of our carrier information, and we are even protected if your data gets lost - we have insurance that covers us in all those scenarios. Now, Exchange server, do you have an Exchange server, well you

---

may or may not know, well how do you get your mail right now?

Marco: *I use Outlook.*

Gary: Okay, so are you using any shared calendars when you do that? Do you have shared calendaring in your infrastructure right now?

Marco: *No.*

Gary: Okay and you said earlier that you're not getting a lot of spam, we said viruses, what about spam, did I ask you about spam earlier?

Marco: *Spam is a problem. I get about 500 spam messages a day. Joe set up the computer in such a way that all the spam goes into the junk mail folder, but I still have some messages in there that are from customers that I want to get. So I would like to be able to eliminate all that spam from the junk folder, I don't even want to see that, I just want to see the mail I'm interested in, and nothing else.*

Gary: Okay, yeah, that's usually the case, so, well that's interesting, and so I'll talk to him about that. Our clients today live in a non-spam, non-virus, non-spyware world; they just don't have those problems.

Marco: *How do you fix that?*

Gary: I am not a technical guy; it's just a software application that we are using. And we constantly change that based on the best practices that are out there, so if we're using a spyware program that is not as good as the new one, we switch to the new one and roll it out to our clients. So they're using the most current stuff that we are using. Personally I don't have spam problems or any of those things, because our network is maintained by our technicians that we offer to our clients.

Marco: *Okay.*

Gary: Certainly when I come back we'll talk about that. So you're not aware if you have an Exchange server here or whether or not you guys are using what they call pop mail, which means you're using another carrier to host your mail?

Marco: *I don't know I just open Outlook and my mail is there.*

Gary: I see, okay, so we don't know about any hosting issues there. Now how about it being down? How often is your mail down?

Marco: *I haven't had any problems with that. It's running fine.*

Gary: So it's never been down?

Marco: *The main problem is the amount of spam, and going through those messages and wasting a lot of time.*

Gary: If you're spending time doing that, then I imagine your other 20 users are spending the same amount of time or some version of time. How long does it take you to get through there, and clean that stuff up, you know drag and drop over and delete it and all that stuff?

Marco: *Over the course of a day? I probably spend a good 20 minutes going through that.*

Gary: Yes, especially when the numbers are really high. Alright so that makes sense, so routers, that's probably a Joe topic but I'm sure you've got one. Do you know if you have a T1, Internet T1, or are you guys using DSL?

Marco: *Yes I know we have a T1 because I know we signed up with a company called Mpower Communications, they do our phones, our phone lines and also our connections to the Internet so I know it's going through some kind of T1.*

Gary: Do you recall how much it is per month average?

Marco: *We are paying about $600 a month.*

Gary: Okay. Now what is your line of business application here that you use to run your business predominately?

Marco: *We use a tax preparation program called* LaCerte, *another tax preparation program called* Pro System Effects, *I use another program called* Accountants Trial Balances, *we use a lot of* Microsoft Excel *to do our auditing, and we use a document management system called* LaserFiche.

Gary: Good, I was going to ask you about document imaging. What about the support on those pieces when those programs are not working or updates or upgrades or what have you, I'm assuming Joe handles all of that?

Marco: *Yes*

Gary: Okay and what about CRM, are you using Microsoft CRM or some version of another CRM application?

Marco: *No we are using Outlook; all of our contacts are in Outlook, that's how we keep track of that.*

Gary: Are you running Microsoft Office with the whole suite of programs?

Marco: *Yes we are.*

Gary: Do you know what version by chance?

Marco: *I know I use Outlook 2003 so I would say that would are using Microsoft Office 2003.*

Gary: Okay, now the Telco stuff, do you have any call accounting - software account codes where people put in account codes to dial?

Marco: *No.*

Gary: What about your phone system? I can see here on your desk it's Nortel. How long have you had it?

Marco: *We've had it for about 5 years.*

Gary: Are you happy with it?

Marco: *It works very well it's just a bit complicated, I'm not a technical person so I really don't know how to use it that well.*

Gary: What about the voicemail - is it working fine?

Marco: *Its working fine, if we have a power outage, it takes about an hour to bring it back up and that creates problems sometimes.*

Selling Managed Services – 1st Appointment

Gary: Have you looked into upgrading it, well you said you are happy with it a second ago.

Marco: *We haven't looked into upgrading it; maybe we are going to wait a few more years.*

Gary: Okay. You said Mpower was your T-1 provider, and your phone bill is about $600 a month.

Marco: *And that includes internet.*

Gary: Okay that's a pretty good deal for 20 people on the phones; you must have got a great rate with them.

Marco: *I think we got a good deal on that.*

Gary: Well Marco that's pretty much everything I need today, let me just go through my notes and make sure I covered everything. Now you said you don't have any downtime on your email - what about your downtime on your servers?

Marco: *Well when we have a power outage, the server sometimes doesn't come back up right away, so that creates a problem. Joe has been dealing with that. We've been down for about 46 hours one time.*

Gary: Wow. In the last month or so, how long would you say you've been down, one or two times per month or?

Marco: *I'd say about 5 months ago we were down for about 5 hours.*

Gary: Okay and how often do you travel?

Marco: *I travel about 5 times every quarter. I go visit my clients in other states.*

Gary: So you have a nationwide presence.

Marco: *Well we do auditing and have to do engagements all over the place, so we have clients with offices in different locations, so sometimes we have to go to different states like New York and we have an auditing engagement there.*

Gary: That's great business. Now, other than Joe, he handles the I.T. stuff, what about other vendors do you engage like Mpower, your copier guy, your Telco guy who does your phone systems, who handles all those guys, does Joe handle all that?

Marco: *No it's Laurie, the office manager, she the person who is in charge of that.*

Gary: Okay. What I need to do before I leave, if they have a couple minutes now that would be great, if not then I can schedule another time to come back and see them because I need more specific information from them so that I can put together a cost savings analysis for you.

Marco: *How much time are you going to need?*

Gary: About five minutes each.

Marco: *Okay you can talk to them right after we're done here.*

Gary: Perfect. Now your phone bill looks pretty good, because at $600 a month they probably have you on some kind of flat rate deal. I usually offer to audit your phone bills to see if you're getting the best rates available because we have relationships with about 30 different phone service providers, but at $600 a month with 20 I think you're probably okay there, but I'll find out with Laurie what she thinks and if she thinks it is worth looking at then we'll look at that. So what I need to do now is set up a day to come back and talk to you, so can you pull your calendar up so that we can see what your next availability might be?

Marco: *Sure, let me see here.*

Gary: So today is Thursday, I'm going to need two or three days to look this stuff through and work with my team on it, so if you're available next Wednesday or Thursday that would be great.

Marco: *Thursday at 8:00 in the morning would work for me.*

Gary: Okay so Thursday at 8:00 it is, and our guys will send you out another one of those appointment confirmation cards we sent you, to make sure that everyone is on the same page and the email that you got before. I want to thank you for your time, I appreciate you and I appreciate what your business is about and I'm looking forward to us working together.

Marco: *Great thank you.*

Gary: Thank you.

As you can see, this appointment was handled in a very conversational manner, and touched on many of the points in our process. Obviously, Gary believes Marco's company would be a great client, and has moved forward to pre-arrange the second appointment at the end of the meeting.

Selling Managed Services – Before the 2nd Appointment

So we've now decided to move forward and allocate time and resources to developing a business partnership with our prospect Marco. What we're going to do next is schedule a technician to crawl Marco's network and perform a network analysis, and document it. This information will be brought back and we'll use it to prepare a quote to bring the network up to our certified network standard. I cannot remember a network that was in such good shape that we didn't have to do absolutely anything to it in order to begin delivering our services, so always go in expecting to create a quote for some sort of service or remediation, in addition to your Managed Services Proposal and Agreement.

We're also going to visit with Laurie, Marco's office manager, in order to get the information from her in order to complete the vendor management portion of our cost savings analysis, and Joe, the accountant who sounds like he's doing more I.T. work than accounting work. In the previous appointment, Gary asked Marco if he could speak with Laurie and Joe while he was there, right after the first appointment ended, saving himself another trip. I would assume that Marco would offer up the payroll information we would need in order to provide us the last bit of data for our cost savings analysis, or direct us to the person we could get that information from.

The objectives we will meet before the second appointment are:

- Gather data for cost savings analysis

The Best I.T. Sales & Marketing BOOK EVER!

Selling Managed Services – Before the 2nd Appointment

- Perform a network analysis and create network documentation

Some of the following is excerpted from *The Guide to a Successful Managed Services Practice.*

Managed Services Cost Savings Analysis	
Gross Revenue	
Organization's Gross Revenue	$1,000,000.00
Productivity Loss To Staff Managing Vendors	
Number of Vendors Managed by Client	12
Number of Hours Spent Managing Vendors Per Month	12
Manager's Average Hourly Rate	$45.00
Productivity Lost Annually To Managing Vendors	$6,480.00
Productivity Loss To Staff Performing IT Functions	
Number of Hours Spent Performing IT Functions Per Month	12
Staff Member's Average Hourly Rate	$35.00
Productivity Lost Annually To Performing IT Functions	$5,040.00
Productivity Loss To Network Downtime	
Number of Users On Client Network	20
Number of Servers At Client Location	1
Network Downtime	Hours
Email Services Down per Month	4
Internet Connection Down per Month	4
Server or Desktops Down per Month	2
Total Hours Network is Down Monthly	10
Total Hours Network is Down Annually	120
Labor Costs	
Average Salary Per Employee	$30,000.00
Total Employee Yearly Payroll	$600,000.00
Average Annual Employee Hours	2080
Total Annual Employee Hours	41600
Average Hourly Labor Cost Per Employee	$14.42
Productivity Lost To Downtime Annually	$34,615.38
Gross Revenue Loss To Network Downtime	
Individual Employee Hourly Contribution To Gross Revenue	$24.04
Gross Revenue Lost To Downtime Annually	$57,692.31
Existing Annual IT Costs	$10,000.00
Unlimited Remote Helpdesk Support For All Client Servers	*Included*
Unlimited Remote Helpdesk Support For All Client Desktops	*Included*
Unlimited Remote Helpdesk Support For All Client Printers	*Included*
Unlimited Remote Helpdesk Support For All Client Scanners	*Included*
Unlimited Remote Helpdesk Support For All Client Copiers	*Included*
Unlimited Remote Monitoring Support 24/7/365	
Unlimited Remote Monitoring For All Client Servers	*Included*
Unlimited Remote Monitoring For All Client Routers	*Included*
Unlimited Remote Monitoring For All Client Broadband	*Included*
Unlimited Remote Monitoring For All Client VPNs	*Included*
Unlimited Remote Monitoring For All Client Email/Web Services	*Included*
Unlimited Remote Monitoring For All Client SQL/Line Of Business Servers	*Included*
Vendor Management Service	
Unlimited Management For All Client Vendor Support Issues	*Included*
Telecomm Vendors	*Included*
Software Vendors	*Included*
Equipment Vendors	*Included*
Annual Loss of Productivity from Staff Managing Vendors	$6,480.00
Annual Loss of Productivity from Staff Performing IT Functions	$5,040.00
Annual Loss of Productivity Cost from Network Downtime	$34,615.38
Annual Loss of Gross Revenue from Network Downtime	$57,692.31
Projected Existing Annual IT Cost	$10,000.00
Total Existing Annual IT Support Costs	$113,827.69
Proposed Managed Services Cost	$36,000.00
Total Client Savings	**$77,827.69**

Selling Managed Services – Before the 2nd Appointment

Collecting the information required, and completing the cost savings analysis is very simple.

In addition to leveraging the cost savings that managing Marco's vendors will provide him, the cost savings analysis tool will also reflect the losses Marco incurs by having an in-house staff person such as Joe perform lightweight I.T. duties before receiving authorization to call in their existing reactive I.T service provider.

The cost savings analysis also *dollarizes* what downtime really costs Marco in terms of lost productivity, as well as lost opportunity, and demonstrates all of the additional benefits he will receive by transitioning to proactive Managed Services.

So we're going to meet with Laurie, Marco's office manager, and ask her how many vendors service their organization, and ask her assistance in gathering important vendor data in order to prepare our cost savings analysis.

After we find out who all of the vendors are, we'll ask Laurie which piece of equipment, 3rd-party line-of-business application, or vendor service they spend the most time troubleshooting .

There will invariably be a problem piece of equipment (such as a network copier) or 3rd-party line of business software application that they will volunteer, and let you know just how frustrated they are from having to deal with it.

Hopefully, Laurie will provide us with enough examples like this that it won't be difficult to illustrate for her, or Marco, the value of our vendor management service.

The Best I.T. Sales & Marketing BOOK EVER!

Selling Managed Services – Before the 2nd Appointment

Now that we've let the Laurie vent a while, we're going to ask her how many hours per week she thinks is spent, on average, managing all of their vendors. We're going to list each and every Infrastructure or software vendor that supports the entire organization:

- Telco Service Vendor
- Telco System Vendor
- Broadband Service Vendor
- Copier Vendor
- Printer Vendor
- Fax Vendor
- Hardware Vendor
- Line-of-Business Application Vendor
- Web Hosting Vendor
- Co-Lo Vendor
- Cellular Vendor
- POS Vendor
- All Other Infrastructure Vendors

Okay, so let's say Laurie tells us there are 12 vendors. We enter this information on the cost savings analysis form under "Number of Vendors Managed by Client".

A copy of the cost savings analysis is included on the CD in the back of this book – launch it and follow along.

Laurie then informs us that she spends about 3 hours per week (12 hours per month) dealing with all of these vendors (we always ask for weekly hours, they always seem higher than when we ask for monthly hours).

The Best I.T. Sales & Marketing BOOK EVER!

Selling Managed Services – Before the 2nd Appointment

We now enter this information on the cost savings analysis form under "Number of Hours Spent Managing Vendors per Month".

We then find out from Marco what Laurie's salary is, including bonuses, benefits, sick leave and vacation time, and calculate what her hourly pay is.

We enter this data on the cost savings analysis form as well, under "Manager's Average Hourly Rate", which will then be used to calculate how much revenue (not to mention productivity) Marco is losing per year by having Laurie perform these duties.

So let's say we've calculated Laurie's true hourly rate to be $45.00 per hour. Our cost savings analysis form will reflect a value of $6,480.00 per year ($45.00 per hour x 12 hours per month x 12 Months) as "Revenue Lost Annually to Managing Vendors". Using this formula, we can extrapolate a loss of more than $32,000.00 over a 5 year period for Marco. These are real dollars impacting his bottom line!

We are now going to speak to Joe, the "lightweight I.T person in Marco's company. We conduct the same type of interview with Joe that we did with Laurie.

First we'll ask Joe which PC's are the most problematic in the environment. Joe will promptly identify them, and with a little coaxing, proceed to vent to us how much time performing these additional "I.T." duties is robbing from his productivity.

It's a simple task, at this point, to ask how many hours a week Joe spends performing these additional tasks. Let's say Joe

Selling Managed Services – Before the 2nd Appointment

---

tells us he spends 3 hours per week (12 hours per month) "keeping things running".

We now enter this information on the cost savings analysis form under "Number of Hours Spent Performing IT Functions per Month".

We then find out from Marco what Joe's salary is, including bonuses, benefits, sick leave and vacation time, and calculate what his hourly pay is.

We then enter this data on the cost savings analysis form as well, under "Staff Member's Average Hourly Rate", which will then be used to calculate how much revenue (not to mention productivity) Marco is losing per year by having Joe perform these duties.

So let's say we've calculated Joe's true hourly rate to be $35.00 per hour. Our cost savings analysis form will reflect a value of $5,040.00 per year ($35.00 per hour x 12 hours per month x 12 Months) as "Revenue Lost Annually to Performing IT Functions". Using this formula, we can extrapolate a loss of more than $25,000.00 over a 5 year period for Marco. Once again - these are real dollars impacting Marco's bottom line!

Next, we're going to find out how many users and servers exist in Marco's environment, and enter this data in the appropriate fields on the cost savings analysis form. In this example, let's say there are 20 Users and 1 Server in the environment.

Now we're going to find out how many hours of downtime the environment experiences in regards to email, broadband connectivity, servers and desktops. We enter this information

---

Selling Managed Services – Before the 2nd Appointment

in the appropriate fields on the cost savings analysis form as well, which will calculate a yearly value for network downtime.

So even though in our example, Marco answered differently, let's assume we've been told that Marco experiences about an hour of downtime per week for email and the same for the broadband connection, and about an hour every other week that the server is down for one reason or another.

This adds up to about 10 hours per month, and is reflected on the cost savings analysis as 120 hours per year. Okay, now we're going to ask Marco what his average Salary is per employee. Let's say this is $30,000 – this value goes in the "Average Salary per Employee" field. The cost savings analysis now calculates this value against the number of users, and reflects a "Total Employee Yearly Payroll" of $600,000.00. The cost savings analysis tool now calculates "Average Annual Employee Hours", "Total Annual Employee Hours", and "Average Hourly Labor Cost per Employee". In this example, the average Hourly Labor Cost per Employee is $14.42.

The Savings Analysis now takes $14.42 and multiplies it by 20 Users, and then again by 120 hours of Downtime, for a total Yearly Downtime Cost of $34,615.38.

We're now going to ask Marco how much he spent on his existing Reactive IT Provider last year - $10,000.00, and enter that value in the "Existing Annual IT Costs" field.

We're also going to ask Marco what his average yearly revenue is, and again, even though in our example 1st appointment, Marco gave another figure, we're going to use one million dollars a year in our example. This goes in the

The Best I.T. Sales & Marketing BOOK EVER!

Selling Managed Services – Before the 2nd Appointment

"Organization's Gross Revenue" field at the very top of the cost savings analysis form. This number is used to calculate the value in the "Individual Employee's Contribution to Gross Revenue" field, as well as the "Gross Revenue Lost to Downtime Annually" field. The cost savings analysis uses a similar calculation to derive these values as it does for the labor cost and downtime calculations.

The Managed Services New Client Savings Analysis tool now brings all of the following values down to the bottom of the form:

Annual Loss of Productivity from Client Vendor Manager

$6,480.00

Annual Loss of Productivity from Staff Performing IT Functions

$5,040.00

Annual Loss of Productivity Cost from Network Downtime

$34,615.00

Annual Loss of Gross Revenue from Network Downtime

$57,692.31

Total Existing Annual IT Cost

$10,000.00

The Savings Analysis now totals all of these values and displays:

Selling Managed Services – Before the 2nd Appointment

Total Existing Annual IT Support Costs

$113,827.69

Let's take a moment to fully comprehend and appreciate the awesome power behind this Sales Technique...

I'll guarantee to you that most prospects have never seen this type of sales approach from an I.T. Company before. They are used to having "break-fix" companies come in, count up the equipment, and provide a quote to support it. When a prospect is dealt with in that manner, they can't help but perceive this type of quote as an *expense* – and rightly so. And expenses always negatively impact the bottom line – right?

So what we accomplish with our cost savings analysis approach is to differentiate ourselves from any other "break-fix" I.T. provider the prospect has ever dealt with in the past. We *begin* the client relationship from a 50,000 foot "Trusted Advisor" level, setting the appropriate tone and expectation with the prospect right from the initial meeting.

As the prospect realizes that we are looking after *their bottom line* – and how we can help to improve it, they are extremely motivated to enlist our services, as we have performed an excellent job of illustrating how much money they are losing each and every month that they *do not* sign our Managed Services Agreement.

Okay – back to our example.

We've now gathered all of the information we need in order to quote a value in the "Proposed Managed Services Cost" field on the Savings Analysis. We are going to quote $36,000.00,

---

or $3,000.00 per month, for Marco. When this value is entered into the "Proposed Managed Services Cost" field on the Analysis, it will reflect a "Total Client Savings" of $77,827.69, or nearly $6,500.00 per month!

Why would we quote only $3,000.00 per month, if we could quote $4,000.00 per month, and have an excellent chance of getting it? Well, because we noted during our network analysis that Marco really needs to replace his aging Server, as well as 5 PC's with new Desktops.

So what we're going to do is prepare a quote to perform these infrastructure upgrades, and present it at the same time we present our Managed Services Agreement for signature. We use this technique to illustrate to our prospects that not only will they benefit from increased uptime, and receive unlimited help desk support as well as vendor management services, but they will also receive an infrastructure upgrade as well – and *it will all still cost less than what they are spending right now!*

When utilized properly, the Managed Services Cost Savings Analysis approach will help you win business over all of the other "break-fix" Proposals you may compete against!

Selling Managed Services –2nd Appointment

As in each phase of our Managed Services sales process, we have several goals we're trying to reach during the 2nd appointment to sell Managed Services:

- Present the client PowerPoint presentation
- Present the results of the cost savings analysis
- Overcome objections

So we're going to arrive, meet the prospect, perform a bit of warm-up, and then sell our prospect on the reasons they should build a business partnership with us by utilizing a short PowerPoint presentation created specifically for this purpose. We'll print it out in color, and have it bound at a local office supply store (it's less than 10 pages), then use it to keep us on point, and make sure we don't forget anything.

PowerPoint Presentation Goal:

Show the Client how to increase profits, decrease costs and mitigate risk by partnering with you to deliver Managed Services and other IT Solutions.

The Client PowerPoint presentation is included on the CD in the back cover of this book.

After we've done the PowerPoint presentation with our prospect, we'll go through the cost savings analysis with them, and finally answer any of their questions and overcome their objections. Here are the client PowerPoint presentation talking points:

- Describe flat-rate IT services and benefits
- Describe Remote Support
- Describe 24x7 Monitoring
- Describe Vendor Management
- Describe your Professional Services
  - Infrastructure
  - Business Continuity Planning
  - Web Development
  - Etc.
- Describe your competencies and vendor relationships
- Validate value of your Services with client

Here are some common objections, and how to overcome them:

- "How much does it cost?" -interruptions during presentation
  - "We're going to get to that in a minute" – Don't be sidetracked, stay with the presentation.
- "I already have someone on staff that can take care of that"
  - "I really want to talk to you about how much productivity and revenue you're losing by having your staff deal with these issues internally" – Validate this during the Cost Savings Analysis presentation
- "What about a physical hardware failure – how do you deal with that?"
  - "In most cases, we'll know when a component is nearing failure, thanks to our 24x7 Monitoring system, and will proactively replace it to avoid work stoppage. The reason we require you to

have a spare PC onsite is so that we can work with your staff to swap a failed PC for us, then we'll remote in and set up the user's profile, so they can get back to work as quickly as possible. We'll then arrange to pick the failed PC up and repair it at our facility, after which it then becomes the new spare."

- "I don't want anyone other than your staff to have access to our internal systems"
  - o "Although our monitoring team is in another country, the only data that they receive from your systems is performance data. They then alert us to issues that need to be dealt with, and we handle it from there. All of our patching, updating and disk optimization activity is handled through scripts that run on your systems automatically. Our help desk, along with the technical staff that will be assisting your organization is based in the United States" – For Clients that are sensitive in this area, implement a strategy that meets their specific needs, rather than employ a "one size fits all" model. For many Clients that understand that just about any Technical Support offered nowadays is delivered from another country, this objection should not surface.

Now let's walk through the 2nd prospect appointment role-playing session we conducted with one of our Partners; Marco Alcala, during a Managed Services Sales Training boot camp.

2nd Prospect Appointment Role-Play Transcript:

Gary: Marco how are you doing?

Marco: *Good and you Gary?*

Gary: Good, good, good, it's good to see you again.

Marco: *You too.*

Gary: So we've done some work since the last time I spoke with you and my team has put some things together that I'm going to go over with you today and see if the fit I think will work, will. Before I get into the numbers, I want to talk a little about our company because when I was here before I didn't spend a lot of time telling you about what we do and how we do it. That meeting is really designed to find out a lot about your organization. I have about 6 or 7 slides that I want to go through here that really talks about our services and what we do, because I think it'll fit nicely with the numbers part of the presentation later.

Gary: So let's talk about flat rate I.T. services, that's our first slide. Flat rate I.T. is a new and upcoming service in our industry, and we liken it to the cell phone industry. You were probably around when cell phones first came out, and it was 47 to 67 cents a minute, you know very expensive, the phones were gigantic and we all had to have them because we wanted a cell phone. But you also had a pager back then so people paged you and then you decided if you wanted to spend the cell phone minutes to call them back, or wait until you got back to the office. So ideally today, for your cell phone you probably have either some buckets of minutes that purchase every month or I know some guys who have unlimited minutes - they pay one fee and talk as much as they want depending on the carrier. Now I am also likening it to your long distance bill today, you probably don't spend, you know, 10 or 11 cents a minute anymore, you buy it in buckets or you're getting an unlimited service. So are you experiencing any services like that?

Marco: *Yes I believe our T1 line has unlimited minutes. So we pay about $600 a month and it's fixed.*

Gary: Perfect that's the concept. Now in I.T. there is no concept like that today. You pay when the guy shows up and there is an exchange of services and he sends an invoice and you pay. Now the problem with that is most of the business owners tell us that they aren't sure how long he was there, and they're not sure if it got fixed. And then they get a bill and what tends to happen is you call up or one of your folks calls up and says, "Hey you were out here two weeks ago, I don't think you were out here for six hours or as long as the invoice says, or you were but you came back the next day because the same problem was not fixed and you came back and then you billed me again." You've probably have had a similar experience. And most business owners don't like that. So we've decided to fix that. Our goal is flat rate service, you use as much as you want from 8 to 5 with unlimited support. So we come onsite and we're there for two hours or we're there for five hours it's on us. You get one bill each month no matter how long we were out there; you can call us as much as you want. So we've applied the same approach to this that the Telco industry has had in respect to just giving the client what they want and most clients say I don't want to have to worry about what the bill is.

Marco: *How much is that going to cost me?*

Gary: We're going to talk about that, that's part of the numbers piece. But I want you to understand the concept here and how we do that. Now, you may say, "How do you guys do that"?

Here's how we do that, it's all remote, predominantly. So, what happens in the remote scenario is you call us up, you have an issue, and you'll open up a ticket through our helpdesk. Now this certainly affects response time, because in the way you do business today, if you call up somebody to come out and roll a truck out here you've got to wait for him to get here. Now if I can give you a response time of 15 minutes to an issue, that's certainly much better than waiting for somebody to roll a truck and you're waiting for the guy to get here. We've found that I.T. companies; you know our brethren out there, take 3 to 4 hours to roll a truck to get out on a call that usually can be fixed in a short amount of time once they arrive.

Marco: *You might recall, Gary, that I have Joe here working for me, we don't have to call anybody, he's here, there's no additional cash out of pocket.*

Gary: Right.

Marco: *All I've got to do is say "Hey Joe why don't you take care of that problem," and he'll take care of it for me. That's why I'm asking you how much is this going to cost because it sounds like I'm going to have to spend additional money to get your service and when I have Joe I don't have to spend any additional money, he's already part of the budget that I have.*

Gary: Well I really want to talk about that because we've got some numbers that are going to scare you about Joe.

Marco: *Oh really?*

Gary: Oh yeah. I appreciate that Joe's here, but I'm certain I remember that you said you didn't hire Joe initially to be your I.T. guy - he is one of your CPA's.

Marco: *Sure.*

Gary: Okay so I am going to show you how technology can give Joe back to you.

Marco: *Okay.*

Gary: Okay so we'll get that done. So, the way we do support today though, we do everything for a fixed fee monthly, we do onsite support as needed, when you need it, but we've figured out a way to do 85 to 90% of all the support that's needed for your network remotely. We connect to your user's desktops, fix whatever problems they have, and actually not have to send someone out here 90% of the time. We have a very proactive approach to providing support. We are not waiting for things to break, and you made a very succinct point to that a second ago, as soon as something breaks, Joe gets involved. Well we want to get to it before it breaks, and we're going to show you how we do that. And that's a significant strategy shift for you in respect on how you do I.T. support, okay?

Marco: Okay.

Gary: So the next piece…

Marco: *Wait a minute, you said remote support, what happens if something breaks and you've got to replace that? Because right now if a hard drive fails on one of my desktops, Joe would just, you know, go to Fry's to buy the hard drive, and come back and replace it, so I mean remotely, how are you going to fix that?*

Gary: Well there are a couple of great things about that. First of all, we're not going to wait for the hard drive to break because of the way we monitor the hard drives. We're never going to get surprised when it breaks. A typical reason why a hard drive fails or becomes unreliable or slow is, it maxes out in capacity, and nobody's watching the capacity. And all of a sudden, someone went on iTunes and downloaded 25 videos and maxed out your server's hard drive and it crashes. Well we're monitoring that stuff, and we'll talk about monitoring in a second. So we come to you proactively and say "Hey the PC in such and such office, is at a point where the drive needs to be replaced, and we proactively do that, and on top of that we have a remote PC sitting in a closet here, so if a hard drive should fail for whatever reason unexpectedly, we can get that user back up in 15 to 20 minutes. And Joe can't do that right now. Because I'm certain that it takes time for Joe to go to Fry's, and there is a user down the entire time that is taking place. We have a complete process to make sure that downtime is minimized when a drive is fails, but we try to address it proactively.

Marco: *You're telling me that, if a hard drive fails, you can get that desktop up and running in 15 minutes?*

Gary: 30 minutes tops. Back on the network, same profile and back to work.

Marco: *Remotely?*

Gary: Not remotely, now remotely we can support it, but Joe being the smart guy that he is, he'll just grab the PC from the closet, put it in there, connect it up, and we'll do the rest.

Marco: *I see.*

Gary: Okay? And so it's really easy. We do it all the time

Marco: *okay, go ahead.*

Gary: With our old model we had to send somebody out when the company didn't have a Joe, take the PC, take it back to the office, they were down, send them a bill for $800, I mean it was a really bad situation for the users.

Marco: *I see.*

Gary: But that's gone away. Okay now let's talk about monitoring. Now this is a huge piece in our business now that we didn't do five years ago. Okay we didn't do it three years ago. Now let me give you an example of this. Imagine your company, you walk in; pretend for a second that you didn't have a Joe and even with Joe here, the example is still applicable. You come in the office at 8:30, 9:00, and for the sake of this discussion, your email server has gone down, but you don't realize it. So you launch Outlook, it's up, but you don't notice in the bottom right hand corner that it's disconnected. So you're taking some meetings, you're talking to folks on the phone, you're not paying attention. So 9:30 or so you figure out you haven't been receiving email. You haven't tried to send any either yet, to realize that it is down. But now you realize that it is down. And let's say for the sake of this example that Joe is not technical enough to solve this particular problem. So you've got to call the guy that you call occasionally that you spend a couple hundred dollars a month on. So it's 9:30, 10:00, he can't get out here, his response time is best case, 2 to 4 hours. And your email is down. So he gets out here around 1:00 or 2:00 to fix it, now he figures out whatever it is and he brings you back up. Now, not only you, but your entire organization is down for this entire time, so 4 or 5 hours. Now some company's emails are critical to them, and they can't afford to be down for that long. So in that case, how

---

can we fix that? Well here's how we fix it - monitoring. Now if your server went down at 3:00 in the morning, and you didn't realize that, our system says "Ahh look at that, the Exchange server went down, why we don't restart the services". And that's all it needed in this particular case. Or if it's something more serious than that, we have live support now where we are in fact monitoring it 24/7 and we can fix it remotely 24/7.

Marco: *How are you going monitor our servers Gary?*

Gary: We load a small agent on every device here, pc's and servers, and every time your server has a problem, it sends an alert to, what is called, an event log. So it tells us that it's sick. All we're doing now is monitoring those event logs. And when that happens, it tells our system, that this is the problem, the system says "I recognize this event log alert: do the following things". And if all it takes is a simple restart to fix, and a lot of the time that's all it is, the services come back up, you walk in at 8:30, 9:00, and you don't know the difference, but your Exchange server is working now. Compare that to the previous example, when the Exchange server went down and nobody was monitoring it at all, including Joe. The reality is you won't walk into the office at 8:30-9:00 in the morning and your Exchange server is down.

Marco: *Now the people that get those alerts, where are those people?*

Gary: Well we have a couple people that do that, we have people at our shop that do it, and we have a team that we work with that's in India that does it for us as well.

Marco: *So you're telling me that some people in India are looking at my tax returns?*

Gary: No just the alerts, period - that's it. Nothing else. All they do is look at the alerts and they contact us by phone and say, "Hey you have a server down in Pasadena" they call one of our technicians, who are on call at 2 in the morning if it's that big of an issue.

Marco: *How do you control those people in India? You know, I'm very concerned about that. We have very confidential information, what if those guys start stealing social security numbers and start selling them over the internet?*

Gary: They can't. All they have access to is the alerts, that's it. We have security to screen that; we'll show you a demonstration on how that works so you can have confidence there.

Marco: *Okay.*

Gary: So we've got that covered. Now you see the value in monitoring? So if this happens on a Saturday, happens on a Sunday, happens on a holiday, we're watching your servers and your desktops 24/7, and we're monitoring. And we also do patches and updates remotely, because we found when we roll trucks on a client's site, the first thing we do when we get there is start patching and updating the pc's and servers. And that would usually fix a lot of the problems that we were having. So we take care of that stuff at 2:00 in the morning for every PC and server, so that proactively these things get patched automatically. So we don't sit around and wait for this stuff to break and wait for it to get slow and wait for the patches to get old and then show up here and charge you for 8 hours to do that for all your pc's and servers, it gets done remotely , it's done after hours and it's proactive.

Marco: Okay

Gary: Okay so you can see that on a weekend or holiday, whenever that might be, if there's any issues going on we are tracking this stuff 24/7.

Marco: Okay

Gary: Okay? So we believe in the proactive, not reactive, approach. And we found by doing that, our clients' servers don't fail unexpectedly anymore, to the point where we'll guarantee you that if your server crashes and has to be restored, we'll restore it at our cost, if it takes us 10 hours to do it, 20 hours to do it, we have whatever technical team on the ground here to bring your server back up to its original configuration, at our cost.

Marco: Okay

Gary: That's how confident we are in it. So the one point I want to read to you on this slide is that we ensure maximum uptime for critical equipment. What we found on this part of our service, clients need their servers to be up all the time. There's never any good time for them to be down, so we make sure that they're up. Now in exchange for that, when we come out to talk to you in the future, saying, "Hey your backup device needs to be upgraded because you guys have outgrown it." Then we give you a price to come out and put that in when that makes sense. When drive space on your servers get to a point where they're too maxed at 90%, we need to look at bringing in new drives. So we're making sure that all this stuff is done proactively so we don't wait for anything to break, and then come out and tell you "well, it's broken now, so we need to fix it", maximizing uptime, the

---

proactive approach. Okay? Now our third service here, which is very popular, is our vendor management service and this is a big relief for Laurie, okay? We really have experts at our company working with vendors, and I think we looked at your vendor count; you had about 7 or 8 vendors that Laurie and other staff are working with monthly.

Marco: Okay

Gary: We found that business owners are spending a lot of time messing with this, no one has a vendor management person on staff that they've hired specifically for this job in their company. People just inherit that job and Laurie is doing a little bit of it, Joe is doing a little bit of it, so what we've found now is that we have the technical expertise to engage all your vendors more efficiently than you do. A lot of clients like the value of this service because what happens is you've got four major applications that you run right now, and when those applications break, someone's got to call the tech support at those vendors and talk to those folks. Now, Joe's a smart guy, there's no question, I've spent some time with him, but our technicians are just as good at working with that software, if not better, than he is, because we do it for more than one CPA. So we can fix the stuff without even having to call the vendor because we know the software. And we also build a knowledgebase in respect to your software. Every time we fix a problem we log it. So what happens is when a call comes in from one of the users about one of the software applications, we search our own knowledgebase first, and see if we have seen this situation before, and if we have then we quickly fix it for them and get them back online. Sometimes with third party vendors, it takes a long time to connect with their tech support and your user is down the whole time just waiting to speak to someone.

Selling Managed Services – 2nd Appointment

Marco: *How many technicians do you have on staff?*

Gary: We have 5 right now.

Marco: *You do?*

Gary: Yes, and two of them are completely trained in all of your software applications

Marco: *They are?*

Gary: They know them as well as your folks or Joe does, if not better.

Marco: *I see so, when we have a question, we're going to be talking to your people, you're not going to send me to India right? Because we used to deal with a company that before I hired Joe, I used to be in charge of the backup, and the company that made our backup software was Computer Associates. One time I had a problem with that backup program and, I called for tech support and they transferred me to India and that person was a total jerk, I talked to different people over there and I was very unsatisfied with the service, and I switched. Not only do we not use that software anymore, we switched to another company called Veritas, and of course I had Joe deal with that because I was tired of dealing with those people over there. They were a pain in the neck.*

Gary: Right.

Marco: *So if you told me my helpdesk was going to be in India, I don't want to do business with you.*

Selling Managed Services – 2nd Appointment

Gary: It is not, all those guys do for us is manage alerts, okay? Period. Let me explain that a little bit because you seem to have a concern about India so let's address it.

Marco: *Okay.*

Gary: Okay. Our whole point here is this, for me to have a guy sit at our help desk and just watch for alerts, well you can imagine what an IT team costs today.

Marco: *Okay.*

Gary: And we had a guy doing that, so we found a way for us to scale that. What's great about it is they are 12 hours ahead of us, so they're literally watching those alerts from midnight to 8 in the morning while we're all sleeping. So that's all they do, and they have very instructions for watching those alerts only, and calling us directly when there's an issue. You'll never talk to them, ever. Okay? So all of your direct support is done by English speaking staff in our local offices here.

Marco: *Okay, good.*

Gary: So they work with your users directly, period. So you'll never hear about the Indian guys. All we've found is that the cost for us to watch the alerts ourselves went to less than half when we asked those guys to do it. And that's all they do for us. It gives us the ability to monitor more pc's and more servers without having to expand our staff, because if I had to do it the way we're doing it now, I'd have to have 5 engineers sitting there watching that stuff. Because we watch it 24/7, holidays, weekends, all the time. So you don't have to walk into your office on Monday morning or after a holiday weekend and find your servers down.

Selling Managed Services – 2nd Appointment

Marco: *I see.*

Gary: Okay and that's the value of that piece, it helps all of us out to protect you when you're not there. If your server had crashed and we couldn't recover it remotely, we'll be sitting out in front of your office, at 8:00 when you get here.

Marco: *Okay.*

Gary: And somebody would have called you at home and say, "Hey our team is on the ground there at your place and we'll be there until somebody opens up 'cause we need to get in".

Marco: *Okay good, how much is this going to cost me?*

Gary: We're going to get to that.

Marco: *Okay*

Gary: That's the best part by the way.

Marco: *Oh it is?*

Gary: Yes it is, so vendor management is our way of managing all of your vendors and this includes SBC, Verizon, all your telco vendors, your phone vendor, guys that fix your copy machine, everybody, we have a philosophy we go by here, this gives us the ability to give you one throat to choke, you make one call to one company to deal with any issue with all your vendors, and your team isn't spending man hours anymore to support this. I give those hours back to those guys. So now they're still engaged and part of the process, but they are not spending as much time as they've been spending on it. And I'm going to show you that on a spreadsheet in a second -

---

---

how much time we're going to give back to you, some of Joe's time and some of Laurie's time because we can handle these vendors much faster.

Marco: *Okay.*

Gary: Okay so this is one of our most popular services, it gives you a chance to focus on your business now, not focus on managing your vendors.

Marco: *Okay.*

Gary: Okay? Alright now professional services, if you should engage us down the line to do projects for you, I want to talk you through how we do projects uniquely different than most I.T. companies. And this is a very important piece because what happens is if you decide that you want to change your line of business applications to something more robust than what you have today, you say, "Hey Gary we've been looking to expand into this software piece or what have you". And you start having those guys calling you. I want to become your Trusted Advisor from an I.T. perspective. You say, "Hey can you interview some folks for me, this is the application that we like, we've seen it before." What I would do now is I would go call those guys, I'll have my technical people engage them, we'll look at your hardware backend piece, we'll see if it's compatible with what you have on the ground now, to a point where, I'll have them give me a presentation and do a quote if you would like, before you even meet with them. I'll screen them out for you. If you want to get three quotes, I'll get three people to talk to me, I'll even talk to their existing clients who have the exact software and make sure they've had a positive experience with it before you even get engaged.

Marco: *And this is included as part of the services?*

Gary: Absolutely.

Marco: *So you're not going to bill me for calling all these people?*

Gary: Absolutely not, it's all part of our service. It's part of the vendor management piece because I am now managing and supporting vendors for you. So if you want a new accounting package or a new line of business application or there's a CRM application you want to look at, what I'm going to do for you is make sure you don't make a bad technology decision because you can't figure out the technology 'gobbledy-goop'. I've had clients who bought $40,000 accounting packages and found out it wouldn't run on their server, and they had to go spend $20,000 on a new server, and they would have loved to have known this ahead of time, but now they're $60,000 into it and it's truly not what they signed up for. And then it turns out that it's not even the best software application for them. So we take care of that. And when we land projects for you, we believe in proof of concept, so in this case if I brought in the application and told you, "Hey I like this software application, I think it's the right one for you guys", we'll test that on our servers, we'll duplicate your environment in our lab in our office, we'll run it for a week or so and make sure that the new application will talk to all of your other applications without crashing your pc's or crashing your server before we land it on your site. Now once we're ready to land it we produce a complete project plan of how long it's going to take from beginning to end, we'll assign a project manager to your project, give you timelines, and we face that out so you can see it and create monthly and/or weekly conference calls with our project manager and you, or whoever you have assigned

---

to the project to make sure you stay informed, because we found that clients really hate it when they're not informed about the status of our projects.

Marco: *Okay*

Gary: So we really do a great job of proving the concept, thinning out the vendors and then giving you solid communication with the project manager on where the project is, and staying on budget, which is the most important piece. When we give you a price for a project, that's the price. Unless you change the scope of work, the price won't change, so if I quote you 40 hours I think it will take to do this project, if it takes me 47 hours, I eat the 7 hours.

Marco: *I see.*

Gary: Okay and we're really serious about that piece so I want to talk to you about that, because who knows what kind of project we might do along the line, I want you to understand our philosophy about projects and how we do those going forward.

Marco: *Good.*

Gary: Okay? Now disaster recovery, you know you don't have a disaster recovery plan, we talked to Joe about that, that's a serious piece to our business. We want to talk to you some more down the line about putting together a solid plan, so if you walked in here tomorrow and the place was on fire, we and you would know what to do the very next second. So if you call me up and say, "Gary my buildings on fire" I say "Let's go into plan bravo", and we know what plan bravo is, you know you've got a copy of it in your safe deposit box, one at home, and your staff knows, everybody knows what to do and we get your business up and running. That's a serious piece of your business if you've been building it for as long as you've been building it, and you would hate to lose it over a fire because you were not prepared.

Marco: *Okay.*

Gary: Okay? Now I'm going to talk to you later about co-location services because that's a huge part of that and a huge part of our business as well. Okay?

Marco: *Okay. Last time we met you mentioned that you were going to help us make money with our website, and that, this is all very nice, but how are you guys going to help us make money with our website?*

Gary: You keep jumping ahead of me; I'm going to show you that Marco.

Marco: *Okay.*

Gary: We're going to talk about that in a minute, and I know you're excited about it; I'm excited about it too. So we're going to talk about it okay? Now software development, I don't see a need for this service with you today, from what I've seen, your line of business applications seem to be straightforward, but down the line if you ever find a need or we collaborate together and decide we want to customize something specific for your business, and specific to you, and link all of your applications into one application, we can do that for you. Okay? So I just want to show you that because I wanted you to know that if you ever get to that point we can make it web enabled, we can do anything you want with it, but these are huge financial engagements, so it's one of the last things we do for clients who really want to do that, but I wanted you to know we have the expertise to do it.

Marco: *Okay.*

Gary: Okay? Now here's a recap of how all of these services link together, we talked about flat rate, we talked about managing your vendors, we talked about the monitoring piece to this and professional services and this is how we see ourselves totally. Now these are some of our vendor relationships. We're a Microsoft Gold Partner.

Marco: *What does that mean?*

Gary: What that means is in the Microsoft world there's several hundred thousand partners, and there's only 1900 Gold partners and we're one of them. So we have to do a lot of things from a competency standpoint to qualify for that. So what it essentially means is we know what we're doing, and Microsoft essentially blessed that. Now, we're a Citrix partner, I don't know if you've had any relationship with Citrix, but it's an application that, you know, clients use to connect to their data remotely from different locations. Cisco, you know who Cisco is, we're Cisco certified so we can handle all the router relationships with that if that should be engaged down the line. From a hardware perspective, we deal with Dell and we deal with HP. Now this is a significant piece, we don't buy hardware for clients anymore. There's no money to be made in that business, if we decide you need new hardware, we set you up with a cart respectively with those two organizations, you purchase the hardware, if it's something we have to configure you ship it to our lab and we'll configure it for you. So that way you get the best possible price available and you pay for it directly.

Marco: *Okay.*

Gary: WTG is our Telco vendor, we have a relationship with about 33 phone companies nationwide, so we can meet any phone company needs you have. I know you told me before, that you are with Mpower?

Marco: *Yes.*

Gary: And we're Mpower partners so, we're going to look at your bills a little bit, we did pull those from your accounting folks, because we just want to take one look and make sure you're getting the best program or package that they have today. So what we do on this piece, I have a person in our office whose sole job is to edit and audit these once a quarter. So if there's a new promotion with Mpower that can save you 20 bucks or a hundred bucks a month we come tell you about it.

Marco: *Oh good.*

Gary: That way you don't have to worry about having those guys calling you and telling you what the new promotion is, when your contract terms end with your T1, we find the best product, or the best contract offer going forward and we'll come and talk to you about that. We'll make sure you get the best possible deal available.

Marco: *That's great.*

Gary: Okay so to recap, I told you about our saving costs and driving revenue, you can certainly see that by going into a flat rate model on IT support that you can save money because you don't have unpredictable bills going forward. You'll know what the bill is every month, and it will be budgeted and it's something you can anticipate each month. You can certainly see the value of monitoring. I gave you a great example of what monitoring will do for you if you walked in Monday, right along with Joe, your server is down, you and him would learn that together and you'd have to try to bring it back up before too much of the work day was lost. This would eliminate that. Vendor management you can see how if I can give Joe and Laurie back to you; and I'm going to dollarize that for you in a minute, the value of them being able to give you more production time, because of their not having to wrestle with SBC, Verizon, the phone guy, you know the copier people, and all those folks, we're doing that and also your line of business applications as well. You can see how there might be some cost savings for you there as well. Certainly you'll agree that the professional services approach we have is probably unique in the experience you've had with an I.T. company, the proactive plan, vetting out vendor relationships you want to get into, us doing that front-end piece so you don't get into a relationship that you don't understand or don't like. We'll help you make better I.T. decisions with future projects, future relationships. We did talk about the software piece but that's not relevant today, but you can certainly see the cost saving opportunities here right?

Marco: *Well I need to see some numbers, I'm an accountant and, do you have any number with you that we could look at, I want to get an idea of how much money I'm going to save if we sign up with you.*

Selling Managed Services – 2nd Appointment

Gary: I'm going to show you that, but in principal, the points I'm making, you can see their value, right?

Marco: *I can, yes.*

Gary: Okay that's what I wanted to make sure of. Okay so we're going to get ready to go into the numbers now, and I have a cost savings analysis form that I'm going to walk through with you, and these are the numbers that you've been dying to see that I'm going to show you.

Marco: *Okay good.*

Gary: Okay.

You can see during this exchange that Gary does a great job of controlling the appointment, and selling on value. No matter how many times Marco interrupts Gary and asks what the service is going to cost, Gary never gives in, because he wants to make certain that he completes his entire presentation, which is designed to illustrate the value of our services. Gary knows that if he does not complete the presentation, and simply gives Marco the price he keeps asking for, that the value of our services will be lost on Marco, and Gary would have simply commoditized our services to him. This engagement is a classic example of maintaining the consultative, Trusted Advisor approach and demeanor during a sometimes hot, sometimes challenging engagement with a prospect. Marco does a good job of throwing out every objection he can think of and trying to wear Gary down, but as a true consultant, Gary stays the course. How would you have handled this situation?

Selling Managed Services – 2nd Appointment

We're now ready to explore the cost savings analysis presentation.

Cost Savings Analysis Goal:

Illustrate to the client in a dollarized manner exactly how much productivity and opportunity is currently being lost by their organization, and how to increase profits, decrease costs and mitigate risk by partnering with you.

Talking Points:

- Describe method used to gather data, and persons in client's organization who assisted
- Walk through Cost Savings Analysis with Client
    - Describe the dollarized amount of lost productivity experienced by the Client due to internal staff managing Vendors
    - Describe the dollarized amount of lost productivity experienced by the Client due to internal staff conducting "lightweight" IT activity
    - Describe the dollarized amount of lost productivity experienced by the Client due to network and service downtime
    - Describe the dollarized amount of lost opportunity experienced by the Client due to all of the above
    - Dollarize how much lost productivity and opportunity revenue you can regain for the Client through your flat-rate Remote Help Desk,

24x7 Network Monitoring and Vendor Management Services
- o Reinforce the concepts of increased uptime and reduced risk the client will experience as a result of partnering with you to receive your Services.

Here are some common objections, and how to overcome them:

- "Do we really spend that much time on (Vendor Management, Lightweight IT, etc)?"
  - o "This is the information we received from your staff" – Refer Client to specific staff member for verification.
- "So if we have trouble with any of our Vendor-supported hardware or services, you will fix it?"
  - o "We will work with your existing Vendors to resolve these issues as quickly as possible. In cases where remote problem solving does not address the issue, and a Vendor onsite visit is required, we coordinate and schedule that activity." – Reinforce the concept of "one Service Request to your organization to deal with any infrastructure issue"
- "It seems like the losses you're showing me are really soft costs from the Vendor Management, Lightweight IT and Downtime perspective…"
  - o "This may be true, but you are losing productivity, which directly affects your revenue. All of the hours that your staff is devoting to managing your Vendors, performing lightweight IT functions, or otherwise experiencing

Selling Managed Services – 2nd Appointment

---

            downtime negatively impacts their contribution to your organization's Gross Revenue."

- "So are you saying that you will guarantee our uptime?"
  - "While neither we, nor anyone else, can guarantee your uptime, it stands to reason that if we are monitoring your network, critical devices and services proactively 24x7, and are conducting Patch Management, Anti-Virus and Anti-Spam Updates and System Optimization according to a consistent schedule, your systems will operate more efficiently and you will experience increased uptime." – Make sure to emphasize that the Client's systems have probably never received such proactive maintenance in the past.

Now let's walk through the second half of the 2nd prospect appointment role-playing session we conducted with one of our Partners; Marco Alcala, during a Managed Services Sales Training boot camp.

2nd Prospect Appointment Role-Play Transcript Part 2:

Marco: So you're going to show me some numbers huh Gary?

Gary: Yeah Marco, I've got the numbers here. We've just finished the PowerPoint and I think that all made sense to you, but let me show you what I found out.

Marco: Okay.

Gary: And these numbers are provided by your staff. I spent a little time with Joe and a couple of other folks to find out...

Marco: Did you talk to Laurie too?

Gary: I talked to Laurie too, and apparently she's your in house vendor manager.

Marco: She is.

Gary: Let me walk you through this. There was a time when we used to go through and use industry statistics on the times that clients your size would spend on managing vendors, and the times they'd spend on managing the I.T. We found that not every client was the same, the stats don't always apply, so we decided to talk to the people in the environment who are actually doing the work, and get this data from directly. Now, no clients we've worked with have hired folks just so they could manage their vendors - they usually assign that job to somebody as an additional duty, but they are usually surprised to find out how much time they really spend doing this stuff. Now that is one of the reasons why we offer the vendor management services, when it makes the most sense. In your case, you have 12 vendors, that's a lot of vendors. Laurie mentioned to us that she spends 12 hours a month managing vendors. Now, we estimate her salary, talking to HR, as about 45 bucks an hour. Okay?

Marco: That sounds about right.

Gary: Okay, so in that example, you're spending $6480.00 a year on vendor time for her.

Marco: Okay.

Gary: Now, if you look at her annual salary against that, I'm certain that you did not plan on having her spend that much of her time working with vendors. These are vendors that we work with all the time and we support directly, and we're going to give that time back to you. Okay? I'm going to sum that up for you in the end.

Marco: So 12 hours a month?

Gary: 12 hours a month.

Marco: Okay.

Gary: So it adds up. Now, we wanted to talk to you about the guy doing your IT stuff, and he's doing 12 hours a month. There's some great industry stats about this too. We found that clients your size, spend about 40% of their time solving I.T. issues before they call their I.T. service company, and the reason they don't want to call is because the guy is going to come out and give you a bill. So they have somebody internally mess with those issues. Going forward with our program, you remember me telling you about our 8 to 5 unlimited remote and onsite support, call right away, don't wait around. We can take care of the issues a lot faster than your having to wait for somebody to roll a truck out here. So, we're going to give you back Joe, and his time was 35 bucks an hour, so another $5,000 a year that your losing by having Joe do IT stuff. Granted, I want to be clear about this. Going forward we're going to probably still use him as our onsite eyes and ears when we need that kind of support, because he know the environment, he knows the users, so he'll still partner with us going forward to help us with things on the ground so we don't have to send somebody out here some of the time. He likes doing I.T., we just don't want him to spend 12 hours a month doing it and I'm sure you don't want him to do that as well.

Marco: So if we sign up with you guys, how many hours a month do you think he's going to be spending assisting you guys and resolving problems for us?

Gary: Well it will probably be more minutes than hours now.

Marco: It will be minutes?

Gary: Yes, because we're doing everything proactively. There might be a situation where we say, go up to the server and do a hard reboot or something or there's some software we're looking for, and he knows where the discs are in respect to the user, or something like that. For the most part we should be able to give him back to you.

Marco: Okay.

Gary: I talked to you about putting a pc in the closet for when we have a failure on a hard drive on a pc, he can go grab that PC for us, bring it out of the closet, put it in front of the user, connect it up and then we've got the ball from there and he's clear.

Marco: Okay

Gary: So you should have more of his time back than you've ever had before.

Marco: Okay, I see.

Gary: So then let me talk you through these numbers, you've got 20 users, one server. We've also talked to you about the downtime and you and I discussed this a little in our needs analysis, you gave me some of these numbers but I got the email downtime from Joe as well, he told me about that, the Internet connectivity, both he and Laurie knew about the Internet connectivity downtime, there were 4 hours there.

Marco: Okay

Gary: You had some server and desktop downtime on average about 2 hours a month, not too bad, but the total was 10 a month that's still more hours down than you need.

Marco: I see.

Gary: Because we like to dollarize everything as you have probably noticed here to make sure you understand what these things are costing you.

Marco: Okay.

Gary: So we averaged your payroll on 20 employees a year at about $30,000, would you agree with that is about close to your average?

Marco: $30,000, let's see. What's my yearly gross payroll?

Gary: Yearly at about $600k, are we in the ball park there?

Marco: Yes that seems about right.

Gary: Okay, so basically doing that math we found that you are losing $34,000 a year to downtime. I always ask every business owner what they think the employees are doing when email is down, or the server is down or the Internet is down, what do you think they are physically doing at their desk when that happens?

Selling Managed Services – 2nd Appointment

Marco: I see, well we typically tell them to work on something else that doesn't require the computer, some filing or things like that.

Gary: Well how much of that do you think they're really doing a lot of times, I mean it's the least productive time ever. And if the Internet is down and you use the Internet a lot, or the server is down, and they're thinking it's going to come back up at any moment now, it really just doesn't happen that fast most of the time. It's non-productive time that you cannot get back and we want to make sure going forward that our monitoring services and some other things that we've talked about from a proactive approach insure that you don't have any downtime like this.

Marco: I see.

Gary: Your accounting folks told me that you guys spent last year about $10,000 on I.T. from the outside vendor you're using right now.

Marco: I see. We're spending about $200 a month on that.

Gary: This is the number they gave us back and this is minus the hardware you purchased, by the way.

Marco: Oh it is?

Gary: Yes, we had them take that out to make sure we're clear on that.

Marco: Oh, okay.

Selling Managed Services – 2nd Appointment

Gary: So I'm going to put this together for you at the end to show you how this fits together. What I want you to really focus on right here are all the services we support going forward with you; unlimited remote help desk for client servers, desktops and printer/scanners and copiers. So from 8 to 5 you call us and we'll take care of all this stuff remotely, it's all a part of our service.

Marco: So if our copier breaks down, you're going to fix it for us?

Gary: We're not physically going to fix it, we're going to call your copier guy, schedule him, coordinate that with Laurie so that she doesn't have to call him and when he gets out here, we have to support him because you have one of those digital copiers with an IP address assigned to it, so we're going to work with him directly to make sure he can bring it back up.

Marco: I see.

Gary: Now she doesn't have to deal with that part of it at all.

Marco: But I have a service contract with the copiers.

Gary: We realize that and we're going to leverage that when we call him to make sure he doesn't send you a bill to come out and do basic service.

Marco: Okay.

Gary: Because you're going to give us all that information, the warranties, and service agreements you have with each one of your vendors so we can manage it from there.

Marco: You mentioned printer, will you also fix the printers if they break down?

Gary: Yes we will, whatever can be done remotely we'll do remotely but whatever has a warranty, we'll support that too.

Marco: Typically what we do is we have technicians come out and remove rollers and things like that, is that something you guys do as well?

Gary: If you have an agreement with the vendor, we'll just manage that and make sure they come out and do that.

Marco: I see.

Gary: Okay, so we don't physically fix printers themselves, but if the printer won't print and it's related to the network, well then certainly we'll take care of that. But if it's a physical printer repair itself, either we'll have it shipped back to wherever it ships back to or if it's a repair company that you have an agreement with to come out we'll facilitate making that happen.

Marco: Okay.

Gary: Now on the 24 hour monitoring we've talked about the value of that. We're monitoring all your devices here remotely and that's part of our service and that's done 24/7.

Marco: Okay.

Gary: So you can see all the devices here that are covered, your broadband connection, your routers, your servers, everything on your network is monitored by us. And that's what

---

we were talking about earlier - the alerts that we get when your equipment is down, and how we respond to that to make sure that it's back up, restart services, or whatever it takes to make that happen.

Marco: Okay.

Gary: Now the vendor management piece here, we've been talking about that quite a bit. We also handle that piece with your telco vendor, your software vendors and your equipment vendors. These are all the people that touch any part of your network, Telco or just the network itself, so all that is covered in our fees here.

Marco: Okay.

Gary: So let me recap here a little bit and cover these numbers and put this all into perspective for you. So up here at the top we talked about the $6480 of lost productivity from internal vendor management.

Marco: Okay

Gary: $5040 for what you do with your inside IT guy.

Marco: Okay, we've got $11,000 there.

Gary: So then we've got $34,000 of downtime due to the network being down being it email, Internet, server, or what have you.

Marco: $44,000

Gary: And then another $10,000 is what you're spending right now with your present IT company. So we are at $56,135.

Marco: Okay.

Now our cost to do this service is $36,000.

Marco: I see.

Gary: And you're going to get all of this service, and as you recall, I talked about guaranteed restore of your server back to its original configuration if your server crashes. And that is built into this price right here.

Marco: I see.

Gary: And if you also remember I talked about doing research for you on a new software application, whether it be accounting or a line of business, I'm going to go out and vet that out for you, and that is also included in that price.

Marco: I see.

Gary: So you see the value of the savings here, I've got $20,000 that I'm giving back to you.

Marco: Okay.

Gary: Does that make sense to you?

Marco: Well, I'm having a little problem understanding this, Gary. This money that you say I'm spending, I'm going to spend it no matter what, because I'm paying these people anyway, right? So they seem to be soft costs, they seem to be soft savings, I'm not quite sure this is going to make sense for us or not.

Gary: Well the reality of it is, and I'm going to be clear about this, we cannot guarantee that you are never going to be down. So our proactive approach to all this is to make sure we manage and do everything we can to make sure you don't go down, and to give you control over your network, and make sure you're not worried about these guys not being productive because of something going on with your network and just taking it completely out of the equation. And we are turning these two staff members back to you, to do what you hired them to.

Marco: I see.

Note:

This role-play was recorded before we modified the cost savings analysis form to reflect lost opportunity costs. The way we would answer Marco's question here now would be to address the fact that although he is correct to note that these are soft costs, in reality the downtime is negatively impacting each user's individual contribution to the company's gross revenue, thus making the costs more "hard" and tangible.

Gary: And more importantly this is about me coming in and talking to you about solutions, without your worrying about your network, so this takes care of your network completely. It is out of the equation and you and I can talk about that website we talked about that you really want to get involved with.

Marco: Okay

Gary: So we take this out of the equation and this is how we do that. So we don't have to worry about your server, or your pc's or your Internet connection or your vendor management, and none of that stuff slows us down. So we are focused on things that take technology to drive revenue and reduce your costs, like I told you in the beginning of our first call. So this is what it takes to do that.

Marco: How would you be able to prove to me that you've actually done this for other CPA firms that you've been able to give those employees back to the company in terms of the time savings?

Gary: I can let you talk to a couple of them, because we have done this before and this is a proven model here.

Marco: Okay. If I can talk to a couple of them and they do in fact tell me that you did do as you say here, then I would like to get started.

Gary: Perfect then we are going to get started.

Marco: Good, thank you.

Gary: Thank you.

Again, a great exchange between Marco and Gary, with Marco not giving an inch, and really making Gary work to overcome all of his objections, but in the end, Gary maintained his composure, and overcame all of Marco's objections as the Trusted Advisor.

Selling Managed Services –3rd Appointment

Alright, we're almost home. The last appointment to close the deal will require us to present our Managed Services Proposal and Agreement to the prospect.

3rd Appointment Goals:

- Present Infrastructure Upgrade Proposal if needed
- Present Managed Services Agreement
  - Overcome Objections

Talking Points:

- Describe the term of the Agreement, and any cancellation or termination clause(s)
- Describe the monthly fee, your billing process and date due
- Describe any requirements necessary to bring the environment up to "certified network" status and additional required billing
- Describe hours that Services are available
  - Remote Help Desk
  - Network Monitoring
  - Vendor Management
- Describe additional charges Client may incur should they request Services outside your normal Service hours
- Describe your Service Request Prioritization process
- Describe your Response and Resolution Times

- Describe your Escalation Process or SLA
- Describe your Onsite Response process
- Describe your process to Prep the Client's environment for Services
- Describe your Provisioning process and projected Service start (Turn-Up) date
- Describe all equipment and Services covered under the Agreement
- Describe the difference between "Covered" Services under the Agreement, and illustrate the fact that all requests which fall outside of the Agreement will be considered and billed as Projects
- Describe the monthly reporting that you will be reviewing with the Client, and confirm that they will heed your advice when it comes time to upgrade hardware, or explore new Solutions

Overcome Objections:

- "How often will you have a Technician Onsite?"
    - "As little as possible. Remember, with our proactive Managed Services, we assume all of the risk in maintaining your environment for a flat fee, so we have to make certain that we are doing everything possible from a maintenance perspective to maximize your uptime. In addition, our remote Help Desk can respond much more quickly to any normal day-to-day issues your staff may experience, compared to

> waiting for someone to break free and drive to your location. "

- "So I won't ever be charged more than my monthly fee for your Services?"
  - "Unless something out of the ordinary occurs outside of our normal covered hours of operation, no. Remember, though, that the cost for replacement hardware components for covered equipment is not included in this Agreement, or the cost to open a Trouble Ticket with a Vendor such as Microsoft to resolve complex issues (we've already discussed what constitutes a Project). In any event, we will always receive your authorization before incurring any additional costs on your behalf. "

I recommend taking the time to go over the Managed Services Agreement in detail with the prospect. We've found that taking an extra 30 minutes to do this at the time of signing nearly eliminates any questions or misunderstandings later on.

Now let's walk through the 3rd prospect appointment role-playing session we conducted with one of our Partners; Marco Alcala, during a Managed Services Sales Training boot camp.

Gary: Marco, it looks like we're going to do business together. Let me walk you through our agreement, how are you doing today?

Marco: Good and you?

Gary: I'm doing fabulous. Let's go through this agreement here, this is going to take just a few minutes, but a lot of my clients tend to have such a great relationship with us, they tend to not read these.

Marco: I see, I'd like the read it.

Gary: There are a few things here I want to walk you through. I want to make sure you understand how our agreement works and certainly I want to answer all of your questions in regards to this. It's a pretty straightforward agreement; it explains our services in detail in terms of how we work together.

Marco: Okay.

Gary: And the first piece I want to call to your attention is the three year term. We have a three year term and that is more designed around our price being locked in for you for three years, because right in the next section there is an opportunity for you to cancel with a sixty day notice. And what that means is, if you're not happy with our service, let us know and we'll let you out of our arrangement, so it's not a binding three year agreement, and we do it for that reason because we have to earn your business every month and that's important to us.

Marco: Okay.

Note:

We have since modified the agreement substantially providing us the ability to write long-term agreements with the option to review the agreement periodically for price modifications.

Gary: And right here is our fee, I think it came out to $3000 a month.

Marco: Yeah that's right.

Gary: Okay, and since you're going to be doing some infrastructure upgrade stuff that we talked about, there won't be a setup charge, that's inclusive in that fee so that'll take care of that. Now I want to call attention right here to section 4, where our 8 to 5 unlimited support piece we talked about previously is. We provide you all-you-can-eat support between the hours of 8am and 5pm pacific standard time Monday through Friday, excluding holidays.

Marco: Yeah, you mentioned that.

Gary: I just want to make sure we're clear on that, and that our 24 /7/365 is monitoring only.

Marco: Okay.

Gary: I have clients sometimes get that a little confused so I always like to reiterate that point to make sure that there is no misunderstanding there.

Marco: Okay.

Gary: And I'll give this to you so you can read it in detail afterwards, but I want to at least run you through these areas that I know prompt the most questions.

Marco: Okay.

Selling Managed Services – 3rd Appointment

Gary: Now on this page here, we talked about the service hours being, you know, 8 to 5, that's probably worth mentioning again but here, down here; we talk about the minimum standards for service down in section 6 here. And we've addressed this already in our proposal, but it's important that you understand what we consider to be our, what we call a certified network.

Marco: Okay.

Gary: The reason this is important is as your network changes over the next couple of years, whether it be, you need a new backup tape device or your network is growing and you need bigger backup tapes or bigger hard drives, we have to continue to be able to maintain this level of service with you.

Marco: Okay.

Gary: So we'll be contacting you from time to time when those things need to happen, so we have to maintain the minimum standards required for service, that's important to us. So when my engineers call you up and tell you that it's time to increase those drives in your server, we've got to do it. If they say you need to increase your backup tape device to a larger one to support your network, we got to take care of that as well. Okay so then I want you to understand that by working with us, or signing an agreement with us, you're also committed to making sure your network is maintained all the time.

Marco: Okay.

Gary: Okay? Now I want to get into the excluded stuff, and this is a spot for you to sign, but before you sign, I want to take you through a few other things here that are important. This is a signature page, and we'll come back to that, okay?

Marco: Okay.

Gary: Now here, our response and resolution times, this is important.

Marco: Okay.

Gary: You know, we respond to the down issues first, those are the most important things. Right here we have all of our response. But we prioritize the tickets based on the urgency of the matter itself. Now obviously, if you're down, there is nothing more important than that, and actually when our IT Manager gets on the phone with you a little later, he's going to go through this with you again and make sure you clearly understand it.

Marco: Okay.

Gary: So if a ticket is opened up regarding something small like a printer won't print, not that it's not important, but it's not more important than the network being down.

Marco: Does this mean that if my server is down, you'll be onsite within one hour, or what is that response time mean?

Gary: It means we will respond within one hour – this means that service may be initiated remotely to determine the cause of the problem, but in any case you will be responded to within one hour, and it may escalate to an onsite visit from there.

Marco: Oh.

Gary: Okay? See the next section here?

Marco: Okay.

Gary: So that's our resolution, and this is our response time. And yes, if you were down, priority one, depending on where you are now, obviously, if you're further out than that then that's our response time. But this is more of us responding to your call.

Marco: Oh I see like a call back?

Gary: Yeah exactly, so obviously a priority one ticket is a down related issue that you're down, okay? So tier one to tier two to tier three are how tickets are escalated based on severity and how long they go unresolved. And tier three engages a vendor, a third party vendor. For example if you have time slips or whatever your other software might be, we won't just pass the issue along to time slips or whoever the software vendor might be, we actually engage them directly and resolve the issue so that its completely taken care of and not just passed on to someone else to take care of it, like some of our competitors.

Marco: Okay.

Gary: Now here's an example of this escalation process and how we push through it. This is our process in terms of how we deliver services.

Marco: That's pretty elaborate.

Gary: It's designed so that you can look at the detail that we put together and in terms of how we process the ticket. Now again, when our IT manager turns up your services he's going to walk you through this in more detail.

Marco: Okay.

Gary: Because it is important that you understand this so we build a proper expectation because if after this meeting is over and you signed up with us and you think that someone called up with an issue and we didn't respond fast enough, I want you to remember part of this conversation in terms of what the issue was and how quickly we respond based on that issue.

Marco: I see.

Gary: It's an important process to build the proper expectation because if not you might want us to respond to something within thirty minutes and we just made it clear that even in a priority one issue it still might takes us an hour's response.

Marco: Okay.

Gary: Now we have a nice graphic here of the but it's basically a graphic representation of what you just saw here.

Marco: Okay.

Gary: Now right here, we talked earlier about all the things we do to your network from a maintenance perspective and how often we do it. This breaks that out in some detail.

Marco: Okay.

Gary: These are all the things that are being done to your network, you know, some of these things are being done at night when you're not around. We are constantly working on your hardware and your environment to make sure that it's maintained. This should almost be like you're sitting in your car in your garage at night and somebody coming into your garage at night and changing the oil, checking the air filters and doing all those things that are being done at night and in the morning drive your car out it's all ready to go.

Marco: That's nice.

Gary: So there's a lot of work being done behind the scenes to keep your network maintained. This is all based on preemptive, proactive support.

Marco: And who's doing all that work?

Gary: Our engineers.

Marco: Okay.

Gary: We write scripts that contact your PC at night and runs the virus protection software and all that type of stuff while you guys are away doing various things. Obviously sleeping, not at the office, right?

Marco: Yeah.

Gary: So, this is an extension of that stuff and if you want to go through this and I suggest that you do, but this is all the detailed service that we provide for you.

Marco: Okay.

Selling Managed Services – 3rd Appointment

Gary: Now here comes my favorite page. Now this page, we've run through a couple of times already, but this covers our cost here, for remote pc management from the helpdesk from 8 to 5, it's included.

Marco: Okay.

Gary: It doesn't cost you anything, vendor management, network management same thing. And notice these are 8 to 5, Monday through Friday. The monitoring is part of it as we talked about already, the lab labor if we do some work for you in the lab during these hours or onsite, is included.

Marco: Okay.

Gary: So as much as you want during those times, it's included. Now where it gets interesting is when you call us after that.

Marco: Okay.

Gary: You can see right here, for remote PC management, from 5:01 p.m. to 9:00 p.m. is $250 bucks an hour.

Marco: I see.

Gary: So don't do that, don't call us.

Marco: Well I don't want to do that; it's a little too expensive.

Gary: Onsite labor from 5 to 9 is $325.

Marco: Okay.

Gary: Lab labor is $125 from 5 to 9. Okay, now it gets really fascinating when you call in any other times like weekends or holidays; onsite is 425 bucks.

Marco: I see.

Gary: So don't call unless it's really an emergency.

Marco: Oh we won't.

Gary: So if you something is not working, if it can wait until Monday, let it wait.

Marco: Okay.

Gary: And if we're doing this proactively, taking care of things, these issues should not ride up over the weekend and most people are not at work on the weekends anyway, and most clients are not working after 5:00, you know, with some small exception. So obviously if you need us then call us but this is what it's going to cost when you do.

Marco: Okay.

Gary: We found that clients who operate between the 8 to 5 window usually don't have a reason to call after hours.

Marco: Okay and how quickly can you have us up and running with the remote monitoring software, that solution you mentioned?

Gary: It will take a couple, three days, let me talk to the help desk guys and see where they are but it won't take that long to get you setup and your network.

Selling Managed Services – 3rd Appointment

Marco: Are you going to have my guy, are you going to give him access to that system so that he can see the tickets and all of that?

Gary: Yeah, if he wants to, sure we can share that with him.

Marco: Okay.

Gary: Now down here we have, I want to cover this piece; we have all of your desktops and printers, servers and notebooks covered and we have a 10% variable here. What that means is, if you go up or go down in number of devices 10% our prices don't change.

Marco: I see.

Gary: So plus or minus two or three PC's then we don't worry about it.

Marco: And let's say I have 20 computers right now, so if I get two computers, that's 10%, you don't bill me anymore, right?

Gary: That's right.

Marco: Do they get installed as part of the agreement or is that, is it going to be billed on a time and material basis to come out and install the computers?

Gary: What happens there is you have the computers shipped to us, we can configure them, we'll ship them back out to you, and your IT guy will connect them to the network and we do everything else remotely, so it's part of the service.

Marco: I see.

Marco: Okay, we'll make sure that we ship the computers you.

Gary: Yeah and it's easy to do.

Marco: Okay.

Gary: Okay?

Marco: Great!

Gary: Alright then let me have you sign here and we'll be on our way.

Marco: Excellent!

Gary: Alright thank you.

Marco: You're welcome.

Gary: Oh before I go, do you have the check cut already or should I pick it up from someone else?

Marco: No, I talked to Laurie already and told her we would be signing the agreement, so I'll sign it for you and then she'll give you a check.

Gary: Oh well fantastic! Welcome aboard.

Marco: Thank you.

Gary: Thank you.

Selling Managed Services – 3rd Appointment

Not a lot of mystery here, just a straightforward client review of the agreement, some clarification of key points, and a signature. Right by the numbers…

Appendix A – Forms and Collateral

We've included on the enclosed CD-ROM each and every form, tool and piece of Marketing Collateral discussed in this book – and then some! These include:

- 17 page Managed Services and I.T. Solutions Website Design Comp
- Thank You Postcard Design Comp
- Appointment Setting Postcard Design Comp
- Closing The Deal – 17 Page Managed Services Sales Process And Overcoming Objections
- Cost Savings Analysis Form
- Cost Savings Analysis Example
- Managed Services Agreement Example
- Client PowerPoint Presentation
- Disaster Recovery Messaging Postcard Design Comp
- Disaster Recovery Messaging Postcard Design Comp2
- Disaster Recovery Messaging Postcard Design Comp3
- Flat-Rate I.T. Messaging Postcard Design Comp
- Website SEO Report
- Case Study Questionnaire
- Newsletter Design Comp
- I.T. Service Line Card Design Comp
- HR Interview Checklist for a New Sales Person
- 5 Ways To Evaluate A Sales Person Before They Make A Sale
- Qualifying Call Script
- Lead Calling Script
- Direct Mail Marketing Letter Design Comp

Appendix A – Forms and Collateral

- HTML Email Disaster Recovery Messaging Design Comp
- Managed Services, Your Business Plan and You PowerPoint Presentation
- Managed Services Business Plan Template
- Managed Services Business Plan White Paper
- Bonus – Haas Webcast With Karl Palachuk
- Bonus – Managed Services Business Plan Webcast
- Bonus – Closing The Deal Managed Services Webcast
- Bonus – How To Use The Cost Savings Analysis Webcast
- Bonus – Creating Effective Managed Services Proposals Webcast
- Introduction to MSPU
- MSPU CEO Support Group Webcast
- MSPU Help Desk/NOC Boot Camp Webcast
- MSPU Sales & Marketing Boot Camp Webcast
- MSPU Introduction Webcast

The Best I.T. Sales & Marketing BOOK EVER!

Appendix A – Forms and Collateral

The following section describes each of these forms, tools and marketing materials in detail, and how to use them.

17 page Managed Services and I.T. Solutions Website Design Comp

This professional website design embodies all of the marketing components discussed in this book. Included in the design are newsletter sign-up, case study download, and a company news component. Each page has been specifically designed for look, feel and content to serve as an effective marketing tool for I.T. and Managed Services. Simply forward the design to your web developer for coding.

Thank You Postcard Design Comp

A professionally-prepared postcard design that can be used to thank your Clients after each appointment.

Appointment Setting Postcard Design Comp

A professionally-prepared postcard design that can be used to confirm each and every client appointment.

Closing The Deal – 17 Page Managed Services Sales Process And Overcoming Objections

A 17 page handout covering talking points, overcoming objections, needs analysis and client PowerPoint presentation.

Appendix A – Forms and Collateral

Cost Savings Analysis Form

An extremely effective tool used to dollarize a prospective Client's lost revenue that can be recaptured through a Managed Services program.

Cost Savings Analysis Example

A cost savings analysis form filled in per the example in this book.

Managed Services Agreement Example

A sample Managed Services Agreement included for instructional and informational purposes only, and is not recommended, or warranted for use. Always have your attorney or legal team review any and all agreements or documents that you use in your IT practice. Local laws and liabilities can never be fully covered by any type of generic document, including this sample Managed Services Agreement.

Client PowerPoint Presentation

An extremely effective sales presentation highlighting the benefits of a Managed Services program for the Client. This presentation can be run either as a slideshow, or printed and placed in a flip-book for one-on-one presentations.

Disaster Recovery Messaging Postcard Design Comp

A professionally-prepared postcard design leveraging a disaster recovery marketing message.

Appendix A – Forms and Collateral

Disaster Recovery Messaging Postcard Design Comp2

A professionally-prepared postcard design leveraging a disaster recovery marketing message.

Flat-Rate I.T. Messaging Postcard Design Comp

A professionally-prepared postcard design leveraging a flat-rate I.T. marketing message.

Website SEO Report

A report illustrating the results of SEO tracking for a website, with hit stats, referral data and much more.

Case Study Questionnaire

A questionnaire used to gather the data necessary from a client in order to create the content of a case study.

Newsletter Design Comp

This professional newsletter design embodies all of the marketing components discussed in this book, with hyperlink positioning redirecting readers back to your website. Simply forward the design to your web developer for coding.

I.T. Service Line Card Design Comp

A professionally-prepared I.T. service line card design.

Appendix A – Forms and Collateral

HR Interview Checklist For New Sales Person

A checklist to utilize when interviewing a new sales candidate in person.

5 Ways To Evaluate A Sales Person Before They Make A Sale

A questionnaire to use when interviewing a new sales candidate in person.

Qualifying Call Script

A call-down script used to follow up on prospects after collateral has been delivered to them.

Lead Calling Script

A cold-calling script used on new prospects.

Direct Mail Marketing Letter Design Comp

A professionally-prepared I.T. service marketing letter design.

HTML Email Disaster Recovery Messaging Design Comp

A professionally-prepared email design leveraging a disaster recovery marketing message.

The Best I.T. Sales & Marketing BOOK EVER!

Appendix A – Forms and Collateral

Managed Services, Your Business Plan and You PowerPoint Presentation

The PowerPoint slide deck used in our Managed Services business plan webcast.

Managed Services Business Plan Template

A customized, fill-in-the-blanks business plan template for Managed Services.

Managed Services Business Plan White Paper

An supporting document to the business plan template.

HaaS Webcast With Karl Palachuk

The infamous Hardware As A Service Webcast with our good friend Karl Palachuk.

Managed Services Business Plan Webcast

My fourth webcast with Microsoft's TS2 team focusing on business planning for Managed Services.

Closing The Deal Managed Services Webcast

My fifth webcast with Microsoft's TS2 team focusing on the content in the last section of this book.

Appendix A – Forms and Collateral

How To Use The Cost Savings Analysis Webcast

A webcast focused on the proper utilization of the cost savings analysis.

How To Use The Cost Savings Analysis Webcast

A webcast focused on the proper utilization of the cost savings analysis.

Creating Effective Managed Services Proposals Webcast

A webcast focused on the delivery of effective Managed Services proposals.

Managed Services Proposal Template

A customized, fill-in-the-blanks proposal template for Managed Services.

Introduction To MSPU

Our line card detailing MSPU's products and services.

MSPU Introduction Webcast

Our MSPU Introduction webcast

MSPU CEO Support Group Webcast

Our MSPU CEO Support Group webcast.

Appendix A – Forms and Collateral

MSPU Help Desk/NOC Boot Camp Webcast

Our MSPU Help Desk/NOC Boot Camp webcast.

MSPU Sales & Marketing Boot Camp Webcast

Our MSPU Sales & Marketing Boot Camp webcast.

The Best I.T. Sales & Marketing BOOK EVER!

Appendix A – Forms and Collateral

Managed Services and I.T. Solutions Website

MANAGED SERVICES PROVIDER UNIVERSITY

Focus On Running Your Business...**Not Your Network**

Home | I.T. Solutions | Case Studies | **TotalCare Plan** | Support | FAQ

TotalCare Plan

MSPU delivers proactive maintenance services through our flat fee TotalCare Service Plans. Designed to reduce your costs, increase your profits and mitigate your business risks, we partner with you as your Virtual CIO and IT Department, allowing you to focus on running your business, not your technology.

Our relationship begins with evaluating your current state of technology, including infrastructure, hardware and line-of-business applications and vendors. We work with you to identify your critical business processes, pain points and vulnerabilities, and perform a threat analysis to determine your business risks. Completing this process allows us to design a Technology Plan that aligns with your long-term business goals.

We become an extension of your business, and true Partner. Because our Service Plans are based on a flat monthly fee allowing you the ability to budget your IT costs annually, we assume both the financial and technical risks in our relationship, fueling our commitment to continuously identify and deliver solutions that improve your efficiencies and reduce downtime – as a true Partner should.

Technical Operations Center

- Rapid Response
- Certified Technicians
- Published SLA and Escalation Process

Learn More >

24x7 Network Monitoring

- Monitors health of devices and line of business applications
- Diagnoses problems before they occur
- Immediately alerts technicians of critical issues for immediate response

Learn More >

Vendor Management

- Manages all infrastructure/line of business vendors
- Recaptures your staff's lost productivity
- Allows you to run your business, not your vendors

Learn More >

Call for more info at

888.248.9964

The Best I.T. Sales & Marketing BOOK EVER!

Appendix A – Forms and Collateral

MANAGED SERVICES PROVIDER UNIVERSITY

Focus On Running Your Business...**Not Your Network**

Home | IT Solutions | CaseStudies | **TotalCare Plan** | Support | FAQ

Technical Operations Center

TotalCare Plans >> Technical Operations Center / 24x7 Network Monitoring / Vendor Management

Our Technical Operations Center personnel are Certified to support all Microsoft Network
Operating Systems, Desktop Operating Systems, Microsoft Office applications and all
versions of Outlook, Exchange Server and SQL Server, as well as server and desktop
hardware, printers, network copiers, scanners, Smartphones and PDA's.

In addition, we support industry specific software such as NextGen, Misys, Timeslips, Quickbooks, Peachtree, ProSystem Fx, Visio, Act, and many more.

Just Pick Up The Phone

How much is it worth to your organization to receive help when you need it? Sometimes it is
the difference between getting that task, project or bid completed on time, or missing your
deadline. Face it - that equates to real dollars and cents. Our Technical Operations Center is
available 24 hours a day, 7 days a week, 365 days a year because you never know when
you will need us.

Call for more info at

888.248.9964

Associations | Partnerships | Careers | Contact Us

The Best I.T. Sales & Marketing BOOK EVER!

Appendix A – Forms and Collateral

MANAGED SERVICES PROVIDER UNIVERSITY

Focus On Running Your Business...**Not Your Network**

| Home | IT Solutions | Case Studies | TotalCare Plan | Support | FAQ |

Web, Application and Database Development

Real Testimonial Entered here...
"MSPU provided a variety of solution plans at a monthly flat rate to small and mid-sized businesses. MSPU helps keep the considerable costs of computer ownership and technology maintenance at a minimum."

John Doe
President / CEO
Technology Inc.

Networking and Mobile Computing / Disaster Recovery and Business Continuity Planning / Web, Application and Database Development / Broadband Services / Mobile Services / Voice Over IP Services

Web Development

Let us maximize your web presence and drive revenue to your business. Our creative design team will work with you to develop a clean, exciting web presence with intuitive navigation and a pleasing layout that provides visitors to your website with an effective delivery system for your marketing message and value proposition.

Application Development

We specialize in Workflow Analysis, Process Engineering and Office Automation. Utilizing these disciplines, we can identify bottlenecks, streamline your workflow, and design and implement your office, workflow or process automation application.

Database Development

We can modify or maintain your existing databases. Maybe your database just needs some minor adjustments - adding some additional fields to capture more data, or designing some additional reports. Or maybe it is time to completely re-write your database. Perhaps you need a completely new application. No matter what your specific needs are, we can help.

Associations | Partnerships | Careers | Contact Us

7077 Orangewood Ave. Suite 104, Garden Grove, CA 92841   Copyright © 2007 MSPU. All rights reserved.

www.mspu.us

MANAGED SERVICES PROVIDER UNIVERSITY

Focus On Running Your Business...**Not Your Network**

Home | Solutions | Case Studies | **TotalCare Plan** | Support | FAQ

24x7 Network Monitoring

Real Testimonial Entered here...
"MSPU provided a variety of solution plans at a monthly flat rate to small and mid-sized businesses. MSPU helps keep the considerable costs of computer ownership and technology maintenance at a minimum.

John Doe
President / CEO
Technology Inc

TotalCare Plans >> Technical Operations Center / 24x7 Network Monitoring / Vendor Management

Businesses are continually scrutinizing IT budgets. Service quality and high-availability demands are at an all-time high and the internet has revolutionized how organizations operate, allowing us the ability to proactively monitor your critical devices and services, and predict potential failures before they occur. Our proactive Network Monitoring program addresses your business pain.

24x7x365 Proactive Network Monitoring Never Sleeps

* Monitors the critical health status of devices and line of business applications
* Remotely diagnoses problems before they occur
* Restarts essential Services automatically
* Capacity planning reports for informed IT purchasing and budget decisions
* Minimize network and device downtime that causes lost productivity

Call for more info at

888.248.9964

Associations | Partnerships | Careers | Contact Us

7677 Orangewood Ave. Suite 104. Garden Grove. CA 92841

The Best I.T. Sales & Marketing BOOK EVER!

Appendix A – Forms and Collateral

MANAGED SERVICES PROVIDER UNIVERSITY

Focus On Running Your Business...**Not Your Network**

Home | IT Solutions | Case Studies | TotalCare Plan | Support | FAQ

Broadband Services

Real Testimonial Entered here. "MSPU provided a variety of solution plans at a monthly flat rate to small and mid-sized businesses. MSPU helps keep the considerable costs of computer ownership and technology maintenance at a minimum."

John Doe
President / CEO
Technology Inc.

There is no question that broadband has revolutionized the way—and speed—in which we connect to the Internet.

When it comes to this key service, it helps to have an objective, trusted expert in your corner. **Alchetec's team of broadband specialists have helped hundreds of companies throughout the region:**

- Improve their broadband speed and accessibility
- Consolidate their voice and data plans
- Save money!
- Connect remote offices and users
- Protect their broadband network from hackers, viruses and spyware

Associations | Partnerships | Careers | Contact Us

7077 Orangewood Ave Suite 104 Garden Grove CA 92841   Copyright © 2007 MSPU All rights reserved.

MANAGED SERVICES PROVIDER UNIVERSITY

Focus On Running Your Business...Not Your Network

Home | IT Solutions | Case Studies | Total Care Plan | Support | FAQ

Careers

Real Testimonial Entered here.
"MSPU provided a variety of
solution plans at a monthly flat
rate to small and mid-sized businesses. MSPU helps keep the
considerable costs of computer
ownership and technology maintenance at a minimum.

John Doe
President / CEO
Technology Inc.

Thank you for your interest in a career at MSPU. We are always looking for
bright, energetic people to join our team. If you are looking for an entrepreneurial environment, and you are fanatical about customer service,
we would love to talk with you. Feel free to send us your resume to:

Mail: MSPU
7077 Orangewood Ave, Suite 104
Garden Grove, CA 92841

EMAIL:

Associations | Partnerships | Careers | Contact Us

7077 Orangewood Ave. Suite 104. Garden Grove, CA 92841   Copyright © 2007 MSPU. All rights reserved

The Best I.T. Sales & Marketing BOOK EVER!

Appendix A – Forms and Collateral

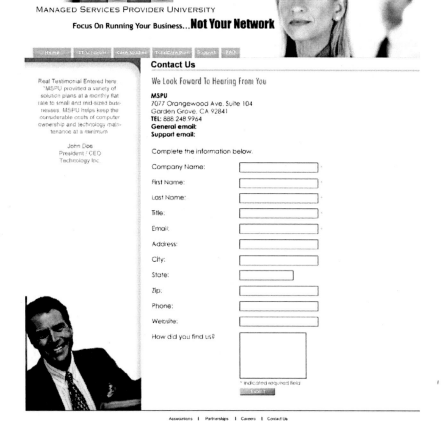

The Best I.T. Sales & Marketing BOOK EVER!

Appendix A – Forms and Collateral

MANAGED SERVICES PROVIDER UNIVERSITY

Focus On Running Your Business...**Not Your Network**

Home   **IT Solutions**   Case Studies   TotalCare Plan   Support   FAQ

Disaster Recovery and Business Continuity Planning

Real Testimonial Entered here...
"MSPU provided a variety of
solution plans at a monthly flat
rate to small and mid-sized businesses. MSPU helps keep the
considerable costs of computer
ownership and technology maintenance at a minimum.

John Doe
President / CEO
Technology Inc

Networking and Mobile Computing / Disaster Recovery and Business Continuity Planning / Web, Application and Database Development / Broadband Services / Voice Services / Voice Over IP Services

Statistics show that on average, over 40% of businesses that do not have a Disaster Recovery Plan go out of business after a major loss like a fire, a break-in, a storm, or sabotage.

A Good Plan Increases Your Chances of Recovery

There is no reason a temporary setback should turn into a permanent failure - if you protect your organization before disaster strikes. The first step is to create a Disaster Recovery, or Business Continuity Plan. We can help you get started right away. We will put together a comprehensive plan for your entire organization, considering key components crucial to your recovery, and establish a formal process to be followed to restore your business continuity when a disaster occurs.

Your Disaster Recovery Plan will be a comprehensive, step-by-step process for you and your staff to follow, covering such items as contacting your local authorities and insurance carriers, re-establishing phone service, sourcing equipment, restoring data, and all essentials needed to restore your organization's operational capability.

Associations | Partnerships | Careers | Contact Us

www.mspu.us

Appendix A – Forms and Collateral

MANAGED SERVICES PROVIDER UNIVERSITY

Focus On Running Your Business...**Not Your Network**

FAQ

Real Testimonial Entered here...
"MSPU provided a variety of solution plans at a monthly flat rate to small and mid-sized businesses. MSPU helps keep the considerable costs of computer ownership and technology maintenance at a minimum."

John Doe
President / CEO
Technology, Inc.

Do you perform support on an as needed basis?

Studies show that proactive maintenance improves equipment longevity, uptime and efficiency, and provides cost savings over time. Since all of our Flat Fee service plans are based on this premise, we do not offer reactive services.

What does your Flat Fee service include?

Proactive maintenance and monitoring for all covered equipment, operating systems and applications:

- Patch Management and Service Pack updates
- Anti-Virus and Anti-Spam management, updates and remediation
- Manage backups and restores
- Disk and memory optimization
- Manage user accounts
- Manage network and internet connectivity
- Manage Firewalls, Routers and Switches

Remote Help Desk, Lab/Bench Service and Onsite Service for all covered equipment, operating systems and applications:

- Servers, PC's, Laptops, Firewalls, Routers and Switches
- Microsoft Windows XP Pro Desktop Operating Systems
- Microsoft Office 2000, 2003 and 2005
- Microsoft Windows Server 2003 and Small Business Server 2003
- Microsoft Exchange Server 2003 and 2007
- Microsoft SQL Server 2000 and 2005

Vendor Management Services: We will manage all of your infrastructure vendors, allowing you and your staff to run your business, not your vendors. Anytime there is a problem with a device or line of business application serviced by a vendor we manage for you, it's one call to us, and we take it from there, and work the problem to resolution with that vendor. We will even schedule any onsite visits required by the vendor, and oversee the successful remediation of the issue at hand.

- Broadband Vendors
- Phone Service Vendors
- Phone Equipment
- Copier/Fax/Scanner/Document Imaging Vendors
- Line of Business Application Vendors

So no matter what happens in my environment, I'll never pay more than one Flat Fee per month?

Examples of items that are not covered under our Flat Fee service plans include the cost of replacement or new hardware, or shipping costs, the cost of software licensing or renewal or upgrade fees, and the cost of any third party vendor or manufacturer support or incident fees. Whenever the potential arises for additional fees outside of our Flat Fee, you will always be notified in advance for approval.

What other services and solutions do you provide?

We can take care of all of your business needs, using technology solutions to reduce your costs, increase your revenues and mitigate your business risks. Some examples of these solutions are:

- Cost-saving Voice and Data T1 and Integrated T1 Solutions
- Productivity-enhancing Voice Over IP services and solutions
- Revenue-generating Web Development solutions that drive clients to your Website
- Disaster Recovery and Business Continuity Planning to mitigate your risks in the event of Disaster
- Efficiency-boosting mobility solutions to keep your mobile workforce connected

How can I get more information and get started with your Services?

Just give us a call at (410) 823-6767, and we'll be happy to schedule an appointment with you to discuss your particular business needs. In order to make certain that we can help your business, our process begins with a Needs Analysis, followed by a Cost-Savings Analysis. We'll examine the results of these in order to determine our best recommendations to meet

Innovations | Partnerships | Careers | Contact Us

The Best I.T. Sales & Marketing BOOK EVER!

Appendix A – Forms and Collateral

MANAGED SERVICES PROVIDER UNIVERSITY

Focus On Running Your Business...**Not Your Network**

Home | **IT Solutions** | Case Studies | Total Care Plan | Support | FAQ

IT Solutions

Real Testimonial Entered here...
"MSPU provided a variety of solution plans at a monthly flat rate to small and mid-sized businesses. MSPU helps keep the considerable costs of computer ownership and technology maintenance at a minimum.

John Doe
President / CEO
Technology Inc.

The experience of our Certified Network Engineers and Technicians combined with our strategic partnerships with technology resources such as Microsoft, Cisco, Citrix, and HP allows us the ability to competently evaluate all of your organization's IT needs. Our solutions are designed to reduce your costs, increase your revenue and mitigate your business risks through their productivity and efficiency enhancing benefits.

Networking and Mobile Computing

Disaster Recovery and Business Continuity Planning

Web, Application and Database Development

Broadband Services

Voice Services

Voice Over IP Services

Associations | Partnerships | Careers | Contact Us

7077 Orangewood Ave. Suite 104, Garden Grove, CA 92841   Copyright © 2007 MSPU. All rights reserved.

---

www.mspu.us

338

The Best I.T. Sales & Marketing BOOK EVER!

Appendix A – Forms and Collateral

MANAGED SERVICES PROVIDER UNIVERSITY

Focus On Running Your Business...**Not Your Network**

| Home | IT Solutions | Case Studies | TotalCare Plan | Support | FAQ |

Networking and Mobile Computing

Networking and Mobile Computing / Disaster Recovery and Business Continuity Planning / Web Applications and Database Development / Broadband Services / Voice services / Voice Over IP Services

Technology and our ability to harness its benefits to improve your organization's productivity has certainly come a long way. High-Speed, secure networking has evolved beyond the Local Area Network to Wide Area Networks, the Internet, Smartphones, PDA's, and beyond.

Local or Remote? Wired or Wireless?

Your ability to remain continually connected is now a reality whether spending time at home, traveling for business, or on vacation. You and others in your organization can increase productivity simply by allowing this type of accessibility.

Speed and Security

With the promise of global connectivity comes the need for speed on your internal network, along with hardened security requirements. Our solutions are designed to guarantee your ability to service your remote users' requests for data quickly and securely, preventing unauthorized intrusion attempts utilizing Intrusion Detection, Virtual Private Networking, and Advanced Firewalling techniques.

Home Office or Branch Office?

Remote locations need a continuous, stable, and secure connection. A Secure VPN provides an inexpensive, secure and reliable method to connect.

Smartphones and PDA's

For the ultimate answer in staying connected, Smartphones and PDA's are the way to go. No longer do Blackberry and PDA owners have exclusive access to functions like Live Email and Calendar access. Smart Cell Phones have now entered the arena with numerous models, each sporting its own set of features and benefits. Let us show you how to take your connectivity needs to the next level with true mobility.

Associations | Partnerships | Careers | Contact Us

The Best I.T. Sales & Marketing BOOK EVER!

Appendix A – Forms and Collateral

MANAGED SERVICES PROVIDER UNIVERSITY

Focus On Running Your Business...**Not Your Network**

Home | IT Solutions | Case Studies | TotalCare 24 | Support | FAQ

Partnerships

Real Testimonial Entered here.
"MSPU provided a variety of
solution plans at a monthly flat
rate to small and mid-sized businesses. MSPU helps keep the
considerable costs of computer
ownership and technology maintenance at a minimum.

John Doe
President / CEO
Technology Inc.

Microsoft
GOLD CERTIFIED
Partner

Microsoft.
Small Business
Specialist

CiTRIX·

Associations | Partnerships | Careers | Contact Us

The Best I.T. Sales & Marketing BOOK EVER!

Appendix A – Forms and Collateral

The Best I.T. Sales & Marketing BOOK EVER!

Appendix A – Forms and Collateral

MANAGED SERVICES PROVIDER UNIVERSITY

Focus On Running Your Business...**Not Your Network**

| Home | IT Solutions | Case Studies | **TotalCare Plan** | Support | FAQ |

Vendor Management

Real Testimonial Entered here...
"MSPU provided a variety of solution plans at a monthly flat rate to small and mid-sized businesses. MSPU helps keep the considerable costs of computer ownership and technology maintenance at a minimum.

John Doe
President / CEO
Technology Inc

TotalCare Plans >> Technical Operations Center / 24x7 Network Monitoring / Vendor Management

Improve productivity and focus on running your organization...

By unloading the burden of you or others in your organization having to deal with multiple vendors, you regain lost productivity - directly impacting your bottom line.

Reap the benefits of a single point of contact...

Think of the productivity you will gain on an organization-wide level by allowing us to be your single point of contact for all of your technology vendors. The days of keeping up with all of the vendors for your phone systems, computer equipment, network scanners, copiers, faxes and all of your line of business applications every time there is a problem are gone. With our Vendor Management Program, you will only need to open up a single Trouble Ticket, and we will manage all vendor issues to resolution for you, no matter what they are, and the number of vendors involved.

Call for more info at
888.248.9964

Associations | Partnerships | Careers | Contact Us

The Best I.T. Sales & Marketing BOOK EVER!

Appendix A – Forms and Collateral

MANAGED SERVICES PROVIDER UNIVERSITY

Focus On Running Your Business...**Not Your Network**

| Home | IT Solutions | Case Studies | TotalCare Plan | Support | FAQ |

Voice Over IP Services

Networking and Mobile Computing / Disaster Recovery and Business Continuity Planning / Web Application and Database Development / Broadband Services / Voice Services / Voice Over IP Services

Thinking about a new Phone System? Let us share with you the benefits of VoIP, and introduce you to features such as Unified Messaging – where all of your voicemails are forwarded to your email for the ability to retrieve and forward messages to and from anywhere to anyone. Or Find Me, Follow Me, where your calls can ring at your office, then your cell phone, then your home office or hotel room while traveling – always maintaining the appearance that you are available to your clients.

Maximum Accessibility

One of our clients' favorite features is the ability to record phone calls and conferences, then email them to individuals that could not attend. There are laptop agents we can install which allow you to place and receive calls directly from your Internet-connected laptop or PC, anywhere in the world – imagine the ability to receive a call on your laptop that was dialed to your office extension!

Associations | Partnerships | Careers | Contact Us

The Best I.T. Sales & Marketing BOOK EVER!

Appendix A – Forms and Collateral

MANAGED SERVICES PROVIDER UNIVERSITY
Focus On Running Your Business...**Not Your Network**

Home | **IT Solutions** | Case Studies | Healthcare pros | Support | FAQ

Voice Services

Real Testimonial Entered here .
"MSPU provided a variety of
solution plans at a monthly flat
rate to small and mid-sized businesses. MSPU helps keep the
considerable costs of computer
ownership and technology maintenance at a minimum.

John Doe
President / CEO
Technology Inc

Networking and Mobile Computing / Disaster Recovery and Business Continuity Planning / Web Application and Database Development / Broadband Services / Voice Services / Voice Over IP Services

Today's businesses and organizations have access to a seemingly endless array of local and long-distance calling plans and options. With all the choices available, how can you be sure your current plan gives you the most value for your money? Is it worth the time and effort to switch providers and/or plans? Do you really need all those calling features?

The answer: integration

From NetQuest's experience helping other companies sort through their calling plan options, we have found that the best solution is integration. With integration, voice and broadband are bundled into one comprehensive, cost-efficient service.

Companies that integrate their voice and broadband services benefit from:

- Improved speed and reliability
- Substantial costs savings (up to 50 percent!)
- One bill from one supplier
- More streamlined, easy-to-manage data and voice services

Associations | Partnerships | Careers | Contact Us

7077 Orangewood Ave. Suite 104, Garden Grove, CA 92841   Copyright © 2007 MSPU All rights reserved.

Thank You Postcard

MANAGED SERVICES PROVIDER UNIVERSITY

THANK YOU

Put our expertise to work for you!

It we can be of service, please call **888.248.9964**

MANAGED SERVICES PROVIDER UNIVERSITY

THANK YOU

Providing high quality, affordable Information Technology Consulting Services for Organizations of all sizes is our goal.

Need a first or second opinion before making a Technology-related business decision? Leverage our expertise, and allow us the opportunity to evaluate your current and future I.T. needs with you. In most cases, we can recommend effective, cost-saving strategies that improve productivity without breaking the bank.

Contact us at (888) 248-9964 and allow us the opportunity to provide you with a Free Consultation to discuss how your Organization could benefit from our Services.

Flat-Rate I.T.
We support and maintain your entire Organization with our revolutionary Flat-Rate I.T. Program - all for a fixed monthly cost.

24x7x365 Network Monitoring
Our Network Monitoring Service never sleeps, and continuously monitors your network to insure maximum uptime. We take action as soon as a problem is detected.

Vendor Management
Quite possibly our most popular cost-saving Service. We manage all of your Vendor relationships, freeing you to focus on running your business. Whether it's an equipment, phone or network problem, we'll manage the issue to resolution.

Any questions visit www.mspu.us or call 888.248.9964

Appointment Postcard

Thank you for scheduling a consultation

If we can be of service visit **www.mspu.us** or call **888-248-9964**

Thank you for scheduling a consultation with:

_____

On:

_____ , __ / __ / __ at ___:___ AM / PM

At:

_____

For more information find us at
www.mspu.us or 888.248.9964

Closing The Deal Handout

MANAGED SERVICES PROVIDER UNIVERSITY

Your Comprehensive Online Managed Services Training Program...

Closing The Deal – How to Make Signing Your Managed Services Agreements Irresistible to Clients...

Goal:

Illustrate to the Client how you can help them use technology to increase profits, decrease costs and mitigate their risks.

Topics:

- Describe the dynamics of a Managed Services Sale
    - 1st Appointment
        - Build rapport
        - Conduct Needs Analysis
    - Before the 2nd Appointment
        - Gather data for Cost Savings Analysis
        - Network Analysis
    - 2nd Appointment
        - Client PowerPoint Presentation
        - Cost Savings Analysis
            - Overcoming Objections
    - 3rd Appointment
        - Infrastructure Upgrade Proposal if needed
        - Managed Services Agreement
            - Overcoming Objections
- Close the deal

Emphasis:

- Get into character – consultative, trusted advisor
- Build rapport
- Control the appointment
- Overcome Objections
- Sell on Value
- Close the deal

The Best I.T. Sales & Marketing BOOK EVER!

Appendix A – Forms and Collateral

Your Comprehensive Online Managed Services Training Program...

Client Needs Analysis Talking Points

Goal:

Build rapport with the Client and determine viability of a relationship. Gather preliminary data in order to present recommendations and/or a quote for Services.

Talking Points:

- Warm-up
- Let Client know you've researched their organization
- Find a common point to build a discussion around
  - Hobbies
  - Sports
  - Family
  - Business
- Learn about Clients business
  - Time in business
  - Type of business
  - Number of Employees
- Learn about Clients Network
  - Infrastructure
  - Number of Servers
  - Number of Desktops
  - Other Network Devices
  - Line of Business Applications
- Learn about Clients Vendors
  - Number of Hardware Vendors
  - Number of Software Vendors
  - Number of Service Vendors
  - Products/Services provided
- Walk through Needs Analysis
  - Collect all necessary data

- Learn about Clients pain points
  - Uptime
  - Security
  - Viruses/Spam
  - Productivity
  - LOBs
  - Equipment
  - Mobility
  - Business Continuity
  - Website
  - Phone System
  - T1 Service/Costs
  - CRM System

MANAGED SERVICES PROVIDER UNIVERSITY

Your Comprehensive Online Managed Services Training Program...

Client PowerPoint Presentation Talking Points

Goal:

Show the Client how to increase profits, decrease costs and mitigate risk by partnering with you to deliver Managed Services and other IT Solutions.

Talking Points:

- Describe flat-rate IT services and benefits
- Describe Remote Support
- Describe 24x7 Monitoring
- Describe Vendor Management
- Describe your Professional Services
  o Infrastructure
  o Business Continuity Planning
  o Web Development
  o Etc.
- Describe your competencies and Vendor relationships
- Validate value of your Services with Client

Overcome Objections:

- "How much does it cost?" - interruptions during presentation
  o "We're going to get to that in a minute" – Don't be sidetacked, stay with the presentation.
- "I already have someone on staff that can take care of that"
  o "I really want to talk to you about how much productivity and revenue you're losing by having your staff deal with these issues internally" – Validate this during the Cost Savings Analysis presentation
- "What about a physical hardware failure – how do you deal with that?"
  o "In most cases, we'll know when a component is nearing failure, thanks to our 24x7 Monitoring system, and will proactively replace it to avoid work stoppage. The reason we require you to have a spare PC onsite is so that we can work with your staff to swap a failed PC for us, then we'll remote in and set up the users profile, so they can get back to work as quickly as possible. We'll then arrange to pick the failed PC up and repair it at our facility, after which it then becomes the new spare."
- "I don't want anyone other than your staff to have access to our internal systems"
  o "Although our monitoring team is in another country, the only data that they receive from your systems is performance data. They then alert us to issues that need to be dealt with, and we handle it from there. All of our patching, updating and disk optimization activity is handled through scripts that run on your systems automatically. Our help desk, along with the technical staff that will be assisting your organization is based in the United States" – For Clients that are sensitive in this area, implement a strategy that meets their specific needs, rather than employ a "one size fits all" model. For many Clients that understand that just about any Technical Support offered nowadays is delivered from another country, this objection should not surface.

The Best I.T. Sales & Marketing BOOK EVER!

Appendix A – Forms and Collateral

Client Cost Savings Analysis Talking Points

Goal:

Illustrate to the Client in a dollarized manner exactly how much productivity and opportunity is currently being lost by their organization, and how to increase profits, decrease costs and mitigate risk by partnering with you.

Talking Points:

- Describe method used to gather data and answers – Client's organization who assisted
- Walk through Cost Savings Analysis with Client
  - Describe the dollarized amount of lost productivity experienced by the Client due to internal staff managing Vendors
  - Describe the dollarized amount of lost productivity experienced by the Client due to internal staff conducting "lightweight" IT activity
  - Describe the dollarized amount of lost productivity experienced by the Client due to network and service downtime
  - Describe the dollarized amount of lost opportunity experienced by the Client due to all of the above
  - Dollarize how much lost productivity and opportunity revenue you can regain for the Client through your flat-rate Service Help Desk, 24x7 Network Monitoring and Vendor Management Services
  - Reinforce the concepts of increased uptime and reduced risk the Client will experience as a result of partnering with you to receive your Services.

Overcome Objections:

- "Do we really spend that much time on [Vendor Management, Lightweight IT, etc]?"
  - "This is the information we received from your staff – Refer Client to specific staff member for verification.
- "So if we have trouble with any of our Vendors associated hardware or services, you will fix it?"
  - "We will work with your existing Vendors to resolve these issues as quickly as possible. In cases where a Vendor is taking too long, and a Vendor issue was resolved, we monitor and schedule this activity." – Reinforce the concept of One Service Resource to your organization to deal with any infrastructure issue."
- "I see on the list the losses you're showing me are really soft costs from the Vendor Management, Lightweight IT and Downtime areas above."
  - "This may be true, but you are losing productivity, which directly affects your revenue. All of the hours that your staff is devoting to managing your Vendors, performing lightweight IT functions, or otherwise experiencing downtime negatively impacts the contribution to your organization's Gross Revenue."
- "So are you saying that you will guarantee our uptime?"
  - "While no one can, nor anyone else can guarantee your uptime, it stands to reason that if we are monitoring your network, crucial devices and servers proactively 24x7, and are conducting Patch Management, Anti-Virus and Anti-Spam updates and System Optimization according to a consistent schedule, your systems will be more reliable, more efficiently and you will experience increased uptime." – Make sure to emphasize that the Client's systems have probably never received such proactive maintenance in the past.

The Best I.T. Sales & Marketing BOOK EVER!

Appendix A – Forms and Collateral

Client Managed Services Agreement Talking Point

Goal:

Describe the Managed Services Agreement to the Client, highlighting important points, and address any final questions or concerns the Client may have prior to signing and receiving payment.

Talking Points:

- Describe the term of the Agreement, and any cancellation or termination clause(s)
- Describe the monthly fee, your billing process and date due
- Describe any equipment necessary to bring the environment up to "Certified Network" status and additional equipment billing
- Describe how services are available
    - Remote Help Desk
    - Network Monitoring
    - Vendor Management
- Describe additional charges Client may incur should they request Services outside your normal Service hours
- Describe your Service Request Escalation process
- Describe your Response and Resolution Times
- Describe your Escalation Process or SLA
- Describe your Device Assurance process
- Describe your process to Flex the Client's environment for Services
- Describe your Provisioning process and proposed Service start (turn-up) date
- Describe all equipment and Services covered under the Agreement
- Describe the difference between "Covered" Services under the Agreement, and illustrate the fact that all requests which fall outside of the Agreement will be considered and billed as Projects
- Describe the monthly reviews that you will be reviewing with the Client, and confirm that they will need your advice when it comes time to upgrade hardware, or explore new Solutions

Overcome Objections:

- "How often will you have a technician Onsite?"
    - "As little as possible. Remember, with our proactive Managed Services, we assure all of the work we manage is giving you resolution for a flat fee, so we have to make certain that we are doing everything possible for a maintained and solid solution to maximize your uptime. In addition, our remote Help Desk can respond much more quickly to any normal day-to-day issues your staff may experience compared to waiting for an Onsite to treat free and drive to your location."
- "So I won't ever be charged more than my monthly fee for your Services?"
    - "Unless something out of the ordinary occurs outside of our normal covered hours of operation, no. Remember, though, that the cost for replacement hardware components for covered components is not included in this Agreement, or the cost to add or Install hardware with a Vendor such as Microsoft in case hardware becomes issues (we've already discussed what constitutes a Project). In any event, we will always secure your authorization before incurring any additional costs on your behalf."

Needs Analysis

Section 1	Server				Proposal Date

How Many Servers					
Server OS	NT4	W2000	W2003	SBS	
Number of Licenses					
Size of Hard drives					
Mirrored/Raid Hard drives	Yes or No				
Server Manufacturer					
Purchase Date					
Server Proposal	Yes or No				

Section 2	Desktops

How Many Desktops				
OS	W98	Win2k	XP Pro	Other
How Many Remote Users				
Spyware Problems	Yes or No			
Virus Problems	Yes or No			
Type of Anti-Virus Software				
Type of Anti-Spyware Software				
Internet Filtering	Yes or No			
Group Policy controls	Yes or No			

Section 3	Back-Up Strategies

Back up Software	Veritas or Other
Back Up Hardware	Internal or External
Back Up Tapes (Type)	
Disaster Recovery	Yes or No
Bio Disaster Recovery	Yes or No

Section 4	Website Information

Does Client Host Site	Yes or No
Domain Name Registered	Yes or No
Hosting Cost per Month	

Section 5	Security			Proposal Date
	Firewall	Yes or No		
	Firewall Hardware			
Section 6	**Exchange Server**			
	Version of Exchange	5.5 2000 2003		
	Version of Outlook			
	Shared Calendars	Yes or No		
	AntiVirus	Yes or No		
	AntiSpam	Yes or No		
	AntiSpyware	Yes or No		
	Does Client Host Email	Yes or No		
	Hosting Costs per Month			
	Proposal for Exchange Server	Yes or No		
Section 7	**Routers and Modems**			
	Router (specify)			
	Does Client own Router	Yes or No		
Section 8	**Company Software**			
	Client Software			
	CRM – Share point			
	Microsoft Office			
	Document Scanning			

Section 8	TELCO	Yes or No Type	How old	User Description
Software	Call Accounting Software			
	Account Codes			
Equipment	Phone System			
	Digital/Analog Cards			
	PRI/Super trunk			

	Telco Providers	Contract Yes or No	Contract Length	Race check/ Service
LEC				
CLEC				
Long Distance				
Equipment Vendor				

The Best I.T. Sales & Marketing BOOK EVER!

Appendix A – Forms and Collateral

Managed Services Savings Analysis - Example

Gross Revenue	
Organization's Gross Revenue	$1,000,000.00
Productivity loss to Staff Managing Vendors	
Number of Vendors Managed by Client	12
Number of Hours Spent Managing Vendors Per Month	12
Manager's Average Hourly Rate	$45.00
Productivity Lost Annually To Managing Vendors	$6,480.00
Productivity loss to Staff Performing IT Functions	
Number of Hours Spent Performing IT Functions Per Month	12
Staff Member's Average Hourly Rate	$15.00
Productivity Lost Annually To Performing IT Functions	$3,040.00
Productivity loss to Network Downtime	
Number of Users On Client Network	20
Number of Servers At Client Location	1
Network Downtime	Hours
Email Services Down per Month	4
Internet Connection Down per Month	4
Server or Desktops Down per Month	2
Total Hours Network Is Down Monthly	10
Total Hours Network Is Down Annually	120
Labor Costs	
Average Salary Per Employee	$50,000.00
Total Employee Yearly Payroll	$600,000.00
Average Annual Employee Hours	2080
Total Annual Employee Hours	41600
Average Hourly Labor Cost Per Employee	$14.42
Productivity Lost To Downtime Annually	$34,615.38
Gross Revenue loss to Network Downtime	
Individual Employee Hourly Contribution To Gross Revenue	$24.04
Gross Revenue Lost To Downtime Annually	$57,692.31
Existing Annual IT Costs	$10,000.00
Unlimited Remote Helpdesk Support For All Client Servers	Included
Unlimited Remote Helpdesk Support For All Client Desktops	Included
Unlimited Remote Helpdesk Support For All Client Printers	Included
Unlimited Remote Helpdesk Support For All Client Scanners	Included
Unlimited Remote Helpdesk Support For All Client Copiers	Included
Unlimited Remote Monitoring Support 24/7/365	
Unlimited Remote Monitoring For All Client Servers	Included
Unlimited Remote Monitoring For All Client Routers	Included
Unlimited Remote Monitoring For All Client Broadband	Included
Unlimited Remote Monitoring For All Client VPN's	Included
Unlimited Remote Monitoring For All Client Email/Web Services	Included
Unlimited Remote Monitoring For All Client SQL/Line Of Business Servers	Included
Vendor Management Services	
Unlimited Management For All Client Vendor Support Teams	Included
Telecomm Vendors	Included
Software Vendors	Included
Equipment Vendors	Included
Annual loss of Productivity from Staff Managing Vendors	$6,480.00
Annual loss of Productivity from Staff Performing IT Functions	$3,040.00
Annual loss of Productivity Cost from Network Downtime	$34,615.38
Annual loss of Gross Revenue from Network Downtime	$57,692.31
Projected Existing Annual IT Cost	$10,000.00
Total Existing Annual IT Support Costs	$111,827.69
Proposed Managed Services Cost	$50,000.00

Total Client Savings $77,827.69

Managed Services Savings Analysis	
Gross Revenue	
Organization's Gross Revenue	
Productivity Loss To Staff Managing Vendors	
Number of Vendors Managed by Client	
Number of Hours Spent Managing Vendors Per Month	
Manager's Average Hourly Rate	
Productivity Lost Annually To Managing Vendors	
Productivity Loss To Staff Performing IT Functions	
Number of Hours Spent Performing IT Functions Per Month	
Staff Member's Average Hourly Rate	
Productivity Lost Annually To Performing IT Functions	
Productivity Loss To Network Downtime	
Number of Users On Client Network	
Number of Servers At Client Location	
Network Downtime	Hours
Email Services Down per Month	
Internet Connection Down per Month	
Server or Desktops Down per Month	
Total Hours Network Is Down Monthly	
Total Hours Network Is Down Annually	
Labor Costs	
Average Salary Per Employee	
Total Employee Yearly Payroll	
Average Annual Employee Hours	
Total Annual Employee Hours	
Average Hourly Labor Cost Per Employee	
Productivity Lost To Downtime Annually	
Gross Revenue Loss To Network Downtime	
Individual Employee Hourly Contribution To Gross Revenue	
Gross Revenue Lost To Downtime Annually	
Incoming Annual IT Costs	
Unlimited Remote Helpdesk Support For All Client Servers	Included
Unlimited Remote Helpdesk Support For All Client Desktops	Included
Unlimited Remote Helpdesk Support For All Client Printers	Included
Unlimited Remote Helpdesk Support For All Client Scanners	Included
Unlimited Remote Helpdesk Support For All Client Copiers	Included
Unlimited Remote Monitoring Support 24/7/365	
Unlimited Remote Monitoring For All Client Servers	Included
Unlimited Remote Monitoring For All Client Routers	Included
Unlimited Remote Monitoring For All Client Broadband	Included
Unlimited Remote Monitoring For All Client VPN's	Included
Unlimited Remote Monitoring For All Client Email/Web Services	Included
Unlimited Remote Monitoring For All Client SQL/Line Of Business Services	Included
Vendor Management Services	
Unlimited Management For All Client Vendor Support Issues	Included
Telecomm Vendors	Included
Software Vendors	Included
Equipment Vendors	Included
Annual Loss of Productivity from Staff Managing Vendors	
Annual Loss of Productivity from Staff Performing IT Functions	
Annual Loss of Productivity Cost From Network Downtime	
Annual Loss of Gross Revenue From Network Downtime	
Projected Incoming Annual IT Cost	
Total Incoming Annual IT Support Costs	
Proposed Managed Services Cost	
Total Client Savings	

---

www.mspu.us

5 Easy Ways to Save $$$ With Technology
-or-
How to Immediately Improve Your Bottom Line

MSPU

1

---

1. Flat-Rate I.T. Services

- Support and maintain your entire Organization Remotely
- Phone Support
- Remote Assistance (Desktop Sharing)
- Live Meeting (Online Collaboration)
- State-Of-The-Art Trouble-Ticketing System
- Automated Escalation Process
- Onsite Support As Needed

All for One Fixed Monthly Cost!

MSPU

2

2. Managed Services

- 24x7x365 Network Monitoring
- Over 255 Events/Services Monitored
- Critical Services Automatically Restarted
- Immediate Alerting
- Automated Trouble-Ticket Generation
- Automated Escalation Process
- Proactive not Reactive

Insures Maximum Uptime for Critical Equipment

MSPU

3

Appendix A – Forms and Collateral

3. Vendor Management

- Our Most Popular $$$-Saving Service
- Manage all Vendor Relationships
- Phone and Internet Service and Providers
- All Voice or Data Network-Connected Equipment
- Phone Systems
- Faxes
- Scanners
- Copiers
- Proprietary Software Applications

Frees You to Focus on Running Your Business – Not Your Vendors

MSPU

4

---

4. Professional Services

- Technology Solution Design and Development
- Proof-of-Concept Lab Testing
- Onsite Implementation
- Project Management
- Disaster Recovery Planning and Response
- Intrusion Detection and Security Testing
- Secure Point-to-Point VPN Design
- Co-Location Services for High-Availability Services

We Create a Technology Plan that Serves Your Mission

MSPU

5

---

5. Software and Application Development

- Custom Database Design and Maintenance
- Custom Application Development
- Web-Enabling Application Services
- Legacy Application Rewrites
- Custom Report Generation
- Hosting Services for High Availability

Existing Data Migration to New Applications

MSPU

6

Appendix A – Forms and Collateral

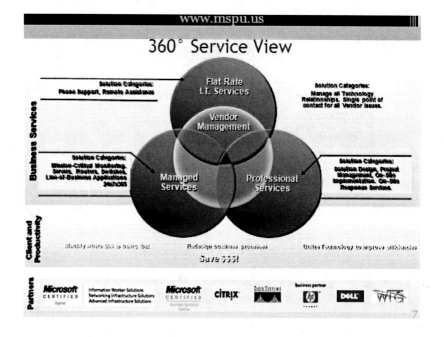

Appendix A – Forms and Collateral

Cost-Saving Services

* Flat-Rate I.T. Services
* Immediate I.T. Savings
* Managed Services
* Proactive Monitoring for Long-Term Savings
* Vendor Management
* Immediate Impact to the Bottom Line
* Professional Services
* We get it right the First Time, Every Time
* Software and Application Development
* Eliminate Redundant Data Entry and Improve Efficiency

You Can't Afford Not to Start Saving $$$ With Us!

MSPU

8

The Best I.T. Sales & Marketing BOOK EVER!

Appendix A – Forms and Collateral

Cost Savings Analysis

Managed Services Savings Analysis	
Gross Revenue	
Organization's Gross Revenue	
Productivity Loss To Staff Managing Vendors	
Number of Vendors Managed by Client	
Number of Hours Spent Managing Vendors Per Month	
Manager's Average Hourly Rate	
Productivity Lost Annually To Managing Vendors	
Productivity Loss To Staff Performing IT Functions	
Number of Hours Spent Performing IT Functions Per Month	
Staff Member's Average Hourly Rate	
Productivity Lost Annually To Performing IT Functions	
Productivity Loss To Network Downtime	
Number of Users On Client Network	
Number of Servers At Client Location	
Network Downtime	Hours
Email Services Down per Month	
Internet Connection Down per Month	
Server or Desktops Down per Month	
Total Hours Network Is Down Monthly	
Total Hours Network Is Down Annually	
Labor Costs	
Average Salary Per Employee	
Total Employees Worth Payroll	
Average Annual Employee Hours	
Total Annual Employee Hours	
Average Hourly Labor Cost Per Employee	
Productivity Lost To Downtime Annually	
Gross Revenue Loss To Network Downtime	
Individual Employee Hourly Contribution To Gross Revenue	
Gross Revenue Lost To Downtime Annually	
Existing Annual IT Costs	
Unlimited Remote Helpdesk Support For All Client Servers	Included
Unlimited Remote Helpdesk Support For All Client Desktops	Included
Unlimited Remote Helpdesk Support For All Client Printers	Included
Unlimited Remote Helpdesk Support For All Client Scanners	Included
Unlimited Remote Helpdesk Support For All Client Copiers	Included
Unlimited Remote Monitoring Support 24/7/365	
Unlimited Remote Monitoring For All Client Servers	Included
Unlimited Remote Monitoring For All Client Routers	Included
Unlimited Remote Monitoring For All Client Broadband	Included
Unlimited Remote Monitoring For All Client VPN's	Included
Unlimited Remote Monitoring For All Client Email/Web Services	Included
Unlimited Remote Monitoring For All Client SQL/Line Of Business Servers	Included
Vendor Management Services	
Unlimited Management For All Client Vendor Support Teams	Included
Telecomm Vendors	Included
Software Vendors	Included
Equipment Vendors	Included
Annual Loss of Productivity from Staff Managing Vendors	
Annual Loss of Productivity from Staff Performing IT Functions	
Annual Loss of Productivity Cost from Network Downtime	
Annual Loss of Gross Revenue from Network Downtime	
Projected Existing Annual IT Cost	
Total Existing Annual IT Service Costs	
Proposed Managed Services Cost	
Total Client Savings	

www.mspu.us

364

Cost Savings Analysis Example

Managed Services Savings Analysis - Example	
Gross Revenue	
Organization's Gross Revenue	$1,000,000.00
Productivity Loss To Staff Managing Vendors	
Number of Vendors Managed by Client	12
Number of Hours Spent Managing Vendors Per Month	12
Manager's Average Hourly Rate	$45.00
Productivity Lost Annually To Managing Vendors	$6,480.00
Productivity Loss To Staff Performing IT Functions	
Number of Hours Spent Performing IT Functions Per Month	12
Staff Member's Average Hourly Rate	$15.00
Productivity Lost Annually To Performing IT Functions	$3,040.00
Productivity Loss To Network Downtime	
Number of Users On Client Network	20
Number of Servers At Client Location	1
Network Downtime	Hours
Email Services Down per Month	4
Internet Connection Down per Month	4
Server or Desktops Down per Month	2
Total Hours Network Is Down Monthly	10
Total Hours Network Is Down Annually	120
Labor Costs	
Average Salary Per Employee	$30,000.00
Total Employee Yearly Payroll	$600,000.00
Average Annual Employee Hours	2080
Total Annual Employee Hours	41600
Average Hourly Labor Cost Per Employee	$14.42
Productivity Lost To Downtime Annually	$34,613.53
Gross Revenue Loss To Network Downtime	
Individual Employee Hourly Contribution To Gross Revenue	$24.04
Gross Revenue Lost To Downtime Annually	$57,692.31
Existing Annual IT Costs	$10,000.00
Unlimited Remote Helpdesk Support For All Client Servers	Included
Unlimited Remote Helpdesk Support For All Client Desktops	Included
Unlimited Remote Helpdesk Support For All Client Printers	Included
Unlimited Remote Helpdesk Support For All Client Scanners	Included
Unlimited Remote Helpdesk Support For All Client Copiers	Included
Unlimited Remote Monitoring Support 24/7/365	
Unlimited Remote Monitoring For All Client Servers	Included
Unlimited Remote Monitoring For All Client Routers	Included
Unlimited Remote Monitoring For All Client Broadband	Included
Unlimited Remote Monitoring For All Client VPN's	Included
Unlimited Remote Monitoring For All Client Email/Web Services	Included
Unlimited Remote Monitoring For All Client SQL/Line Of Business Servers	Included
Vendor Management Services	
Unlimited Management For All Client Vendor Support Issues	Included
Telecomm Vendors	Included
Software Vendors	Included
Equipment Vendors	Included
Annual Loss of Productivity from Staff Managing Vendors	$6,480.00
Annual Loss of Productivity from Staff Performing IT Functions	$3,040.00
Annual Loss of Productivity Cost from Network Downtime	$34,613.53
Annual Loss of Gross Revenue from Network Downtime	$57,692.31
Proposed Existing Annual IT Cost	$10,000.00
Total Existing Annual IT Support Costs	$114,347.69
Proposed Managed Services Cost	$36,000.00
Total Client Savings	**$77,827.69**

Managed Services Agreement Example

This Sample Managed Service Agreement is included for instructional and informational purposes only, and is not recommended, nor warranted for use.

Always have legal counsel review any and all Agreements or Documents that you distribute to your Clients prior to doing so.

Local laws and liabilities can never be fully covered by any type of generic document, including this Sample Managed Service Agreement.

Managed Services Agreement

1.   Term of Agreement

This Agreement between
_____, herein referred to
as Client, and _____,
hereinafter referred to as Service Provider, is effective
upon the date signed, shall remain in force for a period of
three years, and be reviewed annually to address any
necessary adjustments or modifications. Should
adjustments or modifications be required that increase
the monthly fees paid for the services rendered under
this Agreement, these increases will not exceed
_____% of the value of the existing monthly fees due
under this Agreement. The Service Agreement
automatically renews for a subsequent three year term
beginning on the day immediately following the end of
the Initial Term, unless either party gives the other
ninety (90) days prior written notice of its intent not to
renew this Agreement.

   a) This Agreement may be terminated by the Client upon
       ninety (90) days written notice if the Service Provider:
       I.   Fails to fulfill in any material respect its
            obligations under this Agreement and does not
            cure such failure within thirty (30) days of
            receipt of such written notice.
       II. Breaches any material term or condition of this
            Agreement and fails to remedy such breach
            within thirty (30) days of receipt of such written
            notice.

III. Terminates or suspends its business operations, unless it is succeeded by a permitted assignee under this Agreement.

b) This Agreement may be terminated by the Service Provider upon ninety (90) days written notice to the Client.

c) If either party terminates this Agreement, Service Provider will assist Client in the orderly termination of services, including timely transfer of the services to another designated provider. Client agrees to pay Service Provider the actual costs of rendering such assistance.

2. **Fees and Payment Schedule**

Fees will be $_____ per month, invoiced to Client on a Monthly basis, and will become due and payable on the first day of each month. The first month will include an additional one-time setup fee equal to the monthly service fee. Services will be suspended if payment is not received within 5 days following date due. Refer to Appendix B for services covered by the monthly fee under the terms of this Agreement.

It is understood that any and all Services requested by Client that fall outside of the terms of this Agreement will be considered Projects, and will be quoted and billed as separate, individual Services.

3. **Taxes**
It is understood that any Federal, State or Local Taxes applicable shall be added to each invoice for services or materials rendered under this Agreement. Client

---

shall pay any such taxes unless a valid exemption certificate is furnished to Service Provider for the state of use.

4.   Coverage

Remote Helpdesk and Vendor Management of Client's IT networks will be provided to the Client by Service Provider through remote means between the hours of 8:00 am – 5:00 pm Monday through Friday, excluding public holidays. Network Monitoring Services will be provided 24/7/365. All services qualifying under these conditions, as well as Services that fall outside this scope will fall under the provisions of Appendix B. Hardware costs of any kind are not covered under the terms of this Agreement.

Support and Escalation

Service Provider will respond to Client's Trouble Tickets under the provisions of Appendix A, and with best effort after hours or on holidays. Trouble Tickets must be opened by Client's designated I.T. Contact Person, by email to our Help Desk, or by phone if email is unavailable. Each call will be assigned a Trouble Ticket number for tracking. Our escalation process is detailed in Appendix A.

Service outside Normal Working Hours

Emergency services performed outside of the hours of 8:00 am – 5:00 pm Monday through Friday, excluding public holidays, shall be subject to provisions of Appendix B.

Service Calls Where No Trouble is found

> If Client requests onsite service and no problem is found or reproduced, Client shall be billed at the current applicable rates as indicated in Appendix B.

Limitation of Liability

> In no event shall Service Provider be held liable for indirect, special, incidental or consequential damages arising out of service provided hereunder, including but not limited to loss of profits or revenue, loss of use of equipment, lost data, costs of substitute equipment, or other costs.

5.   Additional Maintenance Services

Hardware/System Support

> Service Provider shall provide support of all hardware and systems specified in Appendix B, provided that all Hardware is covered under a currently active Vendor Support Contract; or replaceable parts be readily available, and all Software be Genuine, Currently Licensed and Vendor-Supported. Should any hardware or systems fail to meet these provisions, they will be excluded from this Service Agreement. Should 3rd Party Vendor Support Charges be required in order to resolve any issues, these will be passed on to the Client after first receiving the Client's authorization to incur them.

Appendix A – Forms and Collateral

Virus Recovery for Current, Licensed Antivirus protected systems

> Attempted recovery from damages caused by virus infection not detected and quarantined by the latest Antivirus definitions is covered under the terms of this Agreement. This Service is limited to those systems protected with a currently licensed, Vendor-supported Antivirus solution.

Monitoring Services

> Service Provider will provide ongoing monitoring and security services of all critical devices as indicated in Appendix B. Service Provider will provide monthly reports as well as document critical alerts, scans and event resolutions to Client. Should a problem be discovered during monitoring, Service Provider shall make every attempt to rectify the condition in a timely manner through remote means.

6.   Suitability of Existing Environment

Minimum Standards Required for Services

> In order for Client's existing environment to qualify for Service Provider's Managed Services, the following requirements must be met:

> > 1. All Servers with Microsoft Windows Operating Systems must be running Windows 2000 Server or later, and have all of the latest Microsoft Service Packs and Critical Updates installed.

---

2. All Desktop PC's and Notebooks/Laptops with Microsoft Windows Operating Systems must be running Windows XP Pro or later, and have all of the latest Microsoft Service Packs and Critical Updates installed.
3. All Server and Desktop Software must be Genuine, Licensed and Vendor-Supported.
4. The environment must have a currently licensed, up-to-date and Vendor-Supported Server-based Antivirus Solution protecting all Servers, Desktops, Notebooks/Laptops, and Email.
5. The environment must have a currently licensed, Vendor-Supported Server-based Backup Solution that can be monitored, and send notifications on job failures and successes.
6. The environment must have a currently licensed, Vendor-Supported Hardware Firewall between the Internal Network and the Internet.
7. All Wireless data traffic in the environment must be securely encrypted.
8. There must be an outside static IP address assigned to a network device, allowing RDP or VPN access.

Costs required to bring Client's environment up to these Minimum Standards are not included in this Agreement.

7. Excluded Services

Service rendered under this Agreement does not include:

1) Parts, equipment or software not covered by vendor/manufacturer warranty or support.
2) The cost of any parts, equipment, or shipping charges of any kind.
3) The cost of any Software, Licensing, or Software Renewal or Upgrade Fees of any kind.
4) The cost of any 3rd Party Vendor or Manufacturer Support or Incident Fees of any kind.
5) The cost to bring Client's environment up to minimum standards required for Services.
6) Failure due to acts of God, building modifications, power failures or other adverse environmental conditions or factors.
7) Service and repair made necessary by the alteration or modification of equipment other than that authorized by Service Provider, including alterations, software installations or modifications of equipment made by Client's employees or anyone other than Service Provider.
8) Maintenance of Applications software packages, whether acquired from Service Provider or any other source unless as specified in Appendix B.
9) Programming (modification of software code) and program (software) maintenance unless as specified in Appendix B.
10) Training Services of any kind.

8. **Confidentiality**

Service Provider and its agents will not use or disclose Client information, except as necessary to or consistent with providing the contracted services, and will protect against unauthorized use.

9.   Miscellaneous

This Agreement shall be governed by the laws of the State of _____. It constitutes the entire Agreement between Client and Service Provider for monitoring/maintenance/service of all equipment listed in "Appendix B." Its terms and conditions shall prevail should there be any variance with the terms and conditions of any order submitted by Client.

Service Provider is not responsible for failure to render services due to circumstances beyond its control including, but not limited to, acts of God.

10.   Acceptance of Service Agreement

This Service Agreement covers only those services and equipment listed in "Appendix B." Service Provider must deem any equipment/services Client may want to add to this Agreement after the effective date acceptable. The addition of equipment/services not listed in "Appendix B" at the signing of this Agreement, if acceptable to Service Provider, shall result in an adjustment to the Client's monthly charges.

IN WITNESS WHEREOF, the parties hereto have caused this Service Agreement to be signed by their duly authorized representatives as of the date set forth below.

Accepted by:

Authorized Signature   Date   Service   Provider

Authorized Signature   Date   Client

Managed Services Agreement

Appendix A

Response and Resolution Times

The following table shows the targets of response and

resolution times for each priority level:

Trouble	Priority	Response time (in hours) *	Resolution time (in hours) *	Escalation threshold (in hours)
Service not available (all users and functions unavailable).	1	Within 1 hour	ASAP – Best Effort	2 hours
Significant degradation of service (large number of users or business critical functions affected)	2	Within 4 hours	ASAP – Best Effort	4 hours
Limited degradation of service (limited number of users or functions affected, business process can continue).	3	Within 24 hours	ASAP – Best Effort	48 hours
Small service degradation (business process can continue, one user affected).	4	within 48 hours	ASAP – Best Effort	96 hours

Support Tiers

The following details and describes our Support Tier levels:

Support Tier	Description
Tier 1 Support	All support incidents begin in Tier 1, where the initial trouble ticket is created, the issue is identified and clearly documented, and basic hardware/software troubleshooting is initiated.
Tier 2 Support	All support incidents that cannot be resolved with Tier 1 Support are escalated to Tier 2, where more complex support on hardware/software issues can be provided by more experienced Engineers.
Tier 3 Support	Support Incidents that cannot be resolved by Tier 2 Support are escalated to Tier 3, where support is provided by the most qualified and experienced Engineers who have the ability to collaborate with 3rd Party (Vendor) Support Engineers to resolve the most complex issues.

Managed Services Agreement

Appendix A (cont)

Service Request Escalation Procedure

1. Support Request is Received
2. Trouble Ticket is Created
3. Issue is Identified and documented in Help Desk system
4. Issue is qualified to determine if it can be resolved through Tier 1 Support

If issue can be resolved through Tier 1 Support:

5. Level 1 Resolution - issue is worked to successful resolution
6. Quality Control –Issue is verified to be resolved to Client's satisfaction
7. Trouble Ticket is closed, after complete problem resolution details have been updated in Help Desk system

If issue cannot be resolved through Tier 1 Support:

6. Issue is escalated to Tier 2 Support
7. Issue is qualified to determine if it can be resolved by Tier 2 Support

If issue can be resolved through Tier 2 Support:

8. Level 2 Resolution - issue is worked to successful resolution
9. Quality Control –Issue is verified to be resolved to Client's satisfaction

---

10. Trouble Ticket is closed, after complete problem resolution details have been updated in Help Desk system

If issue cannot be resolved through Tier 2 Support:

9. Issue is escalated to Tier 3 Support
10. Issue is qualified to determine if it can be resolved through Tier 3 Support

If issue can be resolved through Tier 3 Support:

11. Level 3 Resolution - issue is worked to successful resolution
12. Quality Control –Issue is verified to be resolved to Client's satisfaction
13. Trouble Ticket is closed, after complete problem resolution details have been updated in Help Desk system

If issue cannot be resolved through Tier 3 Support:

12. Issue is escalated to Onsite Support
13. Issue is qualified to determine if it can be resolved through Onsite Support

If issue can be resolved through Onsite Support:

14. Onsite Resolution - issue is worked to successful resolution
15. Quality Control –Issue is verified to be resolved to Client's satisfaction
16. Trouble Ticket is closed, after complete problem resolution details have been updated in Help Desk system

If issue cannot be resolved through Onsite Support:

17. I.T. Manager Decision Point – request is updated with complete details of all activity performed

Managed Services Agreement

Appendix A (cont)

The Best I.T. Sales & Marketing BOOK EVER!

Appendix A – Forms and Collateral

HELP DESK SERVICE CALL ROUTING PROCESS

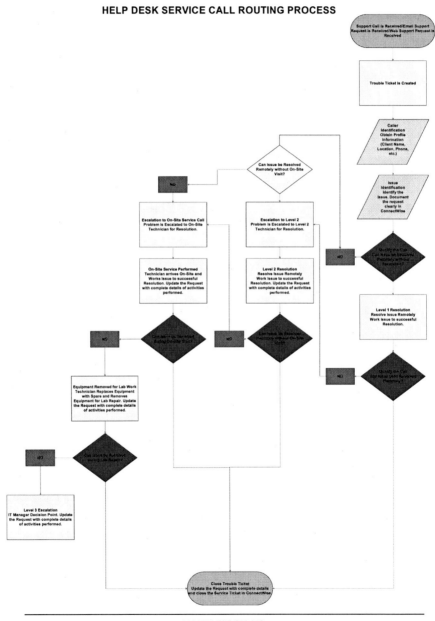

Managed Services Agreement
Appendix B

Description	Frequency	Included in Maintenance
General		
Document software and hardware changes	As performed	YES
Test backups with restores	Monthly	YES
Monthly reports of work accomplished, work in progress, etc.	Monthly	YES
Servers		
Manage Servers	Ongoing	YES
Check print queues	As needed	YES
Monitor all Server services	Ongoing	YES
Keep Service Packs, Patches and Hotfixes current as per company policy	Monthly	YES
Check event log of every server and identify any potential issues	As things appear	YES
Monitor hard drive free space on server	Ongoing	YES
Exchange Server user/mailbox management	As needed	YES
Monitor Active Directory replication	As needed	YES
Monitor WINS replication	As needed	YES
SQL server management	As needed	YES
Reboot servers if needed	As needed	YES
Run defrag and chkdsk on all drives	As needed	YES
Scheduled off time server maintenance	As needed	YES
Install supported software upgrades	As needed	YES
Determine logical directory structure, implement, MAP, and detail	As needed	YES
Set up and maintain groups (accounting, admin, printers, sales warehouse, etc)	As needed	YES
Check status of backups	Daily	YES
Alert Client to dangerous conditions -Memory running low -Hard drive showing sign of failure -Hard drive running out of disk space -Controllers losing interrupts -Network Cards report unusual collision activity	As needed	YES
Educate and correct user errors (deleted files, corrupted files, etc.)	As needed	YES
Clean and prune directory structure, keep efficient and active	As needed	YES
Disaster Recovery		
Disaster Recovery of Server(s)	As Needed	YES

Managed Services Agreement
Appendix B (cont.)

Devices		
Manage Desktops	Ongoing	YES
Manage Network Printers	Ongoing	YES
Manage Other Networked Devices	Ongoing	YES
Manage PDA's/Smartphones.	Ongoing	YES

Networks		
Check router logs	As needed	YES
Performance Monitoring/Capacity Planning	Ongoing	YES
Monitor DSU/TSU, switches, hubs and Internet connectivity, and make sure everything is operational (available for SNMP manageable devices only)	Ongoing	YES
Maintain office connectivity to the Internet	As needed	YES

Security		
Check firewall logs	As needed	YES
Confirm that antivirus virus definition auto updates have occurred	As needed	YES
Confirm that antispyware updates have occurred	As needed	YES
Confirm that backup has been performed on a daily basis	As needed	YES
Create new directories, shares and security groups, new accounts disable/delete old accounts, manage account policies	As needed	YES
Permissions and file system management	As needed	YES
Set up new users including login restrictions, passwords, security applications	As needed	YES
Set up and change security for users and applications	Ongoing	YES
Monitor for unusual activity among users	As needed	YES

Applications		
Ensure Microsoft Office Applications are functioning as designed	As needed	YES
Ensure Microsoft ActiveSync Applications	As needed	YES
Ensure Adobe Acrobat Applications are functioning as designed	As needed	YES
Ensure Symantec Backup Exec Applications are functioning as designed	As needed	YES
Ensure Microsoft NTBackup Applications are functioning as designed	As needed	YES
Ensure Intuit Quickbooks Applications are functioning as designed	As needed	YES

Managed Services Agreement
Appendix B (cont)

Service Rates

Labor	Rate
Remote PC Management/Help Desk 8am-5pm M-F	INCLUDED
Remote Printer Management 8am-5pm M-F	INCLUDED
Remote Network Management 8am-5pm M-F	INCLUDED
Remote Server Management 8am-5pm M-F	INCLUDED
24x7x365 Network Monitoring	INCLUDED
Lab Labor 8am-5pm M-F	INCLUDED
Onsite Labor 8am-5pm M-F	INCLUDED
Remote PC Management/Help Desk 5:01pm-9pm M-F	$_____/hr
Remote Printer Management 5:01pm-9pm M-F	$_____/hr
Remote Network Management 5:01pm-9pm M-F	$_____/hr
Remote Server Management 5:01pm-9pm M-F	$_____/hr
Lab Labor 5:01pm-9pm M-F	$_____/hr
Onsite Labor 5:01pm-9pm M-F	$_____/hr
Remote Labor All Other Times	$_____/hr
Lab Labor All Other Times	$_____/hr
Onsite Labor All Other Times	$_____/hr

Covered Equipment

Managed Desktops:　　　　(Desktops & Notebooks)
Managed Printers:
Managed Networks:
Managed Servers:
Managed Cell/PDA:　　　　(Smart phones & PDAs)

Disaster Recovery Messaging Postcard

Would you be able to continue business
as usual in the event of a disaster?

Do you trust your back-up?

Is your network being monitored every second of every day?

WE CAN BRING YOU PEACE OF MIND!

Disaster Recovery Messaging Postcard2

Flat-Rate I.T. Messaging Postcard

Unlimited Flat-Rate I.T. Remote Support
begins with a phone call...

Did you know...

- Only 6% of companies suffering from a
  catastrophic data loss survive,

- 43% never reopen,

- 51% close within 2 years...

We can bring you a peace of mind

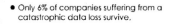

Case Study Questionnaire

1. Background about the client's company- size of system, # of users.

2. What initially brought you to (I.T. Service Provider), and when was this? Did you have an IT company before?

3. What did (I.T. Service Provider) do for your company? Be as detailed as you like. I've had a lot of responses along the lines of 'they upgraded our hardware and software', which is fine, but if you can be more specific that would be very helpful.

4. Do you have system capabilities now that you didn't have before (I.T. Service Provider)?

5. Do you still have an ongoing contract with them for maintenance/upgrades? How is their response time when an onsite call is necessary?

6. How would you grade the ROI- return on investment- you've received from (I.T. Service Provider)?

7. Any other comments you'd like to make about (I.T. Service Provider)- the people who work there, any other aspects of their service or the work they did for you that hasn't been covered already.

The Best I.T. Sales & Marketing BOOK EVER!

Appendix A – Forms and Collateral

Newsletter Design Comp

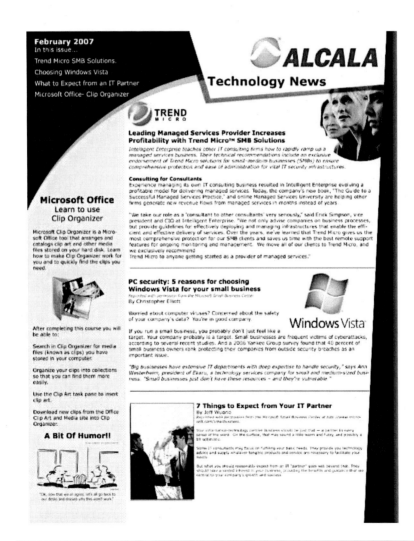

I.T. Services Line Card Comp

ARRC Technology
CharTec

FLAT RATE IT SERVICES

- Support & Maintain Your Entire Organization Remotely
- Unlimited Phone Support
- Remote Assistance
- Onsite Support
- State of the Art Trouble Ticketing System
- Automated Escalation Process
- Parts & Labor for Work Station & Server Repair

MANAGED SERVICES

- 24x7x365 Network Monitoring
- Over 255 Events/Services Monitored
- Critical Services Automatically Restarted
- Immediate Alerting
- Automated Trouble-Ticket Generation
- Patch Management
- Automated Escalation Process
- Proactive & Well Planned Services
- Monthly Reports of Work Performed & Network Health

VENDOR MANAGEMENT

- Manage All Vendor Relationships
  - Phone & Internet Service Providers
  - Copiers
  - Telco
  - Faxes
  - Scanners
  - Web Site Designer & Hosting Company
  - Proprietary Software Applications

PROFESSIONAL SERVICES

- Technology Solution Design & Development
- Proof of Concept Lab Testing
- Onsite Implementation
- Project Management
- Disaster Recovery Planning & Response
- Offsite Backup
- Rental Equipment & Training Facilities
- AMC's & Programming of Customers Existing Telephone Equipment
- C-7 Cabling adds, moves or changes. (AMC's are less than 3 drops at any one time)

COMPLETE HARDWARE SOLUTION

- Custom Servers & Workstations
- Network Printers, Switches, Routers
- Parts & Labor for Life of Contract
- Workstation Upgrades every 2 Years
- Servers every 4 Years or as Required by Applications

The Best I.T. Sales & Marketing BOOK EVER!

Appendix A – Forms and Collateral

HR Interview Checklist For New Sales Person

HR Hiring Checklist for Sales Person

		Completed
1.	Run Sales Ad for Sales person (See ENCLOSED SAMPLE AD)	
2.	Receive and Review Resume	
	• *Detailized Resume, Sales Quotas, Significant Time on Job*	
3.	Conduct Conference Call Interview	
	• *Interview Questions (SEE ENCLOSED QUESTIONS)*	
4.	Email Sales Prospect DISC Behavioral Profile	
5.	Email Sales Prospect Sales Index Survey	
	• *Send Sales Person a copy DISC Profiles Before Interview*	
6.	Schedule In Office Interview	
	• *Complete Job Application and Typing Test*	
	• *Review Disc Profile Questions*	
	• *Review Sales Index Survey*	
	• *Give Sales Person Sales Situations to Answer*	
	• *Review Sales Base and Commission Structure*	
	• *Review Sales Quota/Expectation and Time Line*	
	• *Review Training Process and Timeline~ Verify Sales person CRM Application Skills*	
	• *(3) ways to evaluate a sales person before they make a sale*	
7.	Schedule Second Interview with Partner or Upper Management	
8.	Establish start Date for Sales Person (Set start at least a week out to check references)	
9.	Email Offer Letter to NEW Sales Person (1 Week Window)	
10.	Conduct Criminal Background check	
11.	Schedule Appointment for Drug Screening	
12.	Conduct background check on references from Resume/Application	
13.	New Hire Orientation	
	• *Issue Company Handbook*	
	• *Training Schedule to meet Sales Expectation and Schedule Quarterly Training with Sandler*	
	• *Establish Daily and then Weekly Sales Meeting Times*	
	• *Review and Train on Weekly Sales Stat Requirements*	

---

5 Ways To Evaluate A Sales Person

1. CRM and Sales Tracking Process

- o Does Sales person have a pre-trained process for tracking all prospects and suspects?

- o Do they already track gross calls, Follow ups, are their follow up calls scheduled, no answers, call backs.

- o Can sales person make at least 100 outbound call attempts per day.

- o Does sales person understand the significance of calling Mon-Wed?

- o Does sales person know the average hit ratio of gross calls, net calls to set an appointment?

- o Can sales person easily establish a sales funnel report in either excel or CRM program

- o Have sales person explain the process for negotiating the gatekeeper.

- o Listen to sales persons 30 second pitch to Decision Maker.

2. Does Sales person understand the significance of Product Knowledge vs. Client Relationship

- o Does sales person spend more time on product knowledge than understanding feature and benefits

- o Do you have to convince sales person the importance of being liked by prospects

---

- o Do people tend to like the sales person easily, either on the phone or in person

- o Does sales person make friends easily and does sales person have a lot of friends

3. Can Sales person qualify a prospect on the phone and in a Sales engagement

- o Evaluate sales person's qualifying questions for a prospect in a role playing session

- o Ask sales person the difference between a prospect and a suspect

- o Ask sales person to project sales cycle in terms of initial call to closing deal, once they understand product

4. Can sales person present your product and services effectively

- o Sales Skills Index Survey can help evaluate the sales person presentation ability

- o Has sales person ever attended toast masters

- o Have sales person conduct a PowerPoint presentation recorded with Microsoft One note.

5. Can sales person Close on the phone and in a onsite Sales Engagement

- o Sales Skills Index Survey will give you some idea if the sales person can Close

- o Role play with them once they understand product and see if you would by from them

- o Record all role playing sessions and record them with One Note.

Qualifying Call Script

Hi,

My name is _____ from
_____.

Recently we sent (insert contact name) some information in the mail and I just want to confirm that he/she received it. We sent a giant post card regarding a Microsoft Network Security evaluation. Do you know if (insert contact name) would be the person we should have sent that type of information to? (If not, get new contact info and title)

Maybe you can help me really quick to make sure your company even qualifies for the evaluation. Do you have at least (number of required workstations) computers in your office? Do you have an IT department or do you outsource that work? Is your company using (insert software platform)? Is anyone there having issues with that?

If they qualify:

Great, your company does qualify. Is (insert contact name) available to speak to about the evaluation?

If they do not qualify:

I'm sorry. To qualify for the free evaluation you must have at least (number of required workstations) workstations. Thank you for your time though and have a great day.

If available:

Hello,

My name is _____ and I'm calling from (company name). The reason I'm calling is that we are one of Microsoft's Gold Certified Partners and I have been assigned to offer a Microsoft Network Security Evaluation for your company if you qualify – which in speaking with your assistant, realize that you do qualify. We are conducting these evaluations free of charge and there's no obligation once the evaluation is completed. From what I understand your company is using (insert software platform) correct? Is anyone in your company having issues with that? When is a good time for us to come by and complete the evaluation?

If they have questions:

That's a great question. If you don't mind hold on just one second I can get you to my client-support manager who will be happy to answer that for you.

Lead Calling Script

Hello,

My name is _____ and I'm calling from
_____. Is _____ available?

We calling as your Microsoft Gold Partner and I have been
assigned to offer a Microsoft Network Security Evaluation for
your company if you qualify and I need to speak with (decision
maker) to insure you do qualify.

Decision maker:

Hello,

My name is _____ and I'm calling from
___(company name)___. The reason I'm calling is that we are
your Microsoft Gold Partner and I have been assigned to offer
a Microsoft Network Security Evaluation for your company if
you qualify. We are conducting these evaluations free of
charge and there's no obligation once the evaluation is
completed. So I just had a few questions for you to insure you
qualify, and if so to schedule your appointment.

How many computer work stations you have at your facility?

May I start by asking if you currently have a disaster recovery
plan in place?

Do you have an onsite IT department or do you outsource that
work?

When is the best time for you, your IT department and any other relevant personnel to be available for this evaluation – it usually takes about an hour or so?

Voicemail:

Hello,

My name is _____ and I'm calling from _____. The reason I'm calling is that we are your Microsoft Gold Partner and I have been assigned to offer a Microsoft Network Security Evaluation for your company if you qualify. We are conducting these evaluations free of charge, there is no obligation once completed and the evaluation is to cover Disaster Recovery issues. Please call me at _____ to ensure that your company qualifies for the free evaluation and to set the appointment to complete it. Thank you for your time, we hope you have a great day and we look forward to hearing from you soon.

The Best I.T. Sales & Marketing BOOK EVER!

Appendix A – Forms and Collateral

Direct Mail Marketing Letter

MANAGED SERVICES PROVIDER UNIVERSITY

You Run A Business, We Help Your Business Run!

May 20, 2007

Dear Fellow Business Owner,

Do you ever get frustrated when you need help with your computer systems, printers or Email? Does it ever seem that your systems only act up when you or your staff need them the most? We take the confusion out of your technology. Our goal is to give you IT peace of mind.

The time has come! We introduce clients to new technologies that save them an average of 30% to 50% on technology costs each year. We've proven that proactively managing your network always costs less than reacting to problems after they occur. We believe that your IT infrastructure should be a profit center for your business, not a cost center.

You deserve fast, affordable, professional support. That's why we've bundled our revolutionary Flat-Rate I.T. Support Program with our Proactive Network Monitoring Service, providing you experienced IT Support to maintain and protect your network 24 hours a day, 7 days a week, 365 days a year!

As an added bonus, if you call us right away, you'll be eligible to receive Alchetec's most popular service, Vendor Management, at no additional charge. With Vendor Management, Alchetec becomes the single point of contact for all of your vendor issues, freeing you to focus on running your business, not your vendors.

If you are new to us and would like to learn how to improve your IT support while reducing costs, I'd like to invite you to a **FREE Network and Security Health Checkup**.

One of our Engineers will meet with you, discuss your concerns, and evaluate your network to insure you're getting the most out of the Technology you've already invested in. You'll know exactly where you stand from a Technology perspective after this FREE Service.

We offer this Service to you so that you can get to know us better without any risk, so please call us today!

Name
President/CEO
Email

1 Hour of FREE On-Site Computer Service
Here are just a sample of our available services:

- Hi-Speed Internet Access **DSL** & E-mail
- Local/Wide Area Network Design and Support
- Desktop/Server Troubleshooting
- Long distance at **2 cents** per minute
- Virus Protection and Security
- Home and Remote Access **VPN**

7077 Orangewood Ave. Suite 104. Garden Grove. CA 92841

  citrix

Call Today To Schedule Your FREE On-site Consultation

---

www.mspu.us

HTML Email DR Messaging Comp

MANAGED SERVICES PROVIDER UNIVERSITY

Would you be able to continue business as usual in the event of a disaster?

Is your network being monitored every second of every day?

Do you *trust* your back-up?

Did you know...

- Only 6% of companies suffering from a catastrophic data loss survive,

- 43% never reopen,

- 51% close within 2 years...

WE CAN BRING YOU PEACE OF MIND!

Call now for a FREE consultation

Business Plan PowerPoint Presentation

Today's Presenter

Erick Simpson
Vice President/CIO
Intelligent Enterprise/MSP University

- Author – "The Guide to a Successful Managed Services Practice – *What every SMB IT Service Provider Should Know*"

E-Mail: esimpson@mspu.us

Websites: www.ienterprise.us

www.mspu.us

Intelligent Enterprise   MSPU

2

Who is Intelligent Enterprise?

- We're an IT Service Provider just like you!
- In Business Since 1997
- Microsoft Gold Certified Partner
  - Microsoft Business Solutions Partner
  - Microsoft Small Business Specialist
- Microsoft Competencies:
  - Information Worker Solutions
  - Networking Infrastructure Solutions
  - Advanced Infrastructure Solutions
- HTG Peer Group Member
- ConnectWise Partner
- Zenith Infotech Partner
- Authors: *"The Guide to a Successful Managed Services Practice"*
- Founders: MSP University
  - Training MSP's Since 2005

---

www.mspu.us

Today's Agenda

- Managed Services Business Plan
  - Definition
  - Benefits
  - Purpose
  - Components
  - Tips on Creating your Managed Services Business Plan
  - The Importance of Execution
  - Maintenance
  - Resources
    - Managed Services Business Plan Template Download

Intelligent Enterprise   MSPU

4

Definition of a Business Plan

- A blueprint and communication tool for your business.
- A device to help you, the owner, set out how you intend to operate your business.
- A road map to tell others how you expect to get there.

-The U.S. Small Business Administration
www.sba.gov

Intelligent Enterprise   **MSPU**

5

Benefits

- Confirms the viability of your business venture
- Helps you set realistic goals and expectations, based on the market research you conduct
- Provides a roadmap to your success
- Minimizes business risk

Intelligent Enterprise   MSPU

6

Common Purposes of a Business Plan

- Defines your business
  - Vision
  - Mission
  - Goals
- Identifies your
  - Marketing strategy
  - Sources of Revenue
  - Competition
- Can be used to attract
  - Investment opportunities
  - Business financing

Enterprise   MSPU

7

Strategic Planning

- A precursor to writing your business plan
- Helps you match the strengths of your business offerings to available opportunities by requiring you to:
  - Collect and analyze information about your business environment
  - Clearly understand your business' strengths and weaknesses
  - Develop clear goals and objectives
- Forces you to objectively re-evaluate your business

Intelligent Enterprise   MSPU

8

Appendix A – Forms and Collateral

Traditional Business Plan Components

- Executive Summary
- Vision, Mission & Goals
- Company Overview
- Marketing Plan
- Key Alliances, Partners and Vendors
- Revenue Sources
- Competition
- Financials

Intelligent Enterprise   **MSPU**

9

Executive Summary

- Summary of your business
  - Year of inception, location and areas of expertise
- Company History in the Making
  - Several key highlights in the company's history
- Management
  - A description of your key management team and their backgrounds which qualify them for their positions
- Uniqueness
  - A brief outline of your uniqueness in the industry
- Financials
  - A concise narrative of your current financial position

Intelligent Enterprise   **MSPU**

10

---

www.mspu.us

Vision, Mission & Goals

- Your company's Vision Statement
  - A short, inspiring statement of what the organization intends to become and achieve at some point in the future
    - *"There will be a personal computer on every desk running Microsoft software"* – Bill Gates
- Your company's Mission Statement
  - A short, concise statement of your organization's priorities
    - *"To make people happy"* – Walt Disney
- Your company's Goals
  - Several specific, realistic goals for the organization based upon your Vision and Mission Statements

*Intelligent*Enterprise   MSPU

11

Company Overview

- History
  - Briefly document your company history
- Legal Business Description
  - Briefly describe your legal entity – LLC, S-Corp, etc.
    - *"A privately-held California-based S-Corporation, founded in 1997"*
- Board of Directors
  - Briefly state your Board of Directors, titles and responsibilities
- Company Officers
  - Briefly state your Officers, titles and responsibilities
- Notable Clientele
  - Briefly include a few cornerstone clients

Intelligent Enterprise   MSPU

12

Marketing Plan

- Address the results of your Strategic Planning and Competitive Analysis
  - Your business
  - Your competition
  - Your uniqueness
- Clearly defines your organization's deliverables
  - Managed Services, Project-based work, Application Development
- Identifies your Target Market
- Ilustrates the methods you will utilize in reaching your Market
  - Microsoft Across America-driven events
  - Direct-response marketing

*Intelligent*Enterprise   MSPU

13

---

www.mspu.us

Key Alliances, Partners and Vendors

- Briefly describe the key alliances, partners and vendors that you will leverage in executing your business plan and marketing strategy
  - Microsoft
  - Strategic Fulfillment Partners
  - Other Key Vendors

*Intelligent*Enterprise   MSPU

14

The Best I.T. Sales & Marketing BOOK EVER!

Appendix A – Forms and Collateral

www.mspu.us

Revenue Sources

- Briefly describe all sources of current revenue
  - Project-based Services Revenue
  - Managed Services Contract Revenue
  - Hosting/Co-location Services Revenue
  - Web/Application Development Revenue
  - Other Recurring Revenue from Annuity-Based Solutions such as T1's, Hosted VOIP, etc.
- Briefly describe future revenue sources based on your financial projections
  - SAAS
    - Office Live, Hosted Exchange
  - HAAS

Intelligent Enterprise   MSPU

15

Competition

- General Competitive Analysis
  - Briefly describe 3 (or more) local sources of competition, and their
    - Marketing Strategy
    - Location
    - Strengths
    - Weaknesses
    - Pricing Structure

Intelligent Enterprise   MSPU

16

Financials

- Financial Projections
  - Briefly describe your financial projections, based upon your financial projections spreadsheet
- Spreadsheet
  - Create and include a spreadsheet supporting your financial projections

*Intelligent*Enterprise   MSPU

17

Tips On Creating Your Business Plan

- Don't skimp on your research
- Be brutally honest with yourself and your assumptions
- Sharpen your pencil
- Keep it brief
- Circulate it for review among trusted business associates or a peer group before execution

Intelligent Enterprise

MSPU

18

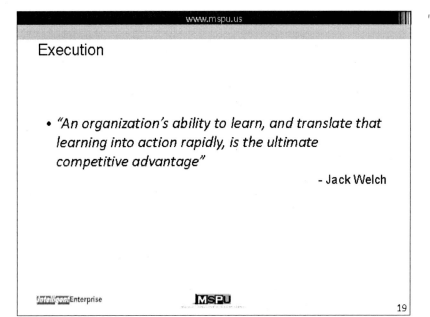

Execution

- *"An organization's ability to learn, and translate that learning into action rapidly, is the ultimate competitive advantage"*

    - Jack Welch

www.mspu.us

Maintenance

- Realize that your business plan is a living document – revisit the plan often for review and revision
- Remember that your business plan is your roadmap – understand that maps must adapt to reflect changing road conditions

*Intelligent*Enterprise   MSPU

20

The Best I.T. Sales & Marketing BOOK EVER!

Appendix A – Forms and Collateral

---

www.mspu.us

Resources

- Visit our website: www.mspu.us
  - Download free Managed Services Webinars
  - Download a sample of *"The Guide to a Successful Managed Services Practice"*
- Attend our next free 1 day Managed Services Workshop
- Email me for:
  - A copy of my white paper on Managed Services Business Planning
  - The complete 11-page Managed Services Business Plan Template we use to train our Partners with

esimpson@mspu.us

Intelligent Enterprise   MSPU   21

Thank You…!
Erick Simpson
esimpson@mspu.us
www.mspu.us
(714) 898-8195

Managed Services Business Plan Template

CONFIDENTIAL BUSINESS PLAN

YOUR COMPANY NAME

This business plan has been prepared solely for the benefit of private shareholders of YOUR COMPANY NAME The information contained herein has been supplied in part from trade and statistical services and publications and from other sources that are reliable. YOUR COMPANY NAME makes no representation or warranty as to the accuracy or completeness of such information. This Business Plan may not be used or reproduced for any other purpose.

Anyone accepting delivery of this Business Plan agrees to maintain the confidentiality of the information contained herein, and, upon request, agrees to return this Business plan and all related documents to YOUR NAME, at the address below. Any questions relating to this Business Plan should be directed to:

YOUR NAME

YOUR COMPANY NAME

YOUR STREET

YOUR CITY, STATE ZIP

YOUR PHONE NUMBER

The inclusion of various other corporate icons in this document is intended solely as a graphic supplement to the Business Plan. These companies should not interpret the use of these logos to convey an express or implied endorsement of this business plan. YOUR COMPANY NAME has no relationship with these companies, other than expressly specified in this document.

I.EXECUTIVE SUMMARY

- **Summary**
- **Company History in the Making**
- **Management**
- **Uniqueness**
- **Financials**

II.VISION, MISSION & GOALS

- **Vision**
- **Mission**
- **Goals**

III.COMPANY OVERVIEW

- **History**
- **Legal Business Description**
- **Board of Directors**
- **Company Officers**
- **Notable Clientele**

Appendix A – Forms and Collateral

IV. MARKETING PLAN

- **Creative Strategies**

V. KEY ALLIANCES

- **Microsoft**
- **Citrix**
- **Cisco**

VI. REVENUE SOURCES

- **Current Revenue Sources**
- **Future Revenue Sources**

VII. COMPETITION

- **General Competitive Analysis**

VIII. FINANCIALS

- **Financial Projections**
- **Financial Charts**

I. Executive Summary

YOUR COMPANY NAME

- Summary
  WRITE A BRIEF SUMMARY OF YOUR BUSINESS – YEAR OF INCEPTION, LOCATION AND AREAS OF EXPERTISE.

  YOUR COMPANY NAME has been providing Information Technology Services and Solutions to the Southern California SMB Market since 1997. Our relationships with partners such as Microsoft, Cisco, Citrix and HP have allowed us the ability to design, scale and implement effective infrastructure solutions for our diverse client base.

  YOUR COMPANY NAME provides Help Desk, 24x7x365 Network Monitoring and Vendor Management Services and Web and Application Development, as well as Network Infrastructure Design, Implementation and Maintenance to a varied Client base, including Small and Medium-

---

Sized Businesses, as well as International Fortune 500 Firms.

- Company History in the Making
WRITE SEVERAL KEY HIGHLIGHTS IN YOUR COMPANY'S HISTORY (3 SENTENCES).

YOUR COMPANY NAME achieved Microsoft Gold Certified Partner status in 2005, as well as Microsoft's Small Business Specialist Competency in 2006. As a result of our successful methodology and delivery of Managed Services, we have been asked to speak and train at high-level Industry functions and Conferences conducted by Microsoft, Intel and others.

- Management
DETAIL COMPANY MANAGEMENT PERSONNEL AND THEIR BACKGROUNDS WHICH QUALIFY THEM FOR THEIR POSITIONS.

Our Management Team is strong and is composed of the following experienced individuals:

YOUR PRESIDENT'S NAME – President and CEO

YOUR PRESIDENT'S NAME draws upon nearly 20 years of strong and diverse management experience in developing strategic operating plans, business modeling and personnel training and development. Oversee the company's day-to-day operations. Maintain clear communication and provide direction to all key personnel in order to achieve company goals and objectives Responsible for customer service and satisfaction. Interface directly with YOUR COMPANY NAME's clients to maintain clear communication and develop methods to address individual client needs, improve relationships and meet expectations.

YOUR VICE PRESIDENT'S NAME – Vice President and CIO

YOUR VICE PRESIDENT'S NAME brings over 16 years of Enterprise-level IT experience to YOUR COMPANY NAME, where he oversees all technical aspects of the organization, determining the strategic direction, development and implementation of YOUR COMPANY NAME's Information Technology services and functions as they apply both internally and to its clients. YOUR VICE PRESIDENT'S NAME's previous experience includes overseeing the design, development and implementation of enterprise-level Help Desks and Call Centers for Fortune 1000 organizations, and

Industry Certifications include Microsoft MCP, Microsoft Business Solutions and Small Business Specialist Certifications, as well as Microsoft Solutions Framework, Networking Infrastructure, Advanced Networking Infrastructure and Information Worker Competencies.

Etc…

Each dynamic individual on the management team reflects years of experience gleaned from previous environments wherein their specific expertise was developed and refined, thus uniquely qualifying them to supervise their respective departments within the Company.

- Uniqueness
  WRITE A BRIEF SUMMARY OF YOUR UNIQUE SELLING PROPOSITION (3 SENTENCES) – THE THINGS THAT DIFFERENTIATE YOU FROM YOUR COMPETITORS.

YOUR COMPANY NAME's Industry-recognized Managed Services Sales, Implementation and Management model sets us apart from all other "break-fix" IT Service Providers. Based and sold on value received, our Managed Services deliverables easily illustrate the benefit to our prospects in doing business with our organization, easily differentiating us from our competition.

- Financials
  DOCUMENT BRIEFLY YOUR CURRENT FINANCIAL POSITION – GROSS SALES, PROFIT, ASSETS AND CASH ON HAND.

YOUR COMPANY NAME's financial position is strong, with gross sales of $_____ for the period ending Q107, reflecting gross profit of $_____, with available cash on hand of $_____. In addition, total company assets are valued at $_____ as of the period ending Q107.

II. Vision, Mission & Goals

- Vision
  WRITE A SHORT, INSPIRING STATEMENT OF WHAT THE ORGANIZATION INTENDS TO BECOME AND ACHIEVE AT SOME POINT IN THE FUTURE.

To become the leading IT Service Provider to Small and Medium Businesses in Southern California.

- Mission
WRITE A SHORT, CONCISE STATEMENT OF YOUR ORGANIZATION'S PRIORITIES.

Our mission is to ease our Clients' Business Pain and increase their productivity and profitability through the use of technology.

- Goals
WRITE DOWN SEVERAL SPECIFIC, REALISTIC GOALS FOR THE ORGANIZATION BASED UPON YOUR VISION AND MISSION STATEMENTS.

  o *Increase Gross Revenues by 20% quarter per quarter*
  o *Maintain and add new Industry Certifications/Competencies with Microsoft, Cisco and Citrix by a minimum of 2 per Vendor per Year*
  o *Hire 3 new Microsoft MCSE's by Q2/07*
  o *Develop relationships with 3 new Fulfillment Partners in Q207 – Web, VOIP and IP Cameras*

- Increased Client Satisfaction by 15% as measured by Microsoft's next quarterly CSAT initiative

III. Company Overview

- History
  BRIEFLY WRITE A COMPANY HISTORY.

- Legal Business Description
  BRIEFLY DESCRIBE YOUR LEGAL ENTITY.

  YOUR COMPANY NAME is a privately-held California-based S-Corporation, founded in 1997.

- Board of Directors
  BRIEFLY STATE YOUR BOARD OF DIRECTORS, TITLES AND RESPONSIBILITIES.

YOUR COMPANY NAME'S Board of Directors includes:

- Company Officers
  BRIEFLY STATE YOUR OFFICERS, TITLES AND RESPONSIBILITIES.

- Notable Clientele
  BRIEFLY INCLUDE A FEW CORNERSTONE CLIENTS

IV. Marketing Plan

- Creative Strategies

YOUR COMPANY NAME has declared as its mission statement to become an industry leader in Information Technology Services. The following proprietary marketing campaign will develop and expand YOUR COMPANY NAME's customer service emphasis; increase the company's client base; enhance relationships with current clients; and grow the company business through measured-response techniques.

The Best I.T. Sales & Marketing BOOK EVER!

Appendix A – Forms and Collateral

The challenges facing YOUR COMPANY NAME are evident: It must attract new business; it must build upon the trust and confidence exhibited by existing clientele; it must brand its customer service ideals among the industry populace, and create an ever-growing "customer pool" from which to develop future business.

YOUR COMPANY NAME has designed a unique marketing plan that will be executed in the following phases:

- *Phase one will be implementation of the small business (1) hour free service review for networking clients. This direct-response marketing campaign will be deployed using DESCRIBE MARKETINGMETHOD HERE. This strategy will yield _____ new client opportunities per month.*

- *Phase two will be the implementation of the Microsoft Across America initiative, which provides a 42-foot truck, fully equipped with the latest innovations from Microsoft, HP, Intel and others; it features complete state of-the-art software and hardware solutions for small and mid-sized business customers, allowing prospects to experience the technology first-hand and discover the many ways to enhance their businesses. The initiative helps build customer relationships and acts as a tool to answer their questions and address their* companies' concerns. This strategy will yield _____ new client opportunities quarterly.

- Phase three will be the implementation of a Direct marketing campaign of YOUR COMPANY NAME's target market i.e. attorneys, accountants, etc. This will be implemented via marketing cold calls from 500-1000 calls per week. This will be supported by a direct mail campaign and email direct-response campaign. This strategy will yield _____ new client opportunities per month.

All three phases will be developed concurrently, commencing on

_____.

YOUR COMPANY NAME's Services:

- Monthly Managed Service Contracts
- Helpdesk
- Network Monitoring
- Vendor Management
- Microsoft Small Business Services
- Back-Up Tape, server upgrades, etc
- Microsoft licenses, software support.

V. Key Alliances

BRIEFLY DESCRIBE YOUR KEY ALLIANCES IN THIS SECTION.

- Microsoft

  YOUR COMPANY NAME is a Microsoft Gold Certified Partner with the following Competencies:

  - *Information Worker Solutions*
  - *Networking Infrastructure Solutions*
  - *Advanced Infrastructure Solutions*
  - *Small Business Specialist (SBSC)*
  - *Microsoft Business Solutions*

- Citrix
  - *Citrix Silver Partner*

- Cisco
  - *Cisco Silver Certified Partner*

VI. Revenue Sources

- Current Revenue Sources
  BRIEFLY DESCRIBE ALL SOURCES OF CURRENT REVENUE.

  YOUR COMPANY NAME currently enjoys the following revenue streams:

  - *Project-based Services Revenue*
  - *Managed Services Contract Revenue*
  - *Hosting/Co-location Services Revenue*
  - *Web/Application Development Revenue*
  - *Other Recurring Revenue from Annuity-Based Solutions such as T1's, Hosted VOIP, etc.*

- Future Revenue Sources
  BRIEFLY DESCRIBE FUTURE REVENUE SOURCES BASED UPON FINANCIAL PROJECTIONS SPREADSHEET.

  YOUR COMPANY NAME will earn additional revenue through the development of additional Annuity-Based Products and Services such as Remote Storage and

Hosted Exchange, as well as Proxy-based Email filtering, Anti-Virus and Anti-Spam Services.

VII. Competition

- General Competitive Analysis
  BRIEFLY DESCRIBE 3 LOCAL SOURCES OF COMPETITION – MARKETING STRATEGY, LOCATION, STRENGTHS, WEAKNESSES AND PRICING STRUCTURE.

Competitor's Name	Do IT Smarter	Alvaka Networks	Bedrock
Location	San Diego, CA	Orange County, CA	Neenah, WI
Methods of Distribution	Events	Website	Events
Promotional Materials	Brochures Presentations	Brochures Website	Brochures Website
Methods of Advertising	Website Events	Website	Website Events
Pricing Structure	$500/Mo Min.	$500/Mo Min.	$500/Mo Min
Market Share	<1%	<1%	<1%
Strengths	Marketing	20 Years in business	Wrote Managed Services White Paper for Microsoft
Weaknesses	Overpriced Small number of Partners	Overpriced Marketing	Expensive High Initial Investment

At this time, there are only a handful of other organizations providing some flavor of Managed Services nationwide. Among these is Do IT Smarter, based in San Diego California, Alvaka Networks, based in Orange County California and Bedrock, based in Neena Wisconsin.

We do not see these organizations as direct competitors in the key sense, as our Services differ dramatically with most of theirs in specific areas, including Core Services, as well as the manner in which we market to our target market. In addition, we maintain a broad menu of Annuity-Based Products and Services that we Market, Sell and Implement. This differentiates us from other Organizations that have a small core of highly-priced Services that they market to their Clients.

Competition market share is growing at this point, and we believe that others will quickly enter this largely untapped market.

In general, the objective reflected by our competitors' services, delivery, training and pricing models skew towards benefiting the competitor more so than the Client. While Core Service offerings such as Network Monitoring and Help Desk vary from competitor to competitor, those that do offer it command a much higher price than our offerings

VIII. Financials

- Financial Projections
  BRIEFLY DESCRIBE YOUR FINANCIAL
  PROJECTIONS, BASED UPON YOUR FINANCIAL
  PROJECTIONS SPREADSHEET.

  *YOUR COMPANY NAME projects Gross Revenue to
  be $_____ for the period ending Q207,
  $_____ for the period ending Q307, and
  $_____ for the period ending Q407, for a total
  Gross Revenue projection of $_____ for FY07,
  with Projected Earnings of $_____.*

- Financial Charts
  ATTACH YOUR FINANCIAL PROJECTIONS
  SPREADSHEET HERE.

Managed Services Business Plan White Paper

Many resellers recognize that there's money to be made in managed services, but in their haste to adopt a new business model they forget a step vital to the success of any new business venture: the business plan. Before you take the plunge into managed services, take the time to update your company's business plan. An effective business plan will help you confirm the viability of your venture, set realistic goals based upon the market research that you conduct, and provide a roadmap to your success while minimizing risk.

A managed services business plan requires special attention to areas that may differ from traditional business plans, such as your marketing strategy and financial projections. If you already have an existing business plan in place, it can make a good template that you can modify to address the managed services-specific sections in your plan.

A well-researched and organized business plan need not be lengthy to be effective. As long as your business plan contains the essential components necessary to realize its desired outcome, the more concise and easy to assimilate it is, the better. Your plan may serve many purposes, from defining your company's vision, mission and goals, to identifying your marketing strategy, sources of revenue, competition and more. Some business plans are written specifically to attract investment opportunities, or to seek business financing.

THE MANAGED SERVICES BUSINESS PLAN

Your business plan should begin with an executive summary, which describes the intent of the business plan, as well as contains brief overviews of your company's history, its management team, its uniqueness in the industry and current financial position.

Subsequent sections of your business plan should address your vision, mission and goals, as well as a company overview, including a legal business description of your company, your Board of Directors and company Officers, and any notable clientele that you may have.

Your marketing strategy is a critical component of your business plan, and will need to address the results of the competitive analysis you conduct and include in your business plan. Your marketing strategy and message need to clearly define your organization's proactive deliverables as the answer to your target market's specific pain points; and illustrate your ability to reduce costs, increase productivity and minimize business risk for your clients.

Your competitive analysis will reflect the research you have performed against your top competitors regarding their services, marketing and pricing strategies. Because of the relatively small number of "pure" managed services providers in existence today, it may be a challenge to identify your direct competitors in your target market. In this case you will need to include other, non-managed service providers in your competitive analysis, and demonstrate what makes your services unique in the space, influencing clients to choose you over your competition and justifying your financial projections.

It's a good idea to incorporate a description of strategic vendor relationships and other key alliances that you will leverage in executing your business plan and marketing strategy.

The final required component of your business plan will be your financial projections over the next five years, and should include a breakdown of your current P&L, if available. Your financial projections should reflect the exponential growth you will experience as a result of selling annuity-based service agreements, which will continue to pay predictable dividends month after month, year after year.

Whether you use your business plan as a strategic roadmap to transition your organization to deliver managed services, or as a vehicle to attract financing opportunities for business startup or growth, the benefits you will reap as a result of its creation will far exceed its intended purpose, as it will help you analyze your business opportunity with your bottom line squarely in mind.

Business Plan Components

An effective business plan is comprised of several key sections. Additional components may be included to address specific needs, and to tailor the plan for a specific outcome. The following items comprise a short list of required topics to include in a basic business plan.

EXECUTIVE SUMMARY

- **A brief summary of the business**
- **Key highlights in the company's history**
- **A description of your key management team**
- **A brief outline of your uniqueness in the industry**
- **A concise narrative of your current financial position**

VISION, MISSION & GOALS

- **Your company's Vision Statement**
- **Your company's Mission Statement**
- **Your company's Goals**

COMPANY OVERVIEW

- **A brief company history**
- **Your company's legal business description (Corporation, LLC, etc.)**
- **Your Board of Directors**

- **Your Company Officers**
- **A brief summary of your notable clientele**

MARKETING PLAN

- **Your creative marketing strategies**

KEY ALLIANCES AND VENDORS

- **An accounting of key relationships that will influence your marketing plan**

REVENUE SOURCES

- **An illustration of your current revenue streams**
- **A description of future revenue streams**

COMPETITION

- **A general competitive analysis**

FINANCIALS

- **A narrative of your financial projections**
- **Your financial charts or spreadsheets**

MSP University

Intelligent Enterprise specializes in providing Managed Services training, workshops, and Boot Camps, as well as Sales and Marketing Services to IT Service Providers, Vendors and Channel Organizations nationwide through our Managed Services Provider University at www.mspu.us.

MSP University is a comprehensive, Vendor-neutral resource whose sole function is to collect and disseminate as much information as possible and mentor its Partners on building, operating and growing a successful Managed Services Practice.

Our Mission: To deliver the finest Managed Services Training and Support Resources available to IT Professionals anywhere.

Our Vision: To be recognized as the premier authority on the development and growth of a successful IT Managed Services Practice.

Our Values: Committed to the highest standards of integrity, we fulfill our responsibilities to our Partners, our staff and their families in an ethical and professional manner.

What you get: A continuing Curriculum dedicated to what every IT Service Provider needs to know about Managed Services!

The Best I.T. Sales & Marketing BOOK EVER!

MSP University

Benefits:
- Access to Over 100 hours of Webinars, TeleSeminars and Live Workshops – *the most MSP Content available anywhere*
- 144 individual MSP Courses and growing!
- Study and participate in these valuable MSP Courses at your own speed
- Unlimited email support
- Participation in 2 live group calls per month
- A complimentary download of **"The Guide to a Successful Managed Services Practice – *What Every SMB IT Service Provider Should Know…"***

Ask about our other MSP Training and Fulfillment Services:
- 3-Day MSP Sales & Marketing Boot Camps
- 2-Day MSP Annuity-based Solution Stack Boot Camps
- 1-Day NOC/Help Desk Boot Camps
- MSP Sales & Marketing Services
- MSP NOC/Help Desk Services
- MSP Sales Engineering Services
- MSP Sales Management Services
- MSP CEO Support Services

What is Managed Services University?

MSP University is the answer for all IT Service Providers either preparing to transition to an Annuity-based Managed Services delivery model, or who are already delivering Managed Services, and wish to increase their knowledge of Managed Services Vendors, Services, Solutions and Business, Technical and Sales and Marketing Best Practices.

Why Managed Services University?

The founders of Managed Services University wished to create a single, comprehensive resource to collect and disseminate as much information as possible about building, operating and growing a successful Managed Services Practice.

What are your qualifications to operate Managed Services University?

We are a subsidiary of Intelligent Enterprise, a Gold Certified Microsoft Partner and operators of a successful IT Services Practice since 1997, who successfully transitioned to a completely Managed Services delivery model in January of 2005.

Since then, we have toured nationwide, speaking at numerous industry events and conferences, and teaching and training IT Service Providers, Vendor Channels and Membership Organizations in our unique Managed Services Methodologies.

In addition to real-world experience, our authorship of "The Guide to a Successful Managed Services Practice – *What Every SMB IT Service Provider Should Know...*", and contributions to numerous publications including Microsoft's Expert Column; as well as a series of Microsoft TS2, Cisco and Intel Webcasts and live, in-the-field events with these clients featuring our Managed Services methodologies, more than qualify us as experts in the field of Managed Services.

The Best I.T. Sales & Marketing BOOK EVER!

MSP University

What can I expect after joining?

You will gain unlimited access to our over 144 Live and Recorded Webinars and TeleSeminars, as well as Live Regional 1-Day Workshops, to guide you - no matter where you are on the path to Managed Services. In addition you will receive unlimited email support from our experienced staff, as well as participation in 2 Live Group Q&A Calls per month to help answer all of your managed services questions.

What types of Courses do you offer?

Unlike other Vendor-Specific Managed Services Training offerings, our University Curriculum has been consciously designed in a completely agnostic and Vendor-neutral manner, allowing us the ability to provide training courses from all MSP Vendors who wish to participate, giving you the best opportunity to experience each Solution or Service to compare head-to-head at your own pace.

In addition to providing access to MSP Vendor Solutions and Services, our Courses are a holistic answer to all facets of operating a successful Managed Services Practice, and include:

- Managed Services Concepts
- MSP Vendor Management
- MSP HR Training
- MSP Marketing Process
- MSP Lead Generation
- MSP Sales Process
- MSP Appointment Setting
- MSP Sales Closing Techniques
- MSP Help Desk Best Practices

The Best I.T. Sales & Marketing BOOK EVER!

MSP University

- MSP Tools
- MSP Service Contracts
- MSP Staffing
- MSP Vendor Solution Partnering
- MSP Additional Annuity-Based Solutions

And more…this is just a small sampling of our Courses…

How are University Courses Conducted?

All of our Managed Services Courses, whether they highlight a specific process such as Sales and Marketing or System Monitoring Best Practices; or spotlight a Managed Services Solution or Vendor, are delivered through Webinars and TeleSeminars, which are recorded for offline access.

We also offer Regional Live Workshops and Boot Camps that deep-dive into specific Advanced Managed Services concepts, as well as One-On-One onsite Consulting Services.

What other benefits will I receive?

As a Managed Services University member, in addition to access to all of our Live and Recorded Courses, Regional Workshops, and email and Group Call support, you will also receive a download of our highly-regarded publication "The Guide to a Successful Managed Services Practice – *What Every SMB IT Service Provider Should Know…*", as well as discounts for all of our Boot Camp training sessions, and other special offers available only to MSPU members.

How long does MSP University take?

It's completely up to you - our MSP University is a Self-Paced program delivered through Webinars, TeleSeminars and all-day Workshops. It's completely up to you to determine how long it will take to meet your specific needs. Since we are continually adding new content to our University as the Managed Services Industry matures and develops, you may wish to maintain your membership indefinitely.

Do you offer any other Partner Services?

In addition to MSP University, we also provide an economical Managed Marketing Service for our Partners, which handles lead-generation activities for new business in a scheduled, consistent manner.

Our Marketing Department sources Marketing Lists, designs and produces Marketing Collateral such as your Website, Letters, Postcards and Emails, performs the Posting and mailing and sets appointments for our Partners – allowing them the ability to do what they do best - deliver their Services.

We also offer affordable marketing collateral creation services – for those Partners who can handle the actual marketing duties themselves, but need help in creating eye-catching collateral, including their website, case studies, white papers, newsletters, line cards, postcards, and developing their marketing message.

The Best I.T. Sales & Marketing BOOK EVER!

MSP University

How much is Tuition for MSPU?

That's the best part – we've made it amazingly affordable to join Managed Services University! For unlimited access to our entire Managed Services Curriculum of 144 Courses (and growing every day!), and FREE attendance to any and all of our Live Regional Workshops, a download of "The Guide to a Successful Managed Services Practice – *What Every SMB IT Service Provider Should Know...*" and email and Group Call support, monthly Tuition is only $99!

Sounds great! How do I join MSPU?

Simply visit our website at www.mspu.us and navigate to the "Registration" tab!

The Best I.T. Sales & Marketing BOOK EVER!

Index

The Best I.T. Sales & Marketing BOOK EVER!

Index

The Best I.T. Sales & Marketing BOOK EVER!

Index

The Best I.T. Sales & Marketing BOOK EVER!

Index

The Best I.T. Sales & Marketing BOOK EVER!

Index

The Best I.T. Sales & Marketing BOOK EVER!

Index

The Best I.T. Sales & Marketing BOOK EVER!

Index

Index

White Papers, 1, 59, 60, 61,
67, 76, 98, 105, 452

Williams, Nancy, 8

Windows Live Search, 58

Win-Wires, 2, 85, 98

Y

Yahoo, 53, 57

Z

ZapData, 37

The Best I.T. Sales & Marketing BOOK EVER!

What's on the CD ROM?

What's on the CD ROM?

- 17 page Managed Services and I.T. Solutions Website Design Comp
- Thank You Postcard Design Comp
- Appointment Setting Postcard Design Comp
- Closing The Deal – 17 Page Managed Services Sales Process And Overcoming Objections
- Cost Savings Analysis Form
- Cost Savings Analysis Example
- Managed Services Agreement Example
- Introduction to MSPU
- Disaster Recovery Messaging Postcard Design Comp
- Disaster Recovery Messaging Postcard Design Comp2
- Disaster Recovery Messaging Postcard Design Comp3
- Flat-Rate I.T. Messaging Postcard Design Comp
- Website SEO Report
- Case Study Questionnaire
- Newsletter Design Comp
- I.T. Service Line Card Design Comp
- HR Interview Checklist For New Sales Person
- 5 Ways To Evaluate A Sales Person Before They Make A Sale
- Qualifying Call Script
- Lead Calling Script
- Direct Mail Marketing Letter Design Comp
- HTML Email Disaster Recovery Messaging Design Comp
- Managed Services, Your Business Plan and You PowerPoint Presentation
- Managed Services Business Plan Template

The Best I.T. Sales & Marketing BOOK EVER!

What's on the CD ROM?

- Managed Services Business Plan Article
- Bonus – Haas Webcast With Karl Palachuk
- Bonus – Closing The Deal Managed Services Webcast
- Bonus – Managed Services Business Plan Webcast
- Bonus – How To Use The Cost Savings Analysis Webcast
- Bonus – Creating Effective Managed Services Proposals Webcast
- MSPU CEO Support Group Webcast
- MSPU Help Desk/NOC Boot Camp Webcast
- MSPU Sales & Marketing Boot Camp Webcast
- MSPU Introduction Webcast

Don't forget to register your copy of The Best I.T. Sales & Marketing BOOK EVER! at www.mspu.us/smbookregistration.htm to receive exclusive additional sales and marketing collateral and valuable webinar training absolutely FREE!